SPEAKING IN PUBLIC

SPEAKING IN PUBLIC

Richard F. Whitman
Ted J. Foster
Ohio University

MACMILLAN PUBLISHING COMPANY *New York*
COLLIER MACMILLAN PUBLISHING *London*

Copyright © Macmillan Publishing Company,
a division of Macmillan, Inc.

Printed in the United States of America

Macmillan Publishing Company
866 Third Avenue, New York, New York 10022

Collier Macmillan Canada, Inc.

Library of Congress Cataloging-in-Publication Data
Whitman, Richard F.
  Speaking in public.

  Includes index.
  1. Public speaking. I. Foster, Ted J. II. Title.
PN4121.W3728 1987   808.5'1   86-16039
ISBN 0-02-427350-3

Printing: 1 2 3 4 5 6 7   7 8 9 0 1 2 3

ISBN 0-02-427350-3

Preface

We wrote *Speaking in Public* because we are firmly committed to the belief that public speaking plays a vital role in our world. Ours is a world in constant flux, in which there is a constant search for solutions to a broad array of complex social, political, and economic problems. Today's college student will soon be called upon to provide new, effective solutions to those problems. Whether their leadership skills will be directed toward the city council, to suburban parent-teacher organizations, to business groups, or even to the heady atmosphere of state and national politics, their public-speaking skills will be a crucial component of effective leadership. We will always need the competent communicator to alert us to societal needs, to educate, to let us know when change is needed, to spur us to action, and to rekindle our beliefs, energy, and enthusiasm. This text will be of assistance to conscientious students attempting to prepare for the leadership role that they soon will assume.

Our Approach

Throughout *Speaking in Public,* we have attempted to strike a proper balance between the *how* and *why* of speechmaking. We know students of public speaking profit from clear and specific advice relating to *how* different activities of the public speaker should be accomplished. We have attempted to advise them on these matters, but we have also tried to go beyond a simple listing of the "do's" and "don'ts" of public speaking. Our teaching experience indicates that although students enjoy learning how to give speeches, they also enjoy discussing and arguing about the bases of the principles they are asked to follow. They want to know how to prepare and give effective speeches. They also want to know why they are following certain rules and procedures. The students who find good reasons for these rules and procedures begin to think of public speaking as an integral part of their education, as vital as algebra, writing, biology, history, or psychology. A knowledge of the reasons for rules arms the students with the information necessary for them to generalize the learning experience to new situations not directly addressed within the public-speaking course. We believe it to be imperative for those who will lead us to have an understanding not only of "how" speeches are given but also of the substance underlying the rules. Striking the proper balance between skill-training and theoretical explanation has been our goal. We hope a meaningful and useful balance is the outcome of our effort.

Our Perspective

We have taught public speaking and related courses for a good many years. Our training and experience within the communication field has been broad and varied. We have studied and taught the theories of classical philosophers and rhetorical theorists and have learned and disseminated the theories, findings, and techniques of the contemporary communication theorist. Our approach, then, to public speaking is an eclectic one. We have drawn on the traditional rhetorical approach to public speaking but have modified it to include research and theory generated by contemporary communication scholars and experts from such related disciplines as psychology, sociology, anthropology, linguistics, and philosophy. In short, we have made our decisions regarding the inclusion of ideas on the merit of the idea, not its source. As a result, this text includes reference to a wide variety of sources, ranging from the works of Aristotle, Cicero, and Quintilian to the research of today's most dyed-in-the-wool experimentalists.

The Plan of the Text

Teaching and learning the substance of public speaking are not without frustration. The nature of the beast leads to the frequent complaint, "I wish there were a way of teaching (studying) all the principles and theory of speeckmaking before actually giving speeches." We too have sometimes felt this concern and have adopted a variety of instructional strategies in an attempt to resolve the difficulty. Generally, we have settled on an approach that mixes the study of skills and theory with practice. The organization of the text and its division of chapters allows for any number of instructional approaches.

The text has five principal divisions: Part I—Getting Started; Part II—Speech Preparation: Initial Considerations; Part III—Basic Principles of Speechmaking; Part IV—Principles to Practice; and Part V—General Considerations. The three chapters of Part I address initial concerns of the student or provide an orientation to the subject matter. Chapter 1 presents a rationale for the study of public speaking. Here we have tempered our true feelings regarding the values to be realized from the study of public speaking. We believe strongly in the merits of public-speaking training and have resisted presenting an overstatement of our case. Chapter 2 helps define speechmaking by recounting its long heritage, illustrating how it is relevant to the contemporary study of communication theory. Chapter 3 acquaints the student with the concept of speech anxiety and gives suggestions about how to deal with it. We prefer to discuss this topic early in the course. The student who knows about it and who understands it is better able to deal with anxiety when it is confronted.

Part II contains three chapters. Chapter 4 discusses general purposes, speech topics, and the specific purpose of a speech (the thesis). Chapter 5 details the speech-preparation process. Chapter 6 discusses principles of audience analysis and techniques relating to audience adaptation.

In Part III we present basic principles of speechmaking. Chapter 7 speaks to the importance of speaker credibility, its component parts, and techniques for achieving favorable perception. Chapter 8 presents principles relating to outlining and organizing speeches; it details a series of organizational techniques and strategies. Chapter 9 defines evidence, provides examples of different types of evidence, and suggests criteria for evaluating evidence. Chapter 10 explains the requirements of good speech introductions and conclusions. Chapter 11 deals with reasoning, illustrating the various forms of reasoning and how the speaker can use them effectively. Chapter 12 covers language. It details the characteristics of effective language, defining and providing examples to illustrate the various characteristics. In Chapter 13 we present principles of effective delivery—the vocal and nonvocal components of delivery.

In Part IV we take the reader from principles to practice. Chapters 14 and 15 are companion chapters, as are Chapters 16 and 17. Chapters 14 and 15 address informative speaking, whereas Chapters 16 and 17 cover persuasive speaking. In the first member of each pair we discuss the nature and function of the speech purpose. The second chapter in each pair suggests how these principles might be applied to the two principal speech purposes—informing and persuading. Chapter 18 details a series of speeches for special occasions and lists the expected requirements of each speech type.

In Part V, we deal with two topics of general interest to the public speaker—humor and listening. Chapter 19 approaches the topic of listening from the speaker's point of view. It alerts the speaker to the listening process employed by audience members, and mentions negative listening habits for which the astute public speaker will compensate. Chapter 20 acquaints the reader with theories of humor and lists a number of guidelines to follow.

Flexibility of Approach

We have ordered the twenty chapters of this text in what we believe to be a logical order. We make no claim that it is the best order. Although our sequence of chapters approximates the order in which we would deal with the many topics, other instructors may find alternative sequences more efficacious. Accordingly, we wrote each chapter as a self-contained unit of instruction. Nevertheless, we recommend that the first six chapters be assigned early in the course. The last fourteen chapters can be taught in the order given or may be sequenced to fit the experience and preference of the instructor.

Throughout the text we attempt to provide cross-references that refer the student to related sections in other chapters. At the same time, we have attempted to avoid redundant discussions.

Instructional Techniques

Each chapter begins with a list of objectives or goals. These are designed to alert the student to the material that follows. We intend for these objectives to produce a learning set within the reader, a set that leads to thorough comprehension of our message. We also close the introduction of chapters with an overview of the topics included within, and have attempted to subdivide the topics of each chapter clearly, with appropriate headings included for each subdivision. Transitions and internal summaries are abundant throughout the text. The chapters end with a summary of the principles covered. These devices provide the student with a clear indication of the concepts involved. Each chapter includes a set of questions and exercises which focus the reader's attention on the important issues raised within the chapter.

R. F. W.
T. J. F.

Contents

PART

I

Getting Started

Courtesy Central Office of Information, London

Why Study Public Speaking?

By the time you finish reading this chapter, you should be able to:

1. Identify a set of communicative skills needed for both speaking and writing.

2. Enumerate college experiences which require public-speaking skills.

3. Explain how skill as a public communicator might equip one to become a better student.

4. Illustrate how public speaking might be considered an approach-avoidance conflict situation.

5. Show the relationship between public-speaking skills and leadership abilities.

6. Know three long-term benefits to be gained from the conscientious study of public speaking.

With the coming of each new academic year, tens of thousands of college students find themselves undertaking the study of public speaking. Now it is your turn. Soon you probably will discover that students in your class represent a cross-section of the university community, coming from such major areas of study as chemistry, engineering, business, the arts, education, agriculture, journalism, English, nursing, or physical education. You also may discover that some of your colleagues have not yet selected a major area of study or established future career goals. Why does such a potentially heterogeneous group of people assemble to study public speaking? To address this question, we will consider the cases of three typical students.

Sally Landon had an active high school career, participating in school plays, debating on the state championship team, and actively seeking out all opportunities for developing her communication skills by participating in a variety of oratorical and writing contests. She completed a rigorous college preparatory program in anticipation of an eventual career in law. Wanting very much to be a successful trial lawyer, Sally eagerly enrolled in public speaking during her first college term because she could see a link between success in her chosen profession and the ability to exert interpersonal influence through public discourse.

Peter Smythers has enrolled in college to become an electrical engineer. In high school, he took many courses in chemistry, physics, and mathematics. He was a member of the science club and a winner in several state science fairs. He has built his own microcomputer from a kit and spends most of his free time writing programs for his computer or designing and implementing modifications in its circuitry. After graduation, Peter hopes to become employed by a major computer manufacturing firm, in new product development, if possible. Peter is surprised to find public speaking as a required course for an electrical engineering degree.

Unlike either Sally or Peter, Alicia Suarez has entered college without a major area of study firmly in mind. Alicia is a respectable student who has experienced some success in high school courses which require very different types of expertise. As Alicia begins her college career, she hopes to choose courses which will be valuable to her and which will suggest career possibilities. Her adviser has suggested she enroll in a public-speaking course.

Why have you decided to undertake speechmaking? Is there anything about the cases of Sally, Peter, or Alicia that reminds you of your own circumstances? We think these three students' reasons for taking public speaking illustrate why the course is a very visible and highly enrolled one in many colleges and universities. Perhaps you have decided to study public speaking because you recognize, as did Sally, a direct link between being an effective oral communication practitioner and achieving a personal goal. Or, as did Peter and Alicia, you may have enrolled because of the advice of parents, friends, or an academic adviser, who felt that it would be beneficial to acquire public-speaking skills.

Whatever your reason for enrolling, you will soon discover that your gains from the study of speechmaking will be no greater than the effort you put into your assignments. Becoming an effective public speaker requires real effort, study, and practice. The ancient Greek orator Demosthenes (384-322 B.C.) is an excellent example of a person who achieved oratorical excellence through hard work and perseverance. A stutterer and weak-voiced, Demosthenes had a great desire to overcome his deficiencies and distinguish himself in the political arena of ancient Greece, so great that he secluded himself in an underground cavern and shaved off half of his hair, presumably to avoid the temptation to return from this voluntary banishment prior to achieving his goal. During Demosthenes' periods of seclusion, it was not uncommon for him to visit the seashore and attempt to speak above the roar of the waves. He also was known to fill his mouth with pebbles and orate while climbing steep hills. So successful was Demosthenes' quest for oratorical excellence that Quintilian, a Roman rhetorical theorist of the first century, A.D., referred to him as the greatest of all Athenian orators, "the sole pattern of oratory."[1]

We are not saying that you have to take up residence somewhere in the bowels of your dormitory, shave your head, or speak with a mouth full of pebbles before you can become a more effective speaker. We are saying

[1] Quintilian, *Institutio Oratoria,* vol. 4, X.1.76, trans. H. E. Butler (Cambridge, Mass.: The Loeb Classical Library, 1961), p. 45.

that if you really wish to enhance your skills as a public speaker, you will have to work hard for a lifetime. Effective speaking results from a thorough knowledge of theory, substantial research efforts, practice, and judicious use of constructive criticism. Such efforts will be rewarded on both a short- and long-term basis. In the remainder of this chapter, benefits which might be accrued from a conscientious study of public speaking are enumerated. Some immediate benefits are described first; then long-term ones are discussed.

Some Immediate Benefits _____

Why do you suppose Alicia Suarez's adviser recommended public speaking as one of her first college courses, even when she had not yet decided on a major area of study? Maybe the adviser recognized the carry-over value of many skills learned in public speaking. These skills should assist Alicia in meeting the continued demands made of her as she progresses through her college career, such as writing papers in various classes, participating and reporting orally in classes, and assuming leadership roles on campus. Let us examine in greater detail a number of immediate benefits that you can realize from the study of public speaking.

Oral to Written Communication

Whether you are a history major, a future physicist, or an aspiring elementary teacher, you are going to be asked to write many essay examinations, term papers, reaction statements, and reports of various kinds throughout your college career. What you learn in your study of public speaking should assist you with these assignments. Research at one Midwestern university indicates that freshmen who took public speaking prior to a first course in writing performed much more effectively as writers than those who did not take it.[2]

Why, you ask, would studying public speaking improve writing skills? Because both modes of communicating require many of the same skills: discovering what should be presented within a particular context; choosing ideas which best advance a cause or explain a position; finding appropriate materials to amplify, clarify, or support a point of view; or choosing those forms of proof most likely to bring about compliance. Once ideas are discovered, speakers as well as writers must order or arrange them appropriately. They also must share a common concern for choosing accurate, clear, proper, economical, and vivid language which will make their ideas compelling. Later you will learn about some

[2]Wayne Wall, *Fundamentals of Outlining: A Self-Teaching Program,* unpublished manuscript, Marietta, Ohio, 1982, p. 3.

FIGURE 1-1   Will your communicative ability be a help when you are looking for employment? Reprinted from *Careers*, a publication of Career Planning and Placement, Athens, Ohio, Ohio University, Spring quarter, 1983.

What employers look for in an employee

The decisions you make about your career will probably be some of the most difficult you will ever have to make. It seems ironic, but a twenty minute interview can have a profound effect on the future of your professional career. You really can't afford to take on-campus interviewing lightly. To perform at your maximum level, you need to know what skills and abilities you have.

That requires some self-evaluation. The College Placement Council has asked top college recruiters what they look for in employees that make them particularly attractive to hire. The following list is their answers. Use this as a starting point. Remember, know yourself; it's necessary before an interviewer can get to know you!

ABILITY TO COMMUNICATE

Do you have the ability to organize your thoughts and ideas effectively? Can you express them clearly when speaking or writing? Can you present your ideas to others in a persuasive way?

INTELLIGENCE

Do you have the ability to understand a job assignment, learn the details of operation, and contribute new, original ideas to your work?

SELF-CONFIDENCE

Do you demonstrate a sense of maturity and direction that enables you to deal positively and effectively with situations and people?

WILLINGNESS TO ACCEPT RESPONSIBILITY

Are you someone who recognizes what needs to be done, and is willing to do it?

INITIATIVE

Do you have the ability to identify purposeful work and to take action?

LEADERSHIP

Can you guide and direct others to obtain a recognized objective?

ENERGY LEVEL

Do you demonstrate a forcefulness and capacity to make things move ahead?

IMAGINATION

Can you confront and deal with problems which may not have standard solutions?

FLEXIBILITY

Are you capable of change, and receptive to new situations and ideas? Do you have the capacity to effectively evaluate a variety of opinions on how to perform a task?

INTERPERSONAL SKILLS

Can you bring out the best efforts of individuals so they become effective, enthusiastic members of a team?

ABILITY TO HANDLE CONFLICT

Can you sucessfully contend with stress situations and antagonisms?

COMPETITIVENESS

Do you have the capacity to compete with others, and a willingness to be measured by your performance in relation to that of the competition?

GOAL ACHIEVEMENT

Do you have the ability to identify, work toward, and obtain specific goals?

VOCATIONAL SKILLS

Do you possess the positive combination of education and skills required for the position you're seeking?

DIRECTION

Have you defined your basic personal needs? Have you determined what type of position will satisfy your knowledge, skills and goals?

SELF KNOWLEDGE

Can you realistically assess your own capabilities? See yourself as others see you?

significant differences between oral and written language, but for now note the similarities. You should always consider how the principles of effective public speaking can be applied to your writing assignments.

Effective Classroom Participation

In many of your college classes, you will have to be more than a passive listener. You will have to be an oral communicator: ask questions, respond to questions, offer opinions, present reports, and advance arguments. A student with the ability to present his or her ideas clearly, forcefully, and enthusiastically will always be at an advantage.

Many of us lack the confidence necessary to volunteer our point of view, to present our viewpoint for public scrutiny. This lack of confidence may result from a simple lack of experience. We also may be reticent about making our ideas known because we lack an understanding of the standards of good speaking practice. What you learn in your public-speaking class can help you become a more effective and active participant in other courses as well, if only you apply your newly acquired public speaking skill to the classroom setting.

Have you ever found yourself sitting in a class listening to a spirited discussion and wanting to take part but holding back and not participating? Frequently, we later reflect back on the event and say, "Why didn't I put in my two cents' worth? Why didn't I say what was on my mind?" If this has ever happened to you, take comfort, because you are not alone. Many people are fearful of speaking in public, of standing up above the crowd and sharing ideas, concerns, and solutions to problems. In a recent survey by R. H. Bruskin Associates, 40.6 percent of 2,543 people expressed a fear of speaking in a group, a fear that is intense.[3] No less a figure than Carol Burnett insists that, although she is not nervous while performing on stage, "the idea of making a speech does more than make me a nervous wreck; it terrifies me. . . .I'd rather scrub floors—without knee pads."[4]

In Chapter 3, you will learn about speech anxiety or speech apprehension in greater detail, but for now note that many people who fear and avoid speaking in public do so because to them it represents the unknown, the unfamiliar. Remember your feeling when you left home for college the first time? Did it present you with what is sometimes called an approach-avoidance conflict? Did you look forward to the independence of college life (approach), but also become apprehensive of your new life, fearful of your forthcoming experience (avoidance), and unsure exactly how you should act and what would be expected of you? If you felt that way, or even continue to feel that way, it is not unusual. As a knowledge of college life is acquired, fears dissipate. So it is with

---

[3]*Spectra* (New York: Speech Communication Association, December 1973), p. 4.

[4]"Ask Them Yourself," *Family Weekly*, January 28, 1979.

public speaking. You will never completely lose those anxieties related to public speaking (in fact, a certain amount of anxiety is useful), but as you acquire knowledge of the theory of speechmaking and receive guided practice, those fears will diminish and become properly channeled.

During your public-speaking course, you will speak on a variety of topics and attempt to achieve a number of goals. You will receive valuable comments and constructive criticisms from your instructor and classmates. You will also be exposed to a number of theories and prescriptions relating to good practice. We believe this new knowledge and practice will make you a better oral communicator in the classroom, a better student; however, you must work at transferring your training to similar experiences outside the public-speaking classroom.

Public Speaking and Leadership

Public-speaking skills will be valuable to those of you who aspire to a leadership role on campus, whether it be a fraternity or sorority officer, member of the student senate, president of the Young Democrats or Republicans, or member of the student activity board. Now is a good time to begin preparation for such a role. It is hard to imagine a student leader, or any leader for that matter, who does not possess the ability to speak in public.

Public speaking does not necessarily guarantee success. All of us can probably point to people who are leaders but who do not very effectively communicate in public. Likewise, we may also know people who are glib, articulate, and fluent who are continually denied leadership positions to which they aspire. There is more to being a good public speaker than demonstrating facility with the language. The kind of speaker you should become is one who demonstrates, through his or her behaviors and discourse, competence, trustworthiness, and the best interest of the audience. These three characteristics are major components of *source credibility,* an attitude or perception the audience has of a source of information, the speaker. Over time, a public speaker will be effective only if he or she is perceived as a trustworthy person well versed in the matter under consideration.

While you cannot be guaranteed a leadership role if you become a skillful speaker, you can be assured that it will help. No "snake oil" solutions, no magic elixirs, no shortcuts to eloquence are peddled in this text. Leadership positions are earned—and only after one has won the respect of a constituency. Quintilian once described the ideal orator as "the good man speaking well." We agree, and would extend Quintilian's thought to the concept of leadership. A good leader is first of all a "good man" (or woman) who is most effective when he or she has the ability to explain ideas clearly and advocate positions when necessary in a persuasive manner.

Some Long-Term Benefits _____

Perhaps you have not thought of it before, but the skills you can acquire within your present study of public speaking will serve you well later in life. Evidence shows that skill in public speaking and communication will enhance your ability to be employed and contribute to job advancement once you have been employed. We believe that training in public speaking has another long-term benefit, a very important one: we can only be active and effective members of a democratic society if we possess the ability and willingness to make ideas known and continually debate the issues facing our society. Let us consider in greater detail, then, some of the long-term benefits to be derived from the study of public speaking.

TABLE 1-1

Among the skills to be acquired through the study of public speaking are:

1. Choosing topics worthy of discussion and debating within a democratic society.
2. Narrowing topics so that they can be meaningfully analyzed.
3. Researching topics thoroughly, making use of the numerous resources available in the college library.
4. Formulating positions on issues and organizing the statement of one's position effectively.
5. Supporting one's position with evidence and reasoning from the evidence in such a way that conclusions are logically justified.
6. Adapting one's ideas and arguments to different types of audiences.
7. Choosing language that forcefully and accurately presents one's ideas.
8. Speaking to others with confidence, enthusiasm, and effectiveness.

Public Speaking and Employability

Pamela M. Birchoff, a counselor at Ramapo College, observed that college experience can enhance initial employability if it helps one "to acquire well-developed communication skills, research capabilities, and analytical abilities"[5]—all skills associated with training in public speaking. To support Birchoff's point, we examine a phenomenon associated with a recent economic recession. The year 1982 was troublesome for many people; double-digit unemployment was rampant across the country. Two cities particularly hard hit by the recession were Detroit and Pittsburgh. It is interesting to note that in spite of the high unemployment rates in these two cities, the Dale Carnegie Institute experienced near-record enrollments in its relatively expensive course entitled Effective Speaking and Human Relations. In fact, the unions of many of the unemployed workers subsidized tuition payments, apparently signifying a belief that communication training will produce an

[5]Pamela M. Birchoff, "Increasing Employability," *Change*, June-July 1978, p. 67.

edge in the job market.[6] Also related to Birchoff's point, Charles Stewart and William B. Cash report that job interviewers consider *inadequate communication skills* to be the most annoying behaviors displayed by job applicants.[7]

The results of numerous surveys further support the link between employability and skill in public communication. In 1978, the engineering college of Colorado State University asked its graduates of the preceding eight years to indicate which of the university's communication courses were of greatest value to an engineering career. Among the courses rated highest in importance was *public speaking.*[8] In the same year, the business administration college at the University of Minnesota conducted a similar study. Alumni with undergraduate and MBA degrees were asked to rate the importance of a variety of skills relevant to careers in business. Again, skill in oral communication was very high on the list of both groups of graduates.[9] Employers are looking for people who have the facility to present information to the many public audiences of the modern organization. The job applicant who can speak clearly, concisely, forcefully, and sensibly will have a decisive edge when it comes to obtaining initial employment.

Public Speaking and Job Advancement

At this point, you may not be thinking a great deal about entering the job market, but the time for job hunting will come more quickly than you might imagine. Naturally, gaining your first position within your chosen career field will be important. It also will be important for you to have the skills necessary to advance within your field. You remember Peter Smythers' surprise when he learned that public speaking was a required course in the electrical engineering curriculum. Peter did not see the connection between being an effective speaker and an effective engineer.

It is fortunate that the professionals who designed Peter's major are well aware of the connection. They know it is not enough to have great ideas; all too often one has to convince others that the ideas are, in fact, great. One large Midwestern university asked a randomly selected group of graduates in a great variety of occupations to rank a group of

[6]Susan Antilla, *USA Today,* February 17, 1983, p. 1B.

[7]Charles J. Stewart and William B. Cash, Jr., *Interviewing: Principles and Practices,* 2nd ed. (Dubuque, Iowa: Brown, 1978), pp. 153-154. See also Charles S. Goetzinger, Jr., *An Analysis of Irritating Factors in Initial Employment Interviews of Male College Graduates,* doctoral dissertation, Purdue University, Lafayette, Ind., 1954.

[8]"Instruction in Communication at Colorado State University" (Fort Collins: College of Engineering, Colorado State University, July 1979). Cited by Samuel L. Becker and Leah R. V. Ekdom, "That Forgotten Basic Skill: Oral Communication," *Association for Communication Administration Bulletin, 33:* 12-25 (1980).

[9]Edward Foster et al., "A Market Study for the College of Business Administration, University of Minnesota, Twin Cities, Minnesota" (Minneapolis and St. Paul: University of Minnesota, November 1978). Cited by Becker and Ekdom, *Association for Communication Administration Bulletin,* pp. 12-25.

communication skills with respect to how important each skill was within their present jobs. The graduates placed *giving information* and *persuading* both individuals and groups high on their list. When the graduates were asked to recommend classroom activities which they regarded as most valuable, impromptu speechmaking, persuasive speech-making, anxiety-reduction exercises, and informative speechmaking were the top four suggested activities.[10] Yet another research study surveyed business college graduates and asked them to list those communication skills they wish they had been taught while a college student. Second only to listening was *public speaking and the presentation of technical information.*[11]

People in business and industry are well aware of the need to have employees who can communicate effectively with one another and with the public. In fact, the business world expends large amounts of money to provide their employees with the same instruction you will receive in your public-speaking class. It is not uncommon for "executive communication schools" to charge as much as $675 per student for a two-day course designed to teach corporate executives how to prepare and deliver an effective public speech.[12]

We are confident you will find the skills of public speaking to be valuable to you now and later as you search for employment, seek to advance within your profession, and assume an important and full-functioning role as a member of a democratic society.

Achieving Social Responsibility

Your college education will serve you even better than it does now if it provides you with the skills and abilities needed to become a full-functioning member of our democratic society—a person with both the willingness and ability to increase our understanding and knowledge of the world, and a person who provides a source of inspiration in times of stress and persuades us to change erroneous beliefs and unproductive attitudes when necessary.

Each of us will undoubtedly perform these roles to varying degrees. Few among us will ever aspire to or achieve public office, but all of us will have the *need,* the *opportunity,* and the *right* to participate in processes of public discussion and debate, which are the major decision-making tools of our society. Should you remain skeptical and think of public speaking as an activity engaged in only by politicians and few others, remember that "real people" do, in fact, give speeches. Kathleen Kendall interviewed over two hundred randomly selected members of the blue-collar population of Albany, New York. Among the questions

[10]James W. Lohr, "Alumni Use of Communicative Activities and Recommended Activities for the Basic Course: A Survey," *The Speech Teacher, 23:* 248-251 (1974).

[11]Vincent DiSalvo, David C. Larsen, and William J. Seiler, "Communication Skills Needed by Persons in Business Organizations," *Communication Education, 25:* 269-275 (1976).

[12]Ron Scherer, "Executives Bone Up on Holding an Audience," *Christian Science Monitor,* August 24, 1979, p. 6.

asked was, "In the last two years, how many times have you spoken to a group of ten or more people at once?" Approximately one-half of the respondents indicated that they had given what can be considered a public speech at least once during the specified time period.[13] Also of interest in the study was the finding that the frequency of public speaking was related to the educational level of the respondent; specifically, as the educational level of the worker increased, so did the frequency with which that person engaged in public speaking. Let's return to Peter Smythers, our aspiring engineer, and see what life might be like for him a few years after graduation. As we rejoin Peter, he has completed his degree and found just the job he had hoped for—a programmer for a major firm specializing in computer software. On Monday of a not unusual week, Peter travels to his company headquarters for purposes of making a formal presentation to senior programmers on a new technique he has devised. When he returns to his office on Tuesday, the boss informs Peter he will be the company's representative at a careers conference sponsored by the local high school. He will be giving a 15-minute speech on careers in computer technology and then responding to students' questions about the field. On Wednesday night, Peter attends a meeting of his church's administrative board. The church has been considering the purchase of a minicomputer to enhance its information management tasks. Some members of the board are not certain the purchase is warranted. Peter is convinced the church should move in this direction and speaks on behalf of purchasing the computer. Our engineer is glad when the meeting adjourns early because he must return home and look over his notes for a presentation he will be making to his Kiwanis Club on Thursday at noon. As campaign chairman for his city's United Appeal, Peter will be explaining the year's campaign plans, and the presentation to fellow Kiwanians will be the first of many such presentations he will be making.

Peter may not be a typical individual, but he is far from being unique. Your opportunities to practice public speaking are and will continue to be practically limitless, whether it be on the job, in clubs and service organizations, in politics, or in our schools and religious institutions.

Summary

1. Public speaking is a pragmatic activity that requires effort, study, and practice.
2. Among the skills that can be acquired through the study of public speaking are the abilities to choose and narrow meaningful topics, research topics, formulate and support positional statements

[13]Kathleen Edgerton Kendall, "Do Real People Ever Give Speeches?" *Central States Speech Journal, 25:* 233-235 (1974).

through evidence and argument, adapt ideas to audiences, choose language that most effectively presents one's views, and speak with confidence, enthusiasm, and effectiveness.

3. The skills associated with the study of public speaking have carry-over value, that is, they assist you in a variety of academic pursuits and leadership roles.

4. Your employability and career advancement opportunities may well be associated with your abilities as a public communicator.

5. All people who live in a democratic society have the need, opportunity, right, and responsibility to participate in public discussion and debate—our principal tools of decision making.

Questions and Exercises _____

1. If public speaking is a required course for you, ask one or more professors who teach within your major field why the course is part of your curriculum. Summarize your findings in a short paper.

2. Talk with several individuals who are practicing professionals in the field for which you are training. How do they use public speaking in their work? How often do they have to give some form of a speech? What kind of speeches do they give? What difficulties do they experience when preparing and presenting a speech? Do they have any advice to offer students?

3. Your authors claim that the study of public speaking can improve written communication. List at least three skills which oral and written communication have in common. Can you think of any skills which are unique to one or the other form of expression?

4. Your text cites a survey which reports fear of public speaking as the main fear of many people. Why do you suppose this is so? What is there about the public-speaking situation which makes the experience so frightful?

5. Explain what Quintilian had in mind when he characterized the orator as "the good man speaking well."

6. Visit a meeting of your local city council or similar body. Who appear to be the most effective members? How did you come to your judgment? How do the public-speaking abilities of the more effective members compare with those who are less effective?

7. Talk with a representative of your college's placement service. Ask the question, "What do employers look for in an employee?" Compare the response with information contained in Table 1-1. What similarities and differences do you observe?

8. Your authors claim that acquiring skill in public speaking is closely linked with what they call "achieving social responsibility." Explain their viewpoint and offer your opinion on the relationship.

Courtesy Gerald R. Ford Library

Public Speaking:
A Process View

OBJECTIVES

By the time you finish reading this chapter, you should be able to:

1. Define *public speaking.*
2. Explain why public speaking was such a vital part of early Greek society.
3. Recall and define the Aristotelian forms of proof.
4. Name the five canons of rhetoric and explain the composition of the subject matter of each.
5. Re-create select models of communication.
6. Identify the ingredients of the communication process in general and the public speaking process in particular, explaining each ingredient's role.
7. Offer definitions for *source, message, channel, receiver, noise, common life space,* and *context.*
8. Explain the concept of circular response and relate it to a process view of public speaking.
9. List three potential purposes that a public speaker might have.
10. Explain how the purpose of a speech cannot be determined apart from a consideration of the audience.

In Chapter 1 we make the claim that many benefits are to be derived from the study of public speaking. Yet we still have not specified the exact subject matter of the area. To do this is not an easy task. Try defining biology, philosophy, or even art. Public speaking presents no exception, and any definition we offer will probably not include all phases of the subject matter. For a starting point and working definition, we will consider public speaking to be *a form of public communication in which one individual (a speaker) intentionally and overtly attempts to affect others (an audience) through sustained oral discourse (a speech).* In the remainder of the present chapter we go beyond this simple definition to recount the rich tradition associated with public speaking. We will place it within the contemporary study of communication, explaining the purposes for which individuals utilize it and identifying its elements and process nature.

Public Speaking: Its Classical Heritage _____

There were public speakers before there were teachers of public speaking or theorists writing on the art and craft of speechmaking. Although no record of the first public speech exists, it probably occurred when some prehistoric hunter or warrior first rose from all fours to exhort compatriots, through a primitive system of grunts and gestures, to unite in order to hunt more efficaciously or to defeat some common foe. The actual study of public speaking began much later, probably in the fifth century B.C., when two Sicilians (Corax and Tisias) were generally credited as the first writers to lay down a systematic treatment of the principles of speaking in public.

Greek Rhetorical Theory

It was not long until the principal study of public speaking shifted from Sicily to Greece—to Athens in particular. Greece of this "Golden Age" (fifth century B.C.) was much like the United States of the twentieth century. Democracy flourished, with all citizens expected to take an active role in the government. Military and domestic decisions were made by the Assembly, a public forum where all citizens were given the right to speak. Free expression abounded in both the Assembly and within the Athenian judicial system. Here all citizens (males over age 30) were potential jurors, and each citizen served as his own attorney. It was a time when the benefits of possessing oratorical excellence were apparent to all. If a person were wrongfully accused of some heinous crime, there were no Clarence Darrows or F. Lee Baileys to whom one might turn. The Athenian was his own defense attorney, his own advocate. Naturally, then, it was in each citizen's best interest to be as skillful and as effective a communicator as possible.

Because of these demands for effective speaking abilities, it was natural that theoreticians and teachers of public discourse should emerge and rise to prominent positions within Athenian society. The Greeks equated the study of public speaking or persuasive oratory with what they called *rhetoric*.

To capture the flavor of the Greek conception of rhetoric, we turn our attention to the work of Aristotle (384-322 B.C.), a student of Plato and a leading, if not the foremost, theorist of his day. In his book entitled *Rhetoric*, considered by many to be among the most significant of all works on speechmaking, Aristotle detailed a three-part analysis of public discourse. To him, rhetoric was "the faculty of observing in any given case the available means of persuasion."[1] In Book I of his work, Aristotle offered a threefold division of public speeches. He classified them as *deliberative*—speeches of the legislative assembly, which dealt

_____

[1]Aristotle, *Rhetoric*, 1.2.1355b, trans. W. Rhys Roberts (New York: The Modern Library, 1954), p. 24.

with propositions relating to present and future courses of action; *forensic*—speeches of the courts of law, which related to issues of guilt, innocence, justice, and injustice; and *epidectic*—speeches devoted to either praising or blaming the political and military leaders of the day. In his first book, Aristotle also detailed the principal means through which speakers give credence to ideas and subsequently gain audience acceptance of their assertions. These forms of proof were three in number; he termed them *ethos* (ethical proof), *pathos* (emotional proof), and *logos* (logical proof). Aristotle observed that with the first type (*ethos*) we comply with the attempts of a speaker because we perceive him or her to be intelligent, of good character, and an individual who has our own best interests at heart. Thus, we respond to what contemporary communication theorists would call *source credibility*. At other times, the influence source gains compliance by stirring our emotions and aligning his or her proposal with our affective responses (*pathos*). Or a speaker can gain acceptance of ideas and compliance with proposals through presenting evidence and the skillful reasoning from that evidence (*logos*). The careful reader will note that these ancient *forms of proof* continue to permeate the study of public speaking and appear in various forms in several chapters of this text.

In Book II, Aristotle established himself as a highly insightful "audience psychologist," presenting a comprehensive analysis of human emotion and establishing the importance of a speaker adapting his or her arguments to the wants and needs of the audience. In the final book, we learn Aristotle's view on the use of delivery (the use of voice and gesture) and language in achieving rhetorical effectiveness.

Our description of Aristotelian rhetorical theory is far from complete; however, it should be apparent that rhetoric (public persuasive speaking) was a principal means by which Greek society sought "truth." Furthermore, rhetoric was a primary medium for disseminating information to the populace, and it was the mechanism through which policies were assessed and future courses of action determined. With some reluctance, we leave this abbreviated discussion of Aristotle. The next section recounts Roman rhetorical tradition, to acquaint you further with the classical heritage of public speaking and to locate the beginnings of many of the pedagogical approaches taken by this text.

Roman Rhetorical Theory

Chief among the Roman rhetorical theorists was Cicero, who lived during the first century B.C. A lawyer and political leader, he was not only a rhetorical theorist but also a practitioner. Many scholars consider him to be the foremost orator of his day and place him among the first who approached his study from what are termed the five canons of rhetoric—*inventio, dispositio, elocutio, pronunciatio-actio,* and *memio.*

A contemporary term for *inventio* is *invention,* or *discovery.* Fundamental tasks of the speaker were to discover what should be said within a particular context, to choose the arguments that would best advance a cause, to find appropriate and persuasive evidence to support those arguments, and to choose those forms of proof most likely to bring about compliance. Once ideas and arguments were discovered, they had to be arranged in a proper order. This was the concern of *dispositio,* or what we today call *organization.* After ideas had been selected and appropriately ordered, language had to be chosen to make those ideas clear and compelling. This was the subject matter of the third canon—*elocutio,* or what we refer to as use of *language* or *style.* A fourth canon, *pronunciatio-actio,* focused on the speaker's use of voice and bodily action in the presentation of a message. *Memio,* or memory (the "treasure house of ideas"), was important to the Romans; they memorized many speeches. Although we no longer place such emphasis on memorization, we still expect the speaker to display command of the subject matter.

These five canons still serve to organize the study of public speaking. Examine the table of contents of this text. Note how the chapter titles and the topics within the chapters relate to the discovery of information, its organization, the use of language, and the delivery of public discourse. Even though our understanding of and approach to communication variables has improved and changed since these early thinkers evolved a theory of speechmaking, many of the concepts remain viable today.

Public Speaking and Contemporary Communication _____

The contemporary approach to the study of public speaking can best be described as an amalgamation of what we have previously presented as a *classical* or *rhetorical* approach and what we now term the *communication theory* perspective. In the mid to late 1940s, certain scientists and engineers formulated principles of communication that were applicable regardless of the context in which the communicative activity occurred.

An Early Communication Model

The traditional rhetorical perspective emphasized the changing of attitudes, beliefs, and behaviors. By contrast, the new approach was concerned with the *fidelity* of a communication system, the ability of the system to produce "outputs" that correlated significantly with "inputs." Claude E. Shannon and Warren Weaver were among the first to schematize the process of communication, identifying the ingredients of the system and visualizing them in a form that resembled an electrician's diagram of a circuit (see Figure 2-1).[2]

[2]Claude E. Shannon and Warren Weaver, *The Mathematical Theory of Communication* (Urbana, Ill.: University of Illinois Press, 1949), p. 5.

FIGURE 2-1 Shannon and Weaver model of communication. (From C. E. Shannon and W. Weaver, *The Mathematical Theory of Communication,* ©1963 by the University of Illinois Press, Champaign, Ill. Reprinted by permission.)

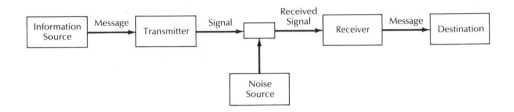

Such a visualization is called a *communication model.* Here we are using the term *model* in a way that may not be familiar to you. Unlike a model of a plane or automobile, a communication model does not stand as a small-scale replica of the object it represents. Rather, as Gerald Miller suggests, a communication model stands "as a kind of classificatory system that enables one to abstract and to categorize potentially relevant parts of the process."[3] You will note that Shannon and Weaver envision communication as a process in which a *source* of information encodes a *message* in the form of a *signal* that is *transmitted* through a *channel* to a *receiver,* where it is subsequently decoded. A key feature of the model is *noise*—stimuli that distort or otherwise interfere with the signal. Static on a telephone line is *noise,* just as lights buzzing and radiators hissing might be *noise* in your classroom. These stimuli compete with a speaker's presentation for your attention and make it difficult for you to receive signals with fidelity. Still other models emphasize different aspects of the communication process.

Communication as Process

Although some representations seem to suggest that communication is linear in nature (moving from a source *to* a receiver), Richard Whitman and Paul Boase suggest a model that emphasizes the *process* nature of communication (see Figure 2-2).[4] They observe that within any communicative activity the parties of the interaction can operate to varying degrees as both sources and receivers of messages. The model creators also incorporate *noise* and a *common life space* (an area of experience shared by the interactants). The Whitman/Boase model stresses that interactants perform encoding and decoding functions, perhaps simultaneously. As a public speaker, you will be primarily a

[3]Gerald R. Miller, *Speech Communication: A Behavioral Approach* (Indianapolis: Bobbs-Merrill, 1966), p. 53.

[4]Richard F. Whitman and Paul H. Boase, *Speech Communication: Principles and Contexts* (New York: Macmillan, 1983), p. 31.

FIGURE 2-2 The Whitman/Boase model of communication. Key: ————— primary message; •—•—•— external self-feedback; — — — internal self-feedback; S = stimulus in external perceptual field; s = stimulus in internal perceptual field. [Reprinted by permission from Richard Whitman and Paul Boase, *Speech Communication* (New York: Macmillan, 1983).]

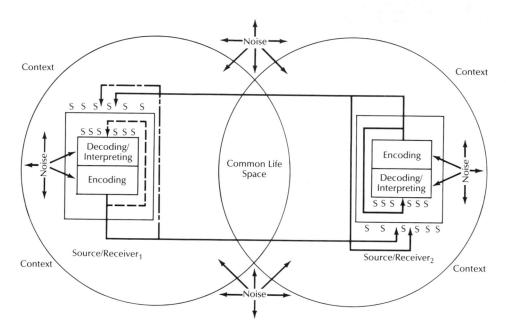

sender or a source (an encoder) of messages, but even as you speak, your audience will be sending you messages (feedback) which you must interpret (decode) as you continue speaking. You will adjust your message, as best you can, to the changing nature of the situation. This model also reminds us that any single message is only one stimulus event within the perceptual field of another party. As a speaker, you should note that there are many things within the immediate environment (external perceptual field) that will compete for your listeners' attention. If you are less than compelling as a speaker, your audience may attend instead to their own thoughts and feelings (stimuli of their internal perceptual field).

There are dangers associated with the use of models. By their very nature, communication models are abstractions. From the complex array of variables that compose communicative interaction, the model-builder selects only a few, presumably those variables most crucial to explaining and understanding the depicted event. In addition, communication is an ongoing process. Two-dimensional pictorial representations do not readily reflect this orientation. Just as a road map represents or displays a certain territory, a communication model holds a similar relationship to the event it represents. A map is not the territory, and a communication model is not the reality that is communication.

Public Speaking: The Ingredients of a Process _____

The communication models we have observed are essentially context-free. By this we mean that they attempt to describe how communication occurs, whether the interactants are members of a dyad, a small group, or an audience. In the section that follows, we are less abstract; we focus on the public-speaking (one-to-many) context, isolating the variables of the communicative event and specifying the role played by its various ingredients. Specifically, we will focus on the speaker, the speech, the audience, the process nature of public speaking, the occasion, and the purposes of speechmaking.

The Speaker (Source)

In many communicative situations it is difficult to determine who is the primary source of information (speaker) and who are the receivers (listeners). The public speaking event is different. Dyadic and small-group communication functions best when the role of speaker and listener constantly shifts. First one individual and then another presents information and ideas, with the former information source assuming the role of listener. Such free exchange typically does not occur in the one-to-many context. Here, the primary source of information is always clear—it is the individual standing at the front of the room, above the crowd, who is the more-or-less constant focus of attention. Under what other circumstances do we so completely reveal ourselves to so many others as when we give a public speech? We stand alone and through our speech reveal some of our attitudes and beliefs, our facility with language, our reasoning process, and numerous other personal characteristics. We give our audience, by the very nature of the event, every opportunity to formulate evaluative judgments of us.

As a speaker, you will discover that your attitudes toward yourself, your message, and your audience are of vital importance. It is imperative to approach the public-speaking situation with self-confidence. Should you find that you lack positive self-regard, note that your confidence can be developed through the type of experience you will have in your public-speaking class. Once you begin to discover what is expected of you and have several opportunities to "test the waters," your confidence will also develop—provided, of course, that you truly make the necessary effort.

It is equally important for you to have confidence in your message. Your effectiveness will be greatly enhanced if you choose topics and approaches that are of real value to your audience. Your classroom audience for each of your speeches will consist of approximately twenty-five people. If you speak 7 minutes, you have approximately 175 minutes at your disposal. Do not waste it!

In Chapter 7 we devote considerable attention to the concept of *source credibility,* a special kind of attitude which receivers of information hold regarding the source of that information. Your effectiveness as a public speaker frequently is dependent on how positively an audience perceives you. Unless you are perceived as both competent to speak on a particular topic and as a messenger worthy of belief, your ability to affect others will be severely limited. Such positive perceptions do not result by chance, but are generated when the speaker approaches the audience with an attitude of respect and concern. Your audience members will not view you as a competent communicator unless you care enough about them to research your speech subjects carefully. It is also unlikely that you will be accorded trustworthiness unless you have the best interest of the audience at heart.

The Speech (Message)

From the communication models we have presented, you may have received the erroneous impression that there is but a single message involved in a communicative interaction. A public speaker is the source of many messages—some of them verbal and others nonverbal, some of them intended and others unintended. Public speaking is a multi-channel communication system, but it primarily involves the senses associated with sight and sound. However, at times the effective speaker will use all five of his or her audience's senses to achieve a particular outcome.

Consider the case of Norm Harris, a student in a public-speaking class. It is Norm's turn to speak. When his instructor calls upon him, Norm shuffles to the front of the room; he lacks vigor and enthusiasm. For four of the seven to ten minutes allotted to him, Norm "hems and haws," and speaks in vague generalities. Then he concludes his speech with the dull phrase, "Well, I guess that's about it," and returns to his seat with the same lack of enthusiasm characterizing his approach to the podium. If we consider *only* the words uttered by Norm (his verbal message), we might decide that his message was "we should oppose all attempts to link student financial aid to draft registration." But when we consider the *total substance* (verbal and nonverbal message) of the presentation, we might come to a different set of conclusions, including that Norm (1) was unprepared, (2) was not very committed to his position, (3) lacked respect for his audience, or (4) really did not care if he gave the speech or not. It is important to note that public speaking is a form of communication in which a speaker consciously and intentionally attempts to create predetermined effects within his or her audience. It is at the same time useful to keep in mind that audiences may assign message value to behaviors and actions not intended by the speaker. Norm did not intend to send the message that he was lackadaisical and unprepared to speak. But his audience perceived a message where none was intended. In Chapter 13 we discuss in detail the various nonverbal codes that might be employed by the public speaker.

The Audience (Receiver)

Many of the decisions you make as a public speaker should be made only after a careful consideration of your audience. The topic selected, the manner in which you approach the topic, the central position you advance, the explanations you offer, the evidence you present, and the arguments you choose to advance all gain effectiveness only to the extent that they are audience-centered. To illustrate this point, let us suppose that one of your classmates has delivered a speech in which he or she has attempted to convince you to buy American-made rather than foreign-made automobiles. To support the position, the speaker argues that the American-made car (1) is more powerful, (2) has more interior room, and (3) is more prestigious. Unless the members of your class are greatly different from the 5,000 car drivers recently surveyed by J. D. Power & Associates (an automotive research firm), such a speech would not be effective. The survey revealed that dependability, initial purchase price, and fuel economy are the top three concerns of today's buyer.[5] The student's speech was, therefore, not well adapted to the concerns of the audience. No matter how artfully such a speech is presented, it will be off the mark if it does not address the concerns important to the audience. Similarly, you may know a great deal about raising chickens in Nigeria, but unless you can adapt such a subject to the needs and interests of your audience, this topic may not be your best choice for a speech.

The effective speaker constantly searches the audience for clues that reveal perception of his or her message. Do the members of the audience understand? Should more be said? Should more evidence be presented? Are the members of the audience enjoying the speech? The audience is usually relatively passive, giving few cues to reveal their evaluation of the speaker's performance. They smile politely, nod occasionally, and even applaud at the end of speeches with which they disagree. Sometimes audience response is obviously either positive or negative, but all too frequently the response is ambiguous and hard to evaluate. Nonetheless, the speaker is well advised to maintain vigilance and to adjust, where possible, to the changing nature of the situation.

The Process

Like communication in general, speechmaking creates a dynamic system in which all ingredients interact to produce an event. Perhaps it is best viewed as a *circular process*. By this we mean that a speaker initiates a message that is subsequently received by audience members

---

[5]Ruth Hamel, "We Still Think Japanese Cars Are a Better Deal," *USA Today*, March 7, 1983, p. 1B.

who, in turn, react or respond. The speaker processes (or assigns some meaning to) the responses of the audience. Then, he or she generates further messages that are adjusted in a manner that better elicits favorable audience response. Study one of your teachers who is particularly skillful. Notice how the circular nature of the speechmaking process operates in his or her classroom. The instructor is undoubtedly acutely aware of students' responses, knowing when the students do not understand and repeating a point or explaining a particularly difficult point in first one way and then in another, if necessary. Notice, too, how audience response shapes the behaviors of the speaker. Stories abound about classes that have "conditioned" the behaviors of their teacher. One such anecdote involves a large introductory psychology class. The topic of study was operant conditioning, a learning theory which argues that behaviors are learned and shaped through applications of positive and negative reinforcement. The class met in a large lecture hall with numerous students in attendance. The course instructor did not realize that the class had collectively agreed to apply what they had learned, with the instructor the subject of their experiment. Every time the professor moved to the left of the room, the class would look puzzled, confused, and be unresponsive to the professor's attempts at humor. But any time the professor made a movement to his right, they displayed interest, understanding, and enthusiasm. They even greeted tired humor with raucous laughter. Where do you suppose the professor found himself positioned as the bell announcing the end of the class rang?—as far to his right as he could get without falling off the stage from which he was speaking. Our story may overdramatize the *circular response* nature of speechmaking, but it does illustrate the process nature of the public-speaking situation.

The Occasion (Context)

Many speeches are given *because* of a specific occasion. Presidents' Day, the 4th of July, and Veterans Day are special occasions that seem to demand speeches as a part of commemorative activity. It is quite unlikely that your speeches, at least in your public-speaking class, will be given in response to such occasions. Yet, it will perhaps be productive for you to think of your speech as occurring in a particular situation—as a part of what communication theorists term the *context of communication.* Joseph DeVito maintains that a communication context has four major dimensions, each interacting with the other.[6] The

_____

[6]Joseph A. DeVito, *Communicology: An Introduction to the Study of Communication* (New York: Harper & Row, 1978), pp. 10-11.

physical dimension is the concrete environment in which the speech occurs. In your immediate circumstances, it will be your classroom, and this will remain relatively constant or controlled during each of your speechmaking efforts. The *social* dimension includes the normative standards and mores operative within the society at the time of your speech. The *psychological* dimension relates to the degree of formality and friendliness of the situation. You will discover that your classmates will usually provide you with a sympathetic and supportive audience. After all, you are "all in the same boat," all taking a turn standing alone. They will empathize with you as you speak and will want you to be successful. But keep in mind that this is not always the case. Frequently, public speakers are in highly hostile, adversarial contexts. Imagine a university president announcing to the faculty senate that all salaries will be cut by 10 percent for the next contract year, or the situation faced by an advocate of abortion on demand speaking to a group of right-to-life advocates. A final dimension of context is *temporal* in nature. All communication occurs at a particular point in time, coexisting with numerous other events and preceding and following still other relevant occurrences.

The context is a highly significant ingredient of the speechmaking process. Topic selection and treatment, choice of arguments, and even word selection become effective only to the extent that they are appropriate to the speaker and audience *in a specific context.*

Purpose

Public speaking is a purposeful act. It does not occur by chance. Public speaking is at its best when it is undertaken to support a central position or *thesis sentence* (see Chapter 4, pp. 48-52). Positional statements are usually stated as simple, declarative sentences, such as "Numerous myths exist regarding herpes," "The voting age should be raised to 21," or "Education is our hope for the future." All such theses are advanced with a particular purpose in mind, a purpose determined primarily through the speaker's analysis of predispositions residing within an intended audience. To Cicero, the aims of speeches were threefold, namely *docere* (to teach), *delectare* (to please), and *movere* (to move). Our position within this text will be similar to this ancient classification. We name the principal purposes as follows: (1) informing (speaking to create or to add to an audience's information base) and (2) persuading (speaking to convince, stimulate, or actuate). Frequently a speaker will have several purposes in mind, but will probably have one primary purpose. In Chapter 18 we detail additional purposes for speechmaking, speaking for what we term "special occasions."

Summary

1. All who live in a democratic society have the need, opportunity, right, and responsibility to participate in public discussion and debate—our principal tools of decision making.
2. Public speaking is a form of communication in which one individual (a speaker) intentionally and overtly attempts to affect others (an audience) through sustained oral discourse (a speech).
3. Public speaking has a rich heritage, with its pedagogical origins in Greece of the fifth century B.C.
4. Many of the doctrines of ancient Greeks and Romans remain useful in the contemporary study of public speaking. Aristotle presented us with *forms of proof,* and the Romans first organized the study of speechmaking around divisions called *canons.*
5. Whereas the ancient Greeks and Romans equated public speaking with persuasion, the contemporary study of speechmaking has a broader base, including both persuasion and fidelity of information exchange.
6. Communication models serve to organize the ingredients of the communication process and to indicate how they operate in combination and as a process.
7. Among the ingredients of speechmaking are the speaker, the speech, and the audience—all operating within a process and context.
8. Public speaking is purposive. It attempts to *create* or *add* to an information base or to persuade (stimulate, convince, or actuate).

Questions and Exercises

1. Explain the Aristotelian notion of "forms of proof," defining *ethos, pathos,* and *logos.*
2. The Roman writers on public speaking introduced what are known as the five canons. List these canons and describe the subject matter associated with each.
3. Examine the table of contents of this book. How many of the chapters can you associate with one or more of the five canons?
4. Within this chapter, you are exposed to a number of communication models. Can you list any benefits that might result from visualizing the communication process in this form? Are there any disadvantages that might result?
5. List what you consider to be the key ingredients of the public-speaking situation. Try arranging the ingredients in the form of a verbal-pictorial model.

6. Examine the Whitman/Boase model of communication presented in Figure 2-2. Why have the creators of the model chosen to call the parties of communicative interaction *source/receivers*?

7. What is meant by the term *source credibility*? What characteristics would you associate with a speaker with high source credibility? With low source credibility?

8. Your authors maintain that an effective public speech can be viewed as producing a *circular response*. Explain this concept by illustrating how it might operate in a public speech.

9. Provide examples of speeches that illustrate the purposes of informing, convincing, stimulating, and actuating.

Photo by William Stempien

3

Developing Confidence as a Speaker

OBJECTIVES

By the time you finish reading this chapter, you should be able to:

1. Identify speech anxiety as a state common to both experienced and inexperienced speakers.

2. Offer a definition of speech anxiety.

3. Describe an approach-avoidance conflict situation, explaining how delivering a speech sometimes fits that classification.

4. Explain how speech anxiety can be overcome through the recognition that it is not an uncommon experience.

5. Explain how shifting the focus of attention from you to your audience and subject can diminish speech anxiety.

6. Explain how a belief in one's subject can lead to diminished speech anxiety.

7. Explain how practice and experience can lead to diminished speech anxiety.

8. Recognize that a certain degree of speech anxiety is desirable if appropriately channeled.

9. Recognize how thorough preparation is the best defense against excessive speech anxiety.

Professional and amateur public speakers share a common problem—speech anxiety. In a recent column, humorist Erma Bombeck assumed the role of the professional lecturer and gave the following advice to all amateur public speakers who would find themselves behind a lectern in the near future:

1. Demand a podium capable of supporting a dead body (yours) up to 187 pounds. Throw yourself over it, being sure to hook your arm over the microphone so you won't slip away.
2. Adhere to the old wives' tale, "Feed a cold crowd, starve a speaker." It cuts down on spitting up.
3. Insist on a table near the restroom. For some unexplained reason, speakers have a kidney wish.
4. Never read a speech. Use note cards which serve a double purpose. You can rearrange them to fit your audience and in the event the person who introduces you uses the jokes on your first eight cards, use the sharp cutting edges on your wrists.[1]

[1]Erma Bombeck, "At Wit's End," *The Messenger,* Athens, Ohio, July 10, 1983, p. B2.

Implicit in Bombeck's advice is the thought that both experienced and inexperienced speakers will approach the public-speaking situation with considerable trepidation. Mark Twain, capable lecturer that he was, remembered how he had felt during the opening of a speech presented early in his career: "The fright which pervaded me from head to foot was paralyzing. It lasted two minutes and was as bitter as death. . . ."[2] Twain considered the experience beneficial, however, and pointed out that experiencing such severe fear "made me immune from timidity before audiences for all time to come."[3] Twain was not alone in his experience. William Jennings Bryan, three times a candidate for the U. S. presidency, indicated that his early efforts at public speaking "called forth more applause from my trembling knees than from the audience."[4] Such initial experience did not deter Bryan, however, who went on to give what has been estimated as 10,000 additional speeches.[5]

No less a speaker than Abraham Lincoln apparently suffered fear of public speaking throughout his career. Witnesses report that for the first few minutes of every address Lincoln "froze in his tracks," "he had a far away prophetic look in his eyes," and "it seemed a real labor to adjust himself to his surroundings."[6] Associating fear with the public-speaking situation is not uncommon. In Chapter 1, we reported on a survey conducted by R. H. Bruskin Associates, which asked people to indicate their greatest fears. Whereas 32 percent reported a fear of heights, 22 percent a fear of financial problems, and 18 percent a fear of sickness or death, over 40 percent reported a fear of speaking in public. In fact, fear of public speaking *headed* the list![7] You should take comfort from the knowledge that speech anxiety is a condition experienced by most public speakers.

Speech Anxiety Defined

If you have ever given a public speech, you probably know what speech anxiety is. You know that as the time for your speech approaches, your heartbeat increases and the adrenalin flows. When your presentation is imminent and you sit in your chair waiting for the person to

[2]Mark Twain, *The Autobiography of Mark Twain,* ed. Charles Neider (New York: Harper, 1959), p. 143.

[3]Twain, p. 143.

[4]Williams Jennings Bryan and Mary Baird Bryan, *Memoirs of William Jennings Bryan* (Philadelphia: John C. Winston, 1925), p. 241. Cited by Myron G. Phillips, "William Jennings Bryan," *History and Criticism of American Public Address,* vol. 2, ed. William Norwood Brigance (New York: Russell & Russell, 1960), p. 894.

[5]Robert T. Oliver, *History of Public Speaking in America* (Boston: Allyn and Bacon, 1965), p. 477.

[6]See Mildred Freburg Berry, "Abraham Lincoln: His Development in the Skills of the Platform," in *History and Criticism,* p. 847.

[7]Reported in *Spectra* (New York: Speech Communication Association, December 1973), p. 4.

introduce you, you are painfully aware that your body does not seem to be enjoying the experience. Your heart is beating fast; you feel uncomfortably warm and sense perspiration on your brow; your stomach sends signals to your brain that it contains a "herd" of butterflies, all struggling to get out. Finally, your name is called and you walk to the podium, vaguely aware of the rubber-like resilience in your legs. You begin to speak. Your voice is higher in pitch than normal, and you have difficulty controlling your breathing. As you reach down to pick up your notecards, you observe a quiver in your hand. Your legs are also trembling. It also occurs to you that you have been staring in the general direction of your audience without "seeing" any single individual. These are the symptoms of speech anxiety.

Scholars have long recognized the existence of this condition, and they have applied various names to this state—stage fright, unwillingness to communicate, apprehension, reticence, shyness, and a term that we prefer, *speech anxiety*. To us, speech anxiety is a condition of intense stimulation, emotional tension, and heightened feeling either brought on by the anticipation of the public-speaking event or manifest during the actual presentation.[8]

Exactly why individuals experience speech anxiety is not altogether clear, but for most of us it probably arises out of a fear of failure. Typically, when we are asked to present a speech, we are flattered. The ego soars at the thought that others are interested in hearing what we think, what we feel, what we consider to be important. If we receive our invitation to speak far enough in advance of the scheduled presentation, we will most likely accept, giving little thought to negative features associated with giving the presentation. But as the day of the speech approaches, we begin to experience building anxiety and ask ourselves, "Why did I agree to do this? What if the audience doesn't like my speech? What if I really bomb out? Who needs this?" What we are experiencing is a classic *approach-avoidance conflict*.[9] More exactly, one feature of our impending event has positive valence associated with it (winning the approval of a particular group of individuals), whereas a second feature of the event has a negative valence (the fear that we will not be well received by the audience). Unless we are able to mitigate this conflict successfully, it is likely that our speech will not be received as we would like it to be. The following suggestions will help make the speech situation more enjoyable for you.

[8]See James C. McCroskey, "Oral Communication Apprehension: A Summary of Recent Theory and Research," *Human Communication Research, 4:* 78-96 (1977); Judie K. Burgoon, "The Unwillingness-to-Communicate Scale: Development and Validation," *Communication Monographs, 43:* 60-69 (1976); Gerald M. Phillips, "Reticence: Pathology of the Normal Speaker," *Speech Monographs, 35:* 39-49 (1968); Philip Zimbardo, *Shyness* (Reading, Mass.: Addison-Wesley, 1977); and Theodore Clevenger, Jr., "A Synthesis of Experimental Research in Stage Fright," *Quarterly Journal of Speech, 45:* 134-145 (1959).

[9]Laurance F. Shaffer and Edward J. Shoben, Jr., *The Psychology of Adjustment* (Boston: Houghton Mifflin, 1956), pp. 110-111.

Overcoming Speech Anxiety Problems _____

Our philosophy of controlling speech anxiety centers on this premise: What has been learned can also be unlearned. We believe that people who experience high levels of speech anxiety have learned to do so and that they can also learn new approaches to speechmaking situations. These new approaches can reduce speech anxiety. While the exact nature of the psychological mechanism accounting for the reduction is not known,[10] the suggestions which follow should help you manage your speech anxiety.

You Are Not Alone

Some public-speaking teachers would suggest that a book of this kind should not include any discussion of speech anxiety. They believe that a discussion of this nature will actually produce fear where it previously did not exist. We do not agree. Certainly, there will be some individuals who may be adversely affected. By and large, however, we believe that the majority of public speakers will experience speech anxiety whether or not they read about it in advance of their presentation. These feelings are common to experienced and inexperienced speakers alike. They are a natural part of the event.

Accurately Appraise the Conditions

It is important to recognize that speech anxiety is not an incapacitating fear. Gerald M. Phillips found in a three-year period at Pennsylvania State University, where about 9,000 students are enrolled in a basic speech communication course, that "only one person . . . required desensitization to get into a frame of mind that permitted instruction."[11] The anxiety associated with presenting a speech may be unpleasant, but it is far from incapacitating. Most people report feeling reduced anxiety toward the end of their introduction, particularly if the introduction elicits some favorable response from the audience. It is also worth noting that we typically see ourselves as more nervous or apprehensive than members of our audience perceive us. Invariably, it is our experience that a student speaker will discuss his or her performance and say something like, "Boy! I was really nervous." On most such occasions, members of the classroom audience will respond with, "It sure didn't seem that way. You appeared very poised and in control." Our experience is not isolated. Research findings generally suggest a weak correlation

_____

[10]William T. Page, "Rhetoritherapy vs. Behavior Therapy: Issues and Evidence," *Communication Education, 29:* 98-99 (1980).

[11]Gerald M. Phillips, "On Apples and Onions: A Reply to Page," *Communication Education, 29:* 107 (1980).

between the degree of stage fright a speaker reports and the degree of fright observed by the audience.[12]

TABLE 3-1 Keys to Overcoming Speech Anxiety

---

1. Recognize that speech anxiety is a common condition, affecting both experienced and inexperienced speakers.
2. Recognize that speech anxiety is not an incapacitating fear.
3. Focus your attention on your message and your desire to communicate, not on yourself.
4. Believe in the content of your speech.
5. Practice and seek out situations that will provide you with needed speaking experience.
6. Prepare thoroughly for any public speech.

Shift the Focus of Your Attention

"I wonder how I look, how I sound. Do they like my ideas? Am I giving a favorable impression to the audience?" If these thoughts are running through your head as you begin to present a speech, the chances are good that the answers to your questions will *not* be favorable. It is important to approach the speaking situation with your focus *not on yourself* but *on your audience*. Remember, you have been invited to speak because someone believed that what you have to say is of value to the audience in question. Your task as a public speaker is to communicate your ideas clearly, forcefully, and effectively. You are not there to impress the audience with your skill and wit. You are there to provide a message of value. Focus your thoughts on your message and your desire to communicate.

Believe in Your Subject

One reason speakers experience high levels of speech anxiety is because they lack confidence in the message they have chosen to present. They suspect that what they have planned will not be of value. Or they suspect a weakness in some of their arguments, a weakness that might not stand up to hostile cross-examination. Either of these situations will produce anxiety, and both can be avoided. If you truly believe in your topic, fear will dissipate. If you are convinced of the value to your audience of what you have to say, you will be less apprehensive. If your arguments are, in fact, sound and well supported with abundant, clear, and recent evidence, you will have less cause for concern. A good salesperson must believe in his or her product. Good speakers must believe in their product, too.

[12]See Clevenger, "A Synthesis of Experimental Research in Stage Fright," pp. 138-193.

Practice and Experience Help

Think back on your first airplane trip. Were you apprehensive days in advance of your scheduled departure? Did your heart beat rapidly as you strapped on your seatbelt? Did you break into a cold sweat as the plane suddenly accelerated down the runway? Did you jump at every strange noise that you heard during flight? Was your relief at landing interrupted by the sound of the sudden and powerful reverse thrust of the engines? These reactions are common to most first-time air travelers and are indicative of a fear of the unknown. For most people, fear of flying dissipates with experience. So it is with public speaking. To inexperienced speakers, the public-speaking situation is an unknown. They do not know what to expect, so they fear the worst. Considerable anecdotal evidence exists to indicate that speech anxiety diminishes with experience and practice. Talk to someone you know who speaks in public frequently—a teacher, a member of the clergy, a lawyer, or an actor. More than likely the person will tell you that with experience will come a reduction (though not an absence) of speech anxiety. It is important to note that a certain degree of speech anxiety is not only normal—it is also desirable. With it, we are more alert and alive. Without it, we may be deadly dull.

Channel Your Nervous Energy

By the time you reach your speaking position behind the lectern, the adrenalin has already begun to flow. Your throat and lips may be dry. Your breathing is likely to be shallow, and your heartbeat strong and rapid. In short, your body is anticipating a task that would require far more energy expenditure than what is needed for the presentation of a speech. Some people release their nervous energy by pacing back and forth for no apparent reason. Others jiggle coins in their pocket. Still others grip the lectern and hang on in what appears to be a "death grip." Why not use your energy to greater advantage? Why not rechannel it into physical activity that amplifies, clarifies, or supports your verbal message? If you find yourself experiencing high levels of tension in the beginning of your speech, think about moving out from behind the lectern and engaging in some physical activity (maybe the display of a visual aid). Release your built-up nervous tension but without attracting undue attention. For the highly apprehensive speaker, here is a cardinal principle: *almost any movement is better than no movement.* As your physical activity drains off tensions, you will find yourself better able to employ meaningful, appropriate action.

Prepare, Prepare, Prepare

The unprepared speaker has reason—very good reason—to be apprehensive, if not downright fearful. Not having researched the subject fully, organized effectively, or rehearsed the phrasing in advance, any speaker, particularly those lacking experience, will approach the speaking situation painfully aware of inadequacies. Out of such awareness undoubtedly will spring a fear of failure and a lack of confidence. Try not to put yourself in such a position. In Chapter 5 we discuss the many phases of the speech-preparation process. Prepare your speech as carefully and extensively as time will permit. Remember, complete preparation involves choosing a topic of value, adapting continually to your audience, organizing clearly and strategically, choosing language that will most effectively express your thought, and continuing to *practice, practice, practice.* There is no substitute for thorough preparation.

Summary

1. Speech anxiety is a condition of intense stimulation, emotional tension, and heightened feeling brought about either by the anticipation of the public speaking event or manifest during the actual speech presentation.
2. Feeling a certain degree of speech anxiety is common to both experienced and inexperienced speakers. It is a natural part of the speaking event.
3. Public speakers typically report feeling a greater degree of speech anxiety than their audience observes.
4. Focusing one's attention on a desire to communicate rather than on one's self can alleviate speech anxiety.
5. A good speaker must believe in his or her message. With confidence in the value of one's message comes diminished speech anxiety.
6. Speech anxiety diminishes with experience and practice, but experiencing a certain degree of it is normal and desirable.
7. Physical activity can help drain off excessive anxiety. It should not, however, attract undue attention.
8. Thorough preparation is the key to controlling speech anxiety effectively. Good preparation leads to self-confidence and confidence in one's message.

Questions and Exercises

1. Interview an individual who gives public speeches frequently. Find out if the individual ever suffers speech anxiety. How does he or she attempt to control it? Have the individual contrast the degree of speech anxiety experienced early in his or her career with the present degree. Is it a fear that has diminished with experience?

2. Think back on your last experience delivering a public speech. Did you suffer from speech anxiety? If you answered "yes," with what physiological changes do you associate feelings of speech anxiety?

3. Speech anxiety is frequently characterized as a classic example of an *approach-avoidance* conflict. Explain what is meant by such a conflict and how public speaking might be so characterized.

4. List three techniques a public speaker might employ in an effort to control speech anxiety.

5. Your authors argue that experiencing a certain degree of speech anxiety can contribute positively to the presentation of a speech. Explain their argument.

6. Do you agree with the authors' assertion that thorough preparation is the best defense against excessive speech anxiety? Why or why not?

7. Observe two public speeches, one by an experienced speaker and one by a person who lacks experience. What behaviors do you associate with speech anxiety? Do you notice more of these behaviors in the inexperienced speaker than in the experienced speaker?

Speech Preparation:
Initial Considerations

Photo by John Tweedle

Choosing a Topic and Purpose

OBJECTIVES

By the time you finish reading this chapter, you should be able to:

1. List three primary general purposes of speeches and explain what is involved within each purpose.

2. Explain how changing an individual's information base might shape future behavior.

3. Differentiate between a speech *to convince* and a speech *to actuate.*

4. Define *affirmation, negation, coercion,* and *persuasion.*

5. Explain the speaker's purpose *to stimulate* within a speech.

6. Define *attitude* and identify its component parts.

7. Illustrate how a speaker might have to both inform and stimulate in order to change a behavior.

8. Provide an example of a speech in which the general purpose of the speaker and the audience's preception of the purpose were at variance.

9. List four factors to consider when selecting a speech topic.

10. Enumerate some resources available within the library that will assist the conscientious speaker/researcher.

11. Differentiate between a speaker's general and specific purposes.

12. Identify two types of statements and their subdivisions that might serve as theses for speeches, providing examples of each.

All communicative activity is purposive or goal-directed. We do not seek out interaction with others at random but do so to meet some objective, to satisfy some need. Sometimes we seek out contact with others for the purposes of gathering information, about ourselves, about others, or about our environment. It is largely through communicative activity that we acquire our self-image, that we develop our self-concept. At other times we seek communicative activity simply because we do not like being alone. We enjoy initiating, developing, and maintaining relationships with our fellow beings. At still other times we communicate simply to avoid or relieve tensions. We have discovered that problems frequently dissipate, or at least appear to, if we just talk about them.

A fundamental purpose of communication in general and public speaking in specific is to influence, to affect others in some way. Communication that has influence as its goals or purpose is termed *instrumental.* Our position throughout this text is that public speaking is an instrumental activity, an activity designed to change some com-bination of knowledge levels, attitudes, beliefs, and behaviors in others.[1]

Determining Your General Purpose _____

If your campus is typical, each week presents numerous opportunities for you to hear public speeches. On Monday of a given week, you might choose to attend a lecture entitled "The Facts and Myths of AIDS." If that subject does not appeal to you, you have only to travel across campus to hear "Who Pays for Crime?" or "Animal Experimentation: A Contemporary Tragedy." On Tuesday you can choose among such topics as "If You Can, Teach," "Plastics as Strong as Steel," and "Draft Registration: The Big Rip-off." Later in the week you can select either an Arab or Jewish account of "The Real Story in the Middle East." At the close of the week, you might have the opportunity to hear "Financing Your College Education Creatively," "Run for Your Life," or "Inner Peace Through Meditation."

Although these topics reflect diverse themes, a close inspection should reveal that each is designed to change some combination of knowledge levels, attitudes, beliefs, and behaviors in others; each has a general purpose of either informing, persuading, or simply entertaining. An important step in the speech-preparation process should be to determine your general purpose. In the classroom situation, this should not be difficult, because your instructor will most likely specify the general purpose for you, prescribing that you present a speech *to inform, to convince, to stimulate, to actuate,* or *to entertain.* Outside the classroom, your general purpose will sometimes be specified for you, but at other times the purpose will be one of your own choosing. It may be that as an employee of a utility company you accept an invitation from a local service club to explain how insulation can cut home energy costs. To assume any general purpose other than informing on such an occasion would violate the terms of your invitation. At other times, the speaker will find greater freedom in his or her choice of general purpose. This is particularly so if a speaker is famous. One typically would not specify a general purpose for a governor, senator, or other dignitary who agrees to speak to a local service club. Rather, one would leave the choice to the speaker, trusting that he or she would address a fundamental, relevant issue. Now let us consider each potential general purpose.

---

[1]For a more comprehensive account of the purposes of communication, see Richard F. Whitman and Paul H. Boase, *Speech Communication: Principles and Contexts* (New York: Macmillan, 1983), pp. 26-30.

Informing: Speaking for Understanding

As a college student, you are probably an expert receiver of informative messages. On an average day, you may learn how to solve quadratic equations, how to prepare a speech, the characteristics of iambic pentameter verse, the difference between a debit and a credit, and the causes of the decline of the Roman Empire. By the time you complete your college education, you most certainly will have heard your share of informative presentations, but you will still retain a constant need to exchange information with others.

The speaker who undertakes the general purpose of informing assumes the sometimes dual burdens of creating an information base in the audience and modifying a preexisting one. On occasion, the speaker will face the situation in which the audience knows little if anything about the chosen topic. Here the task of the speaker is clearly to provide information that, if retained, will be of subsequent value to the various audience members. In Chapter 15 we concentrate on speaking techniques that maximize the amount of learning produced by an informative message. On other occasions, the informative speaker must address what he or she perceives as either an incomplete or erroneous information base. When you add to or modify the information base of another person, you provide the individual with a new way to view the world; you have changed that individual by modifying the information at the individual's disposal as he or she makes choices and arrives at decisions. In other words, to increase or to modify the information base of another is to shape future responses the other is likely to make. To explain clearly to another how to make candles may increase the probability that the individual at some future point actually will make candles or will apply, in a related context, some principle you have taught. Likewise, should you present a speech on alternative energy sources and observe that windmills are not particularly efficient or effective in many sections of the country (because of erratic and low wind speed), that information may guide future decisions of selected audience members. If these members at some future date are tempted to build their own windmill, their decision will undoubtedly be tempered by the data you have added to their information base.

Persuading: Convince, Actuate, and Stimulate

Speeches that seek to modify, change, or reinforce attitudes or behaviors are collectively considered speeches *to persuade*. Traditionally, when the speaker attempts to change or modify an attitude, we classify the general purpose as *to convince*. When the speaker asks for some change of behavior or for a new behavior, we consider the general purpose as *to actuate*. A speech *to stimulate* reinforces attitudes or beliefs already held by the audience. Thus, the speaker who asks an initially hostile audience to accept the position that capital punishment is immoral probably has the general purpose *to convince.* The speaker who calls for us to donate blood to the Red Cross or who seeks money for a political candidate wishes *to actuate.* Finally, a commencement speaker who points to the values of an education is speaking *to stimulate.*

Elsewhere, we give specific advice on how to convince, actuate, and stimulate (see Chapter 17), but here it may be useful to consider how persuasion differs from other forms of interpersonal influence. Suppose your father were to ask you to wash the family car. Chances are that you would seek a reason for not complying with such a request. But what if father "sweetens the pot," saying something like, "If you wash the car for me, you can use it Saturday night?" Your father's chances of having his car washed have improved substantially. But has he persuaded you? What if your father were less benevolent in his approach and said, "Either wash that car or you're not going out of this house until you do." Would your compliance signify that your father has persuaded you? It is our position that such forms of influence, while effective, are not examples of persuasion. In the former case, your father has employed a form of social influence we term *affirmation.* That is, he has sought compliance through the associated promise of a reward. In the latter case, your father has utilized a process somewhat analogous to affirmation but has substituted threats of negative outcome in the place of a promise of reward. This form of social influence we label *negation,* or as some might put it, *coercion.*

The persuader does not bribe or coerce but relies on *mendations* rather than promises, on *warnings* rather than threats, or on the *activation of commitments* to bring about compliance. Here it will be necessary to explain several of our differentiations. We have described the father who sought a clean automobile and *promised,* in one case, its use in return. In another case, the father *threatened* that if the car were not washed, a negative consequence would result. One factor having a bearing on whether such strategies bring about compliance has to be whether the influence source has the power to bestow the promised reward or to carry out the stated threat. Those who employ affirmation, then, offer rewards within their power to confer; those who practice negation suggest threats that they, too, can carry out if compliance does not result.

The persuasive speaker, by contrast, must rely on special kinds of rewards and threats—mendations and warnings. A *mendation* is a type of reward not directly within the power of the influence source to bestow.[2] The persuasive speaker can suggest, for example, that if you

[2]James L. Tedeschi, Barry R. Schlenker, and Svenn Lindskold, "The Exercise of Power and Influence: The Source of Influence," in *The Social Influence Processes,* ed. James T. Tedeschi (Chicago: Aldine-Atherton, 1972), pp. 287-345.

will vote in favor of a tax increase, all of our children will receive a good education. Such a result can be suggested but not guaranteed. Likewise, the persuader can warn that unless we maintain a strong defense, we will be attacked and defeated by the Russians. Here, the speaker can suggest a negative consequence to noncompliance, but cannot guarantee its occurrence.

In addition to utilizing mendations and warnings to bring about compliance, the persuasive speaker has yet another technique at his or her disposal—*the activation of commitments* existing within the target of influence. These commitments are, for the most part, societal norms that individuals do not like to violate. The speaker arguing for euthanasia might suggest that it is morally wrong to prolong life when recovery is not possible, wrong to inflict physical pain on the terminally ill, and wrong to create financial hardships for surviving relatives. To the extent that the audience subscribes to such premises, such an appeal could be effective. Or the speaker favoring the Equal Rights Amendment to the Constitution might suggest that it is unjust to pay equally qualified males and females different salaries for performing the same job. Numerous courts have found this argument persuasive.

Additional General Purposes

Speakers make presentations with yet additional purposes in mind. The speech to entertain, the speech of introduction, of nomination, of acceptance, the speech of goodwill, the speech of welcome and of farewell, and the after-dinner speech are but a few of the special-purpose speeches that scholars have identified. Although our major emphasis in this text is on the more common types of speeches, in Chapter 18 we deal with the expectations associated with special-occasion speeches.

An Intermixture of Purposes

Even if a speech has the *primary* general purpose of *actuating* some behavior, the wise speaker recognizes that before behavioral change will occur it may be necessary to modify attitudes associated with the desired behavior. In a general sense, an attitude can be defined as "a predisposition (or tendency) to respond to stimuli in one way rather than another."[3] Such a definition characterizes an attitude as what social scientists call an intervening variable, an internal state mediating between overt stimuli and observable behavior. Those who assume the existence of attitudes as mediators of behavior take the position that the human organism perceives stimuli and makes an evaluative response to them and that it is this evaluative response which influences subsequent behavior. Thus, the speaker who wishes his or her audience members to

[3]Anita Taylor, Teresa Rosegrant, Arthur Meyer, and B. Thomas Samples, *Communicating* (Englewood Cliffs, N.J.: Prentice-Hall, 1977), p. 125.

make a contribution to the local blood bank first may have to change the listeners' evaluations of the blood-donating process.

But how do you change an attitude? A first step is to recognize that an attitude is a multidimensional construct. Martin Fishbein and Icek Ajzen argue that an attitude is composed of at least three interrelated elements: *affect, cognition,* and *conation.*[4]

Affect refers to one's feelings and evaluations of some person, object, proposition, issue, and so on. *Cognition* describes one's knowledge or beliefs with respect to an attitude object. And finally, *conations* are one's behavioral intentions or degree of response-readiness with respect to or in the presence of the attitude object. This view is what is termed an *information-based theory of attitude.* The implications of such a theory are many. In the present context, it suggests that a speaker may have to change or add to an information base if he or she expects to modify an attitude. Our speaker may discover that people resist donating blood because they hold negative attitudes toward the process, with those negative attitudes rooted in erroneous or incomplete beliefs. For example, the audience may believe that giving blood is time-consuming, painful, and dangerous (*cognitions*). They therefore evaluate (*affect*) those beliefs negatively. If the speaker can modify the information base of the audience, establishing that giving blood can be accomplished quickly, painlessly, and without risk, there is a good chance the attitudes will change and that the desired behavior will result.

In short, a single speech will have one ultimate and primary purpose. To accomplish the purpose might require the formulation of subsidiary purposes. In the case just cited, the speaker had to add to or modify an information base (perhaps reinforcing some preexisting attitudes in the process) and change attitudes before a behavioral change could be accomplished.

Whose Purpose? Yours or the Audience's?

The wise speaker recognizes that what he or she perceives as the general purpose of a speech might not be consistent with the purpose which the audience, or at least some audience members, ascribe to it. Consider the case of the speaker who decides to inform the audience of the benefits of nuclear power and explains that nuclear power is efficient, safe, and plentiful. From the speaker's point of view, the speech is designed as purely informative in nature, with each point developed around "factual" information. But how do you expect an opponent of nuclear power to respond to the speech? It is unlikely that this listener would view it as an innocuous informative lecture. Consequently, we think it is useful to note that different people might assign very different purposes to the same speech.

[4]Martin Fishbein and Icek Ajzen, *Belief, Attitude, Intention and Behavior: An Introduction to Theory and Research* (Reading, Mass.: Addison-Wesley, 1975), p. 12.

Narrowing Your Approach _____

Once you have determined your general purpose, you must decide on a topic for your address. Then you will need to narrow your thoughts down to a specific purpose or *thesis statement*. You will discover that the speech-preparation process is truly dynamic and that a specific purpose can be formulated only when you test it for consistency against the general purpose of the projected speech. You will also have to consider expected audience perceptions and potential reactions. We will come back to this point later, but for now keep in mind that no part of the speech-preparation process is really *completed* until you have presented the address.

Choosing a Topic

Many students, upon receiving a speaking assignment, ask their instructor, "I know I'm supposed to give an informative speech, but what should I talk about?" For a variety of reasons, your instructor cannot be particularly helpful. He or she is unlikely to be aware of your special knowledge or skills, your past experiences, your interests, or your research skills—all factors of potential relevance in topic selection. In general, we think the following questions might be useful to address when you decide on a topic area:

1. How much time do I have to prepare?
2. What special knowledge do I have that is worth sharing with my audience?
3. What topics are of interest to me?
4. What topics appear to be of interest and useful to the members of my audience?
5. What topics will lend themselves to fulfilling the assignment?

Begin Early. Most of us would fail miserably if we waited until mere minutes before our scheduled speech to finalize our topic and ideas. The majority of us appreciate time for preparation. Good speeches, particularly classroom speeches, are the product of considerable preparation and practice. Seldom is a good speech prepared the night before the speaker presents it. Begin your preparation early. Decide on a topic as quickly as possible, and keep in mind that the topic can change as the preparation process unfolds. Many students spend too much time looking for "just the right topic area," and end up with too little time available to develop it. Good speeches go through a maturation process. At the conclusion of one planning session, you may believe that your speech is complete. But when you examine it the next morning, you may find that what seemed clear, fresh, and exciting is now disorganized, mundane, and dull. Allow time for your speech to grow. Mark Twain knew of the efforts associated with speech development. He once remarked that it took him three weeks to prepare a good impromptu (spur-of-the-moment) speech!

Your Special Knowledge. As you search for a speech topic, do not overlook your own experience and special knowledge. Too many students discount what they already know in favor of rushing pell-mell to the library where a "really good" topic might be found. Far be it from us to discourage you from visiting the library, but before making the trip take a few minutes to review and take stock of your existing assets.

Begin with Yourself. Here you may be asking, "What assets? What special knowledge do I have that might suggest a topic?" What about your hobbies, family pets, vacations you have taken, camps you have attended, summer jobs you have held, books you have read, unusual people whom you have met or read about, clubs you have belonged to, sports in which you have participated, parties, workshops, or special courses you have taken? What about your attitudes and beliefs? Do not overlook them. How do you feel about population control, euthanasia, heart and organ implants, the arms race, the federal budget, pornography, capital punishment, unemployment, college athletics, abortion, the electoral college, the Environmental Protection Agency, natural resources, and a host of additional seemingly timeless topics?

What about topics closer at hand? Do you have thoughts, attitudes, and helpful suggestions regarding the policies and practices of your college or university? What about the registration system, general education requirements, the student newspaper, parking regulations, housing regulations, financial charges, financial aid, campus entertainment, library policies, the student code of conduct, the academic calendar, the food service, faculty course evaluations, drop-add policies, academic freedom, faculty tenure, or the procedures for appealing a grade? Do not be guilty of ignoring your immediate environment.

Audience Relevance. Although it is indeed important to draw on your own assets and experiences as you select a speech topic, it is equally important to consider the needs and interests of your audience. You may know more about how to prevent the infestation of parasitic fungi of the order of Uredinales in Canadian wheat than any other person, but unless that topic is of concern to your audience, it is not your best possible choice. As you finalize your selection, it is always a good idea to ask yourself, "Does my audience have a need for this information?" Unless you can come up with an affirmative answer to your query, you would be well advised to continue your search or come up with a way of modifying the topic in question so that it has greater relevance to your audience. In Chapter 19 we will examine how audience members listen. Do not make it even harder for your audience members by asking them to listen to a speech on a topic of little apparent value to them.

Supplementing Your Resources. Many speeches fail because the speaker did not take full advantage of the many resources available to supplement his or her ideas. Begin with your own experience and expertise, but do not be afraid to visit your library, to take advantage of its many sources of information. Encyclopedias, of course, will give you broad information about a topic. More specific information can usually be located within an *index*. Such a work will refer you to articles in specific periodicals relating to your topic. Highly specific facts can frequently be located in almanacs, books of facts, and various statistical abstracts. If you are interested in learning more about a particular person, a biographical reference will be of assistance. Finally, the language-conscious speaker will want to become familiar with various dictionaries and books of quotations. The following is a list of some of the references you may wish to consult:

Encyclopedias

Collier's Encyclopedia
Compton's Encyclopedia and Fact Index
Encyclopedia Americana
Encyclopedia Brittanica
World Book Encyclopedia

Abstracts and Indices

Book Review Digest
Bibliography Index
Business Periodicals Index
Christian Science Monitor Index
Education Index
Humanities Index
Index to Journals in Communication Studies
Psychological Abstracts
Public Affairs Information Service
Reader's Guide to Periodical Literature
Social Science Index
Sociological Abstracts
The New York Times Index
The Wall Street Journal Index
Ulrich's Periodical Dictionary
United Nations Document Index

Almanacs

Information Please Almanac
Reader's Digest Almanac and Yearbook
Statistical Abstract of the United States
The World Almanac and Book of Facts
United Nations Statistical Abstract

Biographical References

Biography Index
Current Biography
Dictionary of American Biography
Dictionary of National Biography
International Who's Who
Leaders in Education
Webster's Biographical Dictionary
Who's Who Among Black Americans
Who's Who in America
Who's Who in Finance and Industry
Who's Who in Law

Dictionaries, Thesauruses, and *Books of Quotations*

A New Dictionary of Quotations on Historical
  Principles from Ancient and Modern Sources
Familiar Quotations
Funk & Wagnall's New Standard Dictionary
Manual of Forensic Quotations
Oxford Dictionary of Quotations
Random House Dictionary of the English Language
Roget's International Thesaurus
Stevenson's Home Book of Quotations
Webster's Third New International Dictionary

Keep in mind that numerous libraries have various special collections and varied information available in what is known as the Vertical File, a repository for pamphlets, brochures, and other publications created by a local librarian. Ask questions! Also keep in mind that many professors and college administrators have abundant information at their command, information they are usually very willing to share if you approach them properly. If you need references on military defense spending, a political science or economics professor can probably assist you. You will also find many authorities in your own community. Are you looking for statistics on crime rates? Why not visit the local police station and see if they can help?

Your Thesis: The Specific Purpose _____

Every good speech will have a single, *simple, declarative sentence* that unifies the entire presentation, subsumes all the ideas of the speech, and serves as the highest-level generality advanced within the speech. This sentence is what is called the *specific purpose* or the *thesis sentence.* How do you get from the general purpose and topic area to a thesis statement? One way is to formulate questions or *problem areas* with respect to the chosen topic. Words such as *what, when, how, why, where, who, by what method, should,* and so on, will provide appropriate questions from which a thesis can be formulated. Let us see what kinds of questions might be generated about the general topic area of photography.

1. What is the best camera to purchase?
2. When did the major innovations in photography occur?
3. How do you take pictures with a 35-mm, single-lens, reflex camera?
4. Why should one learn how to take pictures?
5. Where are the good locations for taking pictures of landscapes?
6. Who are the great sports photographers?
7. By what method is color film developed?
8. Should basic photography be required for the student majoring in news reporting?

We caution that these questions are not examples of thesis statements, but that they are issues (points of some controversy) from which a thesis can be derived. Such questions help you to narrow your research efforts, to focus on the approach that you will be taking in your speech. As you do the preliminary research in your topic area, ask yourself questions beginning with the words *what, when, how, why, where, who,* and so on. The thesis of your speech will be the answer to some question. For example, here are some thesis statements that might follow from the questions on photography:

1. The best camera to purchase is the 35-mm, single-lens reflex.
2. The major innovations in photography occurred over a fifty-year period.
3. There are five steps to effective picture-taking.
4. Picture-taking can be a profitable hobby.
5. Our local area is fertile ground for the amateur photographer.
6. There are three outstanding contemporary sports photographers.
7. New innovations have made it easier for the amateur to develop color film.
8. Basic photography should be required of all news reporting majors.

You will notice that the thesis statement of a speech controls or determines the ideas that are appropriate within the speech itself. If you argue that the 35-mm camera is the best one to purchase, your major ideas should reflect *reasons why.* Should you claim that there are five steps to effective picture-taking, your main points should be *the actual steps* (see Table 4-1).

TABLE 4-1 Theses and Main Points

Thesis: The best camera to purchase is the 35-mm, single-lens reflex.
 	
   I. [Three reasons
  II.   why it
 III.   is best.]
	Thesis: Our local area is fertile ground for the amateur photographer.
	
	   I. [Locations where good
	  II. pictures might
	 III. be taken.]

Thesis: There are five steps to effective picture taking.
 	
   I.
  II.
 III. [The steps involved]
  IV.
   V.
	Thesis: There are three outstanding contemporary sports photographers.
	
	   I.
	  II. [The three photographers.]
	 III.

Thesis: Picture taking can be a profitable hobby.
 	
   I. [Ways you
  II.   can profit
 III.   by taking
  IV.   pictures.]
	Thesis: Basic photography should be required of all news reporting majors.
	
	   I. [Reasons for
	  II. the suggested
	 III. requirement.]

Types of Theses

It also may be useful to note that there are a variety of types of thesis statements. While various authors have come up with differing classification schemes, our approach will be to adopt the system of George W. Ziegelmueller and Charles A. Dause, who classify thesis statements as either *propositions of judgment* or *propositions of policy*.[5]

Judgment. Statements of judgment are descriptions, predictions, or evaluations that assert the past, present, or future existence or worth of something. You will note that propositions of judgment are not facts, but only alleged facts. The following are examples of past, present, and future judgmental propositions.

Past

Francis Bacon wrote the plays currently attributed to William Shakespeare.

Lee Harvey Oswald was an agent of the Russian government.

The Environmental Protection Agency has not yet enforced its own standards.

[5]George W. Ziegelmueller and Charles A. Dause, *Argumentation: Inquiry and Advocacy* (Englewood Cliffs, N.J.: Prentice-Hall, 1975), pp. 14-15.

Present

There are five steps in the speechmaking process.
Russia does not desire war with the United States.
Picture-taking is a profitable hobby.

Future

The Cincinnati Reds will win the World Series this
    year.
The new year will see rapid economic recovery.
A drastic teacher shortage will occur by 1990.

The stated propositions are not facts in the usual sense of the word, for they cannot be proved with certainty. Statements of description (past, present, or future) are really propositions of *fact-probability*—statements the truth of which the speaker can only establish to a limited degree of probability or likelihood.

A second form of the proposition of judgment goes beyond the statement of past, present, or future fact-probability to offer a value judgment, to assert the worth, desirability, fairness, feasibility, and so on of some specified concept. Some examples of such judgmental statements (sometimes called propositions of value) follow:

John Kennedy was a great President.
The Chevrolet Corvette is a better car than the
    Porsche 914.
Capital punishment is immoral.
Modular homes are a good buy.
East Overshoe State is a better university than Old
    Slipshod Prep.

Within these *evaluative propositions of judgment* the speaker must assume dual burdens—establishing appropriate criteria on which a judgment should be made and demonstrating that the object in question possesses the specified criteria. For example, the speaker who would gain his or her audience's acceptance of the proposition that John Kennedy was a great President must convince the audience of (1) the characteristics that make up a great President and (2) the opinion that John Kennedy possessed those characteristics.

Policy. *Propositions of policy* typically call for some change in the *status quo,* our present system, and advocate a course of action that the speaker would like the audience to adopt and follow. In the general sense, these propositions are more complex than propositions of judgment. Typically, the speaker who advocates a change in some system has to describe the present system, demonstrate its inadequacies, propose a more desirable alternative, and show that the proposed policy or course of action is practical and desirable. Some propositions of policy follow:

Congress should be given the power to reverse Supreme Court decisions.

Our university should adopt a pass/fail grading option.

Females should be required to register for the draft.

Conviction for drunk driving should result in a mandatory prison term.

Phrasing the Thesis

When phrasing your thesis, you should keep at least three suggestions in mind: (1) Phrase the thesis as a simple sentence; (2) state the thesis as a declarative sentence; and (3) make the thesis activity-producing. The thesis should be only a single idea that encompasses or concludes your speech. To phrase the thesis as either a complex or compound sentence is to introduce additional ideas that you must defend. In addition, a thesis is a positional statement. Although questions (interrogatives) are useful mechanisms for introducing an idea, they rarely are appropriate thesis statements. Finally, you will discover that it is wise to involve your audience in your topic by asking, where appropriate, that they engage in some activity as a result of your speech. Rather than stating, "Do not support efforts to change our academic calendar to the quarter system," it might be more effective to suggest to your audience, "We *should oppose* efforts to change our calendar to the quarter system." Here you call for involvement rather than inactivity.

Summary _____

1. Speeches *to inform* add to or modify the information base of an audience. When an individual's information base is changed, future behaviors are also "shaped."
2. Speeches *to persuade* attempt to change attitudes (to convince) and behaviors (to actuate) or to reinforce existing attitudes or behavior (to stimulate).
3. The persuasive speaker does not coerce but relies on *mendations* rather than promises, on *warnings* rather than threats, or on the *activation of commitments* to bring about compliance.
4. A speaker might have to accomplish a variety of goals in order to accomplish the primary general purpose of his or her speech. This means that to actuate, one might first have to change knowledge levels and stimulate.
5. An attitude is a "predisposition to response." It is composed of three elements: affect, cognition, and conation.
6. A speaker and an audience might assign very different purposes to the same speech.
7. As you choose a topic for your speech, you should begin early, begin with your own experiences and interests, consider the needs of your

audience, and supplement your personal resources by visiting the library and interviewing experts.

8. The specific purpose of a speech is the thesis statement, a simple, declarative statement that subsumes the entire speech content.

9. Thesis statements are either *statements of judgment* (descriptions, predictions, or evaluations which assert the past, present, or future existence or worth of something) or *statements of policy* (calls for change in the status quo or for a future course of action).

Questions and Exercises _____

1. Explain what is meant by the *general purpose* of a speech. List five of the possible general purposes.

2. Your text maintains that even speeches intended to be informative can influence the behaviors of audience members. Explain this position and offer an example to illustrate the point.

3. Explain how *affirmation* and *negation* differ from *persuasion*. Also differentiate between a *mendation,* a *promise,* and a *warning* as opposed to a *threat*.

4. Speeches frequently have one ultimate general purpose but have an intermixture of subpurposes. Provide an example of a speaking situation that illustrates this viewpoint.

5. List five considerations relevant to the selection of a speech topic.

6. Explain what constitutes a thesis statement. Provide examples of thesis statements appropriate to the general purposes of informing, stimulating, convincing, actuating, and entertaining.

7. Consider the following thesis statements. What errors can you find in the various statements?
   A. The best movies of the year.
   B. What should the United States do about the space program?
   C. Why Federal income taxes should be cut.
   D. Tuition should be frozen at our college, and students should have a greater voice in curricular matters.
   E. The 35-mm, single-lens reflex camera is the best for general use because it is so versatile.

8. Provide examples of past, present, and future judgmental propositions, as well as examples of propositions of policy.

Courtesy of the National Archives/Nixon Project

5

Preparing the Speech

OBJECTIVES

By the time you finish reading this chapter, you should be able to:

1. Contrast the speech-preparation practices of several significant public speakers.

2. List three primary general purposes of speeches and explain what is involved within each purpose.

3. Enumerate some of the demographic characteristics of audiences that will provide useful information to the speaker.

4. Explain how the speaker uses demographic characteristics to make inferences about the audience.

5. Illustrate how "situational demand characteristics" constrain or influence the speaker's choices.

6. Produce a basic speech outline with appropriate symbolization and sub-ordination.

7. List the essential characteristics of good introductions and conclusions.

8. Enumerate a set of guidelines the speaker should follow when responding to questions from the audience.

9. Provide a summary of the steps or phases of the speech-preparation process.

Daniel Webster, undoubtedly among the foremost of all public speakers who have helped to shape our country's history, once referred to his famous "Reply to Hayne" as a speech for which "I have been preparing all my life."[1] In Webster's case, such a statement is only slightly hyperbolic, because the ideas and positions he put forth in that address had, indeed, evolved through his experience, study, and careful thought. As you prepare the assigned speeches of your public-speaking class, Webster's words will take on even greater significance, and you too will discover that your prior learning and experience will be invaluable sources. However, there well may be as many approaches to the actual process of preparing a speech as there are public speakers. In fact, Jonathan Edwards, one of Colonial America's most effective preachers, spent thirteen hours a day researching and preparing sermons. His daily preparations were interrupted only by a brief stint at wood-chopping in the mornings and a horseback ride each afternoon. But

[1]See Robert T. Oliver, *History of Public Speaking in America* (Boston: Allyn and Bacon, 1965), p. 92. Within this speech, Webster makes a strong case for the preservation of the Union.

even as he rode, Edwards continued the preparation process, constantly jotting down ideas that might prove useful for a sermon he was preparing.[2]

Contrasting methods of speech development were employed by "The Shakespeare of the Pulpit," Henry Ward Beecher. An outstanding preacher and a leader in the abolitionist movement, Beecher practiced a relatively unique method of speech preparation, a method that would spell certain disaster for most of us. It was his usual practice to retire to his study an hour before church services were to begin. Only then did he work out the final details of his scheduled sermon. But Beecher should not be considered a complete procrastinator. He explained his method as follows:

> I know what I am going to aim at, but, of course, I don't get down to anything specific. I brood it, and ponder it, and dream over it, and pick up information about one point and another but if I ever think I see the plan opening up to me I don't dare to look at it or put it down on paper. If once I write a thing out, it is almost impossible for me to kindle to it again. I never dare nowadays, to write out a sermon during the week; that is sure to kill it. I have to think around and about it, and get it generally read, and fuse it when the time comes.[3]

There are, obviously, many ways to prepare an effective speech. Nonetheless, within this chapter we recommend just one set of procedures. Many of the topics of this chapter are covered in greater detail elsewhere in this text. Our goal here is to present in one location an overview of all "steps" involved in the creation and presentation of a speech. Specifically, our approach to the speechmaking process centers around five topics: Formulating Your Approach, Anticipating the Situation, Focusing Your Approach, Rehearsing and Presenting Your Presentation, and Responding to Questions. We think you will find our approach somewhat less demanding than what Jonathan Edwards might like but a bit more systematic than the practices of Henry Ward Beecher. The approach is summarized in Table 5-1.

Formulating Your Approach _____

Communicative activity is purposive or goal-directed. Public speaking is no exception. The speaker hopes to affect others in some way through the presentation. We have entitled the first step in the speech-preparation process "Formulating Your Approach." Within this step, the speaker

---

[2]See Orville A. Hitchcock, "Jonathan Edwards," in *A History and Criticism of American Public Address,* vol. 1, ed. William Norwood Brigance (New York: Russell & Russell, 1960), p. 233.

[3]See Lionel Crocker, "Henry Ward Beecher," in *History and Criticism of American Public Address,* vol. 1, p. 279.

TABLE 5-1. An Overview of the Speechmaking Process

Steps in Speech Preparation

I. Formulate your approach.
    A. Decide on a general purpose.
    B. Decide on a topic area.
    C. Select a specific purpose (thesis).

II. Anticipate the situation.
    A. Assess your audience.
        1. Learn their expected composition.
        2. Estimate their expected interest, knowledge level, and attitudes toward the chosen topic as well as their attitude toward you.
    B. Make adjustments, given the nature of the expected audience.
        1. Adjustments in the initially selected general purpose, topic, and specific purpose.
        2. Adjustments that accommodate the expected physical environment and social-historical context.

III. Focus your approach.
    A. Outline the body of the speech.
    B. Prepare the introduction and conclusion.

IV. Rehearse!

V. Give it your best effort.

VI. Respond to questions.

---

makes a number of important decisions regarding how others are to be affected by a speech. Specifically, the speaker decides on the *general purpose* of the speech, the *topic* of the speech, and the *thesis* or central position that the speech will advance. In the classroom setting, your instructor will most likely make one of these decisions for you. Typically, your speech instructor will assign you to speak with a particular general purpose in mind, specifying that you speak to inform, to convince, to actuate, or to stimulate your audience. More than likely, you will be asked to select a topic and to decide on the central position to be advanced.

General Purposes

There are various ways by which speeches might be classified with respect to general purpose. We have selected what might be considered a "traditional" classification system. The two primary general purposes of speechmaking are (1) speaking to inform, and (2) speaking to persuade. Each of these two broad purposes, however, can be further subdivided.

To Inform. When one speaks to *inform,* he or she might do so for a variety of reasons. In general, the informative speaker's goal is to add to the information base of the audience or to create an information base where none existed previously. Sometimes the informative speaker presents what we might call a *process speech.* This form of informative speaking describes how something works, how some task is accomplished, or it alerts the listener to the criteria which might be employed to perform a given task more successfully. Thus, speakers who explain how an internal combustion engine operates, how to employ a word processor effectively, and what to look for when buying a microcomputer are all engaged in informative speaking.

A second way in which the speaker fulfills the general purpose of informing is through the *report.* More than occasionally, you will find yourself in the role of "reporter," called upon to relate your experience—your "findings"—to an audience. As a committee chairperson in your dormitory, you might be asked to investigate and *report* on possible fundraising activities that might be pursued by your living unit. As a delegate to a conference, you may have to relate your perceptions of the conference to your sponsoring organization. Any time you are commissioned to engage in fact-finding on behalf of a larger group of individuals, you will have to report your findings orally.

Yet another form of informative speaking can be classified as *expository.* In a sense, all public speaking might be considered expository, because it attempts to explain or elucidate. However, we utilize the term *expository* in a restricted manner that means *interpretative.* It calls for the speaker to present his or her own definition of a concept or understanding of an event. The speaker who explains "What Academic Freedom Means to Me" or who lectures on "The Evaluation of Conservatism" is engaged in expository speaking.

To Persuade. The persuasive speech has as a general purpose some combination of goals. It aims at changing an attitude present in the audience (to convince), changing a behavior by calling for action by the audience (to actuate), or reinforcing an attitude or behavior already present in the audience (to stimulate). Thus, a speaker who attempts to change the attitude of an audience hostile toward "abortion on demand" speaks to persuade (convince). The speaker who asks us to make a cash contribution to a cause also seeks to persuade (activate). Finally, the speaker who calls for our rededication and commitment to "democratic ideals" engages in persuasive speaking (stimulate).

A single speech might have several purposes. It could try to reinforce some existing attitudes, change some attitudes, and perhaps call for a specific action (see Chapter 4 for a more detailed account of speech purposes). Likewise, many speeches do not fit into the broad categories of general purpose presented here. Speeches of nomination, acceptance, dedication, and so on, are special forms of address. These and other speech types are treated in Chapter 18.

Your Topic

Your instructor is likely to prescribe the general purpose of a speaking assignment. However, it is your own responsibility to specify the topic of your speech. Begin the process of topic selection early. Good speeches are seldom prepared the night before they are to be given; like good wine, they must mature and develop. Keep in mind the understanding that your topic can be changed as the preparation process unfolds.

Strive to find a topic appropriate for you. Evaluate your experience, your special knowledge. What expertise do you possess? What attitudes do you hold? What unusual adventures have you had? What things do you want changed? What is important to you? *You* are your own best source of speech topics.

Specific Purpose

Suppose you have decided that your general purpose is to inform. Your specific topic is "Using Microcomputers." What are you going to say about the use of a microcomputer? Your answer to this question will express the specific purpose of your speech. We call your answer a *thesis statement*: a simple, declarative sentence that expresses the highest level of generality in your speech. It is a statement that the speech attempts to amplify, clarify, or support. Think of the possibilities you might have regarding the topic of "Using Microcomputers." Consider the following possible thesis statements:

1. Microcomputing skills can make you a better student.
2. A knowledge of the disk operating system is vital to any computer user.
3. Floppy disks require special care.
4. Wise selection of peripherals gives you maximum use from your microcomputer.
5. A microcomputer is not for everyone.

Notice how each of the statements relates to using microcomputers. Each statement, however, takes on a very different focus. It is your thesis, then, that "controls" the substance of your speech (see Chapter 4 for a more complete discussion of the thesis).

Anticipating the Situation _____

A second stage in the preparation process is to *anticipate the situation.* Here you attempt to determine the *expected composition* of your audience, their *knowledge level,* their *attitudes toward both you and your projected message.* You also learn if there are *expectations* or *constraints* imposed on you as a result of the context in which you will present your speech. We discuss the process of audience analysis in greater detail in Chapter 6, but for now we will preview some characteristics of audiences.

Audience Characteristics—Demographics

One of the advantages of your classroom public-speaking experience is that you will come to know your audience well, at least if you are a careful listener and observer. Even before your first in-class speech you will have an opportunity to learn much about the composition of your future audience. Many audience characteristics of relevance to the public speaker are either directly observable or easily discerned. These "vital statistics" are frequently referred to as _demographics;_ they can be thought of as group membership variables. Paul D. Holtzman provides a relatively comprehensive listing of the more common groups in which the individuals of your audience will hold membership. They are as follows:

Some Listener Groups

1. Ages
2. Sexes
3. Races
4. Educational levels
5. Occupations
6. Avocational interests
7. Socioeconomic levels
8. Political affiliation
9. Social organizations
10. Religious affiliations
11. Cultural backgrounds
12. Geographical backgrounds
13. Information channels (sources)[4]

To analyze an audience is to make inferences about its members. If you can successfully catalogue and classify the group memberships of your audience, there are a number of conclusions you might draw based on your classification.

Interest and Knowledge-Level Inferences

Audiences are typically kind. They are willing to listen to a speaker until it is apparent that what the speaker has to say is not of particular value. Not long ago, a student in one of our public-speaking classes presented a speech designed to give his audience "tips" on how to buy firewood. Artistically, the speech was excellent—incorporating clear structure, good examples, and appropriate visual aids—but the majority of the audience appeared rather disinterested. This should not have surprised the speaker, for half of the audience was international students who came from countries where it was never cold enough to snow, and

[4]Paul D. Holtzman, _The Psychology of the Speakers' Audiences_ (Glenview, Ill.: Scott, Foresman, 1970), p. 75.

the remainder of the class was dormitory residents, who were not likely to be purchasing firewood. Had the speaker only considered the ages and cultural and geographical backgrounds of his audience, it is likely he would have found his topic, or at least his treatment of it, inappropriate.

Another sure way of losing the attention of your audience is either to provide them with a rehash of something they already know or to employ a vocabulary and level of discussion that only a few can comprehend and follow. But how do you decide on an appropriate information level? One way is to make some inferences from your demographic analysis. How old is your audience? What are their major areas of study? What hobbies do they have? What is their socioeconomic level? What organizations do they belong to? What is their cultural and geographic background? Do the answers to any of these questions suggest the information level of your audiences with respect to the topic you are contemplating? Admittedly, a number of your inferences from demographic information will be incorrect, but what are your alternatives? One alternative would be for the speaker to administer interest inventories or tests of general knowledge in advance of a scheduled presentation, but in practice such careful data-gathering techniques are not available to the speaker. Nevertheless, demographic information can prove to be useful. Do you think international students might know more about air travel than domestic students do? Will seniors know more about the financial aid program of your college than freshmen do? Will students with homes in Iowa and South Dakota know more about agricultural price supports than students from New Jersey and New York? Will females know more about fashion design and interior decorating than males? Are science majors likely to know more about the molecular structure of hydrocarbons than art or music majors do?

Attitude Inferences

One special form of audience analysis is illustrated by the jury selection process. Here both defense and prosecuting attorneys make use of demographic analysis to analyze jurors who might be predisposed in favor of their respective positions. Arthur Miller of Harvard Law School reports that one prominent lawyer always prefers blue-collar and uneducated jurors when representing accident victims, believing that they are likely to ignore legal technicalities because they identify with the victim. In a criminal case, most defense attorneys like highly educated jurors who, they believe, will pay greater attention to the judge's instructions that guilt must be established beyond a reasonable doubt. Miller observes that housewives, particularly white housewives, are favored by prosecutors, who assume the housewife is especially fearful of crime and is most likely to convict.[5]

[5]Arthur Miller, "Picking Jurors: Part Art, Part Guesswork," *USA Today,* March 28, 1983, p. 6D.

One does not have to be an attorney to infer possible audience attitudes from demographic classifications. Will the knowledge that your audience is Roman Catholic affect any of the choices you make in a speech that favors the legalization of abortion or zero population growth? Will a knowledge of your audience's political affiliations influence your choice of arguments when you speak in favor of a national health insurance program? What about the military draft? Will a knowledge of the age distribution present in your audience suggest a general attitude?

The wise speaker is highly concerned about expected audience attitudes toward both the projected topic and the arguments that he or she might advance in support of a specific position. In Chapter 7, we discuss an additional important topic: the influence of the perceived credibility of a speaker on the effectiveness of the speaker's message. The speaker is most effective when perceived as both competent and trustworthy by the audience. Therefore, it will be useful for the speaker to anticipate the degree to which the audience will so perceive him or her.

Situational Demand Characteristics

The careful and thorough speaker also attempts to anticipate the physical environment and social-historical context in which he or she will speak. Will the hour of the day or the day of the week affect audience perception of your message? Do the physical arrangement or characteristics of your speaking environment pose any special problem? Is there a local, national, or religious holiday that you should acknowledge? Is there a ceremonial occasion demanding your recognition? Is the gathering formal or informal? What agenda precedes or follows your speech? What are the time limits for your speech and the meeting? Are there recent happenings (local, state, or national) to which you should allude? These are but a few of the many situational demand characteristics the speaker might consider.

Focusing Your Approach _____

By way of reviewing our discussion, let us consider how one individual's effort at speech preparation might go. Donna Galiano has just received her speaking assignment—a seven-minute informative speech on a topic of her own selection. Donna gets an early start and searches her own knowledge and experience for a suitable topic. Because she is a photographer for the campus newspaper and a part-time worker in a local camera shop, Donna decides that photography would be a good subject for her speech. She realizes that she cannot expect to inform the audience all about photography. Resolved to limit or narrow the topic, Donna sets off for the library, where she quickly locates numerous books and periodicals devoted to different aspects of photography. Several articles remind her that many people avoid the more complicated camera simply because they do not know how to operate it. Donna is relieved when a more specific general purpose occurs to her—"I will inform my audience how to operate a 35-mm, single-lens reflex camera." From here the task becomes easy. Donna decides that she will advance a speech built around the following skeletal outline:

Thesis: Taking pictures with the single-lens reflex camera is as easy as one, two, three.
     I. First, allow for proper exposure.
        A. Set the speed.
        B. Set the aperture opening.
    II. Second, adjust the focus.
   III. "Squeeze off" the shot.

Donna leaves the library, confident that her speech preparation is progressing well. Over the next few days, she mulls the speech over in her mind and begins to consider the characteristics of her intended audience. Then she quickly discovers that she may have made some wrong choices, for she recalls that two class members are fellow campus photographers, three more have mentioned photography as a hobby, three or four more have had cameras with them at past classes, and still others, she remembers, were in a photography class with her during the last quarter. Now it is time to back up—*and adapt.* Based on the new information, Donna decides that other approaches might be more appropriate. Why, she reasons, should she rehash what is already known? Why spend the time covering already familiar ground? Fortunately for Donna, some careful thought and a little research produce a new thesis statement: The choice of the proper filter is the difference between a good and great picture.

Our point here is simple. Do not decide on a final approach to your topic without careful reflections on the interests, knowledge, and attitudes of your audience. But now let us assume that you have given your audience due consideration and are ready to focus your speech for presentation.

Ordering Your Ideas: Outlining the Body

The processes of discovering and ordering information are interrelated. As you formulate ideas intended to serve as amplification and support for your central position, you are also undoubtedly testing different methods for ordering or structuring the information. A good speech will have a clear organization (see Chapter 8 for a complete discussion of organization and outlining) that allows the listener easily and accurately to identify your central position (thesis) and the major ideas you use to advance or develop it. The main points of a speech outline (usually identified with Roman numerals) collectively clarify, amplify, or support the thesis statement—the only point to which they are subordinate. We recommend that ideas of equal levels of subordination be phrased parallel to one another, parallel in both thought and grammatical structure. Notice in Table 5-2 how *each* main point states an "advantage"

TABLE 5.2 The Highest-Level Cell of Information in a Speech

Thesis: Our school should change from the quarter to the semester system.

Materials that clarify, amplify, or support the thesis

    I. The semester system would be more economical.
    II. The semester system would allow for more in-depth study of a subject.
    III. The semester system would provide more favorable vacation periods for the student.

of the quarter system (the points are parallel in thought) and that each statement begins with "The semester system would . . ." (they are parallel in grammatical structure). In Table 5-3 we present a skeletal outline of the thesis, main points, and subpoints of a possible speech.

TABLE 5-3 The Anatomy of a Speech*

Thesis:

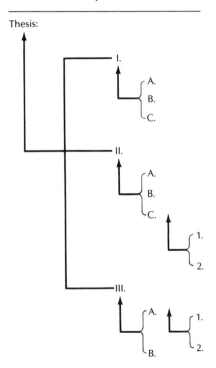

*Bracketed subordinate points clarify, amplify, or support their superordinate counterpart.

Notice how we have bracketed points that collectively relate (amplify, clarify, or support) to their immediately superordinate point—that is, I, II, and III relate to the thesis; A, B, and C relate to a main point; and 1 and 2 relate to a first-degree subpoint. Numerous *patterns of relationship* are possible between two outline points (consult Chapter 8 for more discussion about these patterns). Collectively, the main points and all subordinate points are called the *body* of a speech.

Introductions and Conclusions

Once the thesis and body of a speech are complete, it is appropriate to prepare the introduction and conclusion of the address. These can both be displayed in outline form. When preparing your introduction, keep in mind that it should serve the purpose of creating initial, favorable attention toward you and your message, provide appropriate orientation material that your audience might need to understand your topic or approach, and clearly announce the position you will be taking (your thesis).[6]

The conclusion of a speech has two primary purposes: (1) it summarizes the speech, reminding the audience of the points that were developed; and (2) it restates the thesis of the speech, either verbatim or in a new way—perhaps through an anecdote that stresses the point of the thesis. Table 5-4 depicts a skeletal outline of an entire speech. (See Chapter 9 for a more complete discussion of introductions and conclusions.)

Rehearsing and Presenting Your Speech _____

Once you have formulated your outline, you are ready to rehearse your presentation. At this point, many students are tempted to write out the speech in its entirety and simply practice *reading the speech aloud*. We do not recommend this method. People who read speeches to their audience generally sound like readers—not like communicators. We recommend what is called an *extemporaneous mode of delivery*. By this we mean that the speaker prepares a detailed outline of the speech, without including every word that will be in the final address. Using the outline as a guide or cueing system, the speaker then goes through the speech, depending on the inspiration of the moment for the exact choice of words. Admittedly, there are times when it is desirable for a speaker to read from a completed manuscript. When exact word choice is mandated, such as in a State Department policy statement or a Presidential address, reading from a manuscript may be necessary or even required.

---

[6]Sometimes the thesis does not appear in the introduction but is withheld until arguments in support of it are presented. This is especially true in situations in which the audience is likely to be hostile to the thesis.

TABLE 5-4 The Anatomy of a Speech*

			Title
Thesis:			Introduction
	I.		
		A.	
		B.	
	II.		
		A.	
		B.	
			1.
			2.
			Body
	I.		
		A.	
			1.
			2.
		B.	
			1.
			2.
			3.
	II.		
		A.	
			1.
			2.
			3.
		B.	
			1.
			2.
	III.		
		A.	
			1.
			2.
		B.	
			1.
			2.
			Conclusion
	I.		
		A.	
		B.	
			1.
			2.
	II.	A.	
			1.
			2.
		B.	
			1.
			2.

*A skeleton outline of an entire speech depicting the three major divisions.

But in most situations, audiences seem to expect the less formal and more conversational manner afforded by the extemporaneous mode of delivery.

Do not try to memorize your speech. To do so is to flirt with disaster. Many a speaker has suffered the great embarrassment and the long silence of suddenly "drawing a blank," not remembering what was to come next. Instead, work your way through your detailed outline, experimenting aloud with various word choices. Once you have some phrases in mind, try writing out an abbreviated version—perhaps including only key words—of the detailed outline. Use your abbreviated version for your notes, and continue your practice until you have the speech firmly in your control.

Try practicing in front of a mirror, noting how you might appear to others. At this stage, do not worry about gestures and movement. We believe that planned gestures and physical activity usually end up appearing as planned and artificial. The speaker who is truly involved in a speech and has a fundamental desire to communicate a message soon will discover that words alone are insufficient. Gestures and physical activity that reinforce and supplement the verbal or vocal message will come with involvement. Observe some good conversationalists. What characteristics do they display? Are they enthusiastic, lively, forceful, and sincere? Do their facial expressions, gestures, and vocal inflections add additional meaning to their message? The good speaker emulates the qualities of the good conversationalist but expands upon them to meet the demands of the public platform.

It is also wise to keep in mind that when you give your speech, your perceptions of many aspects of the speaking situation will be at variance with those of your audience. Did you ever appear in a high school play? Perhaps you recall a rehearsal during which the director interrupted one of your fellow actors' speeches with the statement, "I can't hear you back here." What the actor perceived as "shouting" was hardly audible to those in the rear of the auditorium. While in our role of speaker we exaggerate many of our self-perceptions, we are probably not as loud, enthusiastic, forceful, or animated as we think we are. Similarly, those periods of silence, when we are not sure what comes next, will seem longer to the speaker than to the audience. It may be comforting for you to know that the audience is likely to perceive you as more relaxed and free of stage fright or apprehension than you see yourself.[7]

When you are satisfied that the speech is ready for presentation, see if you can convince a roommate, some friends, or even relatives to hear your dress rehearsal. Before you speak to this group, provide them with points for which they might listen and watch. A partial checklist follows:

[7]Theodore Clevenger, Jr., "A Synthesis of Experimental Research in Stage Fright," *Quarterly Journal of Speech, 45:* 134 (1959).

1. Did my introduction create interest in the subject?
2. Was my thesis clear?
3. Did my major ideas emerge clearly?
4. Are my major ideas clearly and adequately developed?
5. Was I conversational and direct?
6. Did I appear enthusiastic and credible?
7. Was my language clear, correct, and otherwise appropriate?
8. Was my conclusion adequate? Did it contain a good summary and restatement of the thesis?

Evaluate the information this audience provides. Then make your final revisions.

Responding to Questions

After your speech, you may be expected to answer questions. In fact, many speakers consider the question-and-answer session to be of major importance. For the speaker, the situation can be both rewarding and threatening. Questions from your audience provide the speaker with valuable feedback. The questions can suggest how the members perceive you as a source of information. The questions show what parts of your address were clear or ambiguous, pleasing or disconcerting, interesting or boring, complete or incomplete, and so forth. But the situation can be threatening for the speaker because it involves the unknown and requires the spontaneous. The following suggestions should prove useful as you participate in the response to questions from your audience:

1. Establish your willingness to answer questions early in your speech. Sometime during the introduction of your speech, you should alert the audience that you will entertain questions regarding your speech. If they know this opportunity will be available to them, audience members will have an additional reason to listen closely to the content of your speech. If you truly want your audience to pose questions about your speech, your expression of willingness must be sincere.
2. Specify early the ground rules for the questioning process—when you will answer them, the type you prefer, the time that will be available, and so forth.
3. Keep in mind that how the audience responds to you during questioning will be a function of the image you generate (your credibility) during the speech.
4. Do not bluff an answer. If you do not know, say so. (Obviously, a law of diminishing returns might be operative here. Not knowing the answer to most questions would produce undesirable results.) If it is practical, you might offer to find the answer to a particular

question and provide it for the questioner at a later date. Should you make such a promise, be sure to carry through.

5. Try to anticipate in advance of your presentation areas of your speech that might produce questions. Rehearse your answers.

6. Be thoroughly prepared. Know far more about your topic than you reveal through your speech. If your speech exhausts all of your knowledge about a given topic, your performance in answering audience questions is unlikely to be effective.

7. Keep your composure. Do not allow the emotions of your questioner to become your emotions. Audiences will come to respect the speaker who can remain calm in moments of adversity.

8. Consistency in your response to questions is important, with *honesty* its best guarantee.

9. Listen carefully to a question and attempt to discover its various complexities. Paraphrase it if necessary. Some of the questions from your audience will be poorly phrased. By rephrasing the questions, you may be able to help other audience members better understand the thrust of the question.

10. Repeat the question, if practical. In many speaking situations the physical environment is such that all audience members may not be able to hear a question. Repeating a question has an additional benefit—it gives you time to think about your answer as you are restating the question.

11. Know when to halt the process. As your audience begins to grow restless or the questions come more slowly, you may want to draw the process to a close with a statement such as, "I think we'll have time for one more question."

12. Conclude the presentation. Many speakers will close their presentation with, "Well, if there are no more questions, I guess that's about it." Such concluding remarks are not appropriate. Once you terminate the questioning process, a brief summary of your position would seem to be in order and will serve to bring the speechmaking event to an effective close.

We encourage you, where it is possible and practical, to allow your audience to participate in your presentation by asking questions. If you frequently speak on the same or a similar topic, you may find it beneficial to keep a log of questions posed by your various audiences. As you plan for each new speech, a reference to the log can help you anticipate questions and possibly suggest topics to be included or perhaps avoided.

A Final Thought _____

We have provided what we believe to be a systematic process leading to effective speeches. We want to emphasize, however, that the speech-preparation process is not completed a step at a time. Each new phase of the process may suggest possibilities requiring some back tracking. Remember how Donna Galiano thought she had her speech topic and main ideas finalized but had to revise after her audience analysis revealed that her initially chosen approach was not appropriate. It may be better to regard the speech-preparation process as composed of *interactive phases* rather than discrete steps. As we conclude this chapter, we are reminded of how we began—by detailing the diverse speech-preparation practices of some truly outstanding speakers. The method of preparation we suggest is only one way of accomplishing the task. There are undoubtedly others that work. If something works for you, keep at it. We ask only that you consider and evaluate our approach, incorporating within your own preparation practices those suggestions that will produce dividends.

Summary

1. Great speakers have used a variety of sometimes very divergent methods to prepare their speeches.
2. There are a number of general purposes for speeches.
3. Speeches *to inform* add to or modify the information base of an audience. When an individual's information base is changed, future behaviors are also shaped.
4. As you choose a topic for your speech, begin early, drawing from your own experiences and interests.
5. The specific purpose of a speech is noted by the thesis statement—a simple, declarative statement that subsumes the entire speech content.
6. Audience analysis is an important step in the speech-preparation process. The wise speaker attempts to determine the expected composition, knowledge level, and attitudes of the audience and adjusts accordingly.
7. Many characteristics of audiences can be inferred by demographic analysis.
8. The physical environment and the nature of a speaking occasion impose additional constraints on the speaker.
9. The speech outline is a valuable preparation tool. With an outline, the speaker can order ideas into meaningful patterns of relationships.
10. A good introduction captures initial, favorable attention, orients the audience, and indicates the focus of a speech.
11. A good conclusion summarizes a speech and restates the central position (thesis).
12. Rehearse your speech before presentation. Work for a fluent and conversational manner of delivery. Do not read your speech to the audience or attempt to recite it from memory.
13. Rehearse!

14. Responding to questions is an important public-speaking activity through which the speaker can learn more regarding audience perception and have an additional opportunity to clarify or reinforce the message of the speech.

Questions and Exercises _____

1. The present chapter suggests a method to be employed in the preparation of a speech, but it also points out that prominent speakers have taken varied approaches to speech preparation. To date, what has been your method of preparing a speech? Have you been more of a Jonathan Edwards or a Henry Ward Beecher?
2. Your text enumerates three types of informative speeches. Recall these three types and provide examples of speeches that illustrate each of them.
3. One step in the preparation process is to anticipate the situation. Explain what is involved in this phase of speech preparation.
4. How does a knowledge of the demographic characteristics of an audience aid the public speaker? List a number of these demographics of interest to the speaker.
5. Explain the relationship between accurately predicting the interest and knowledge level of an audience and preparing an effective speech. On what information would a speaker base predictions of expected audience interest and knowledge with respect to a given topic?
6. Identify a number of situational demand characteristics that the speaker should anticipate in the speech-preparation process.
7. Your authors observe that the processes of discovering and ordering information are assuredly interrelated. Do you agree with this observation, and, if so, can you illustrate through example how the processes interrelate?
8. Pair off with a fellow classmate and select a current speech (perhaps from *Vital Speeches*) for purposes of analysis. Outline the speech and have your classmate do likewise. Do you agree on what constitutes the introduction, body, and conclusion of the speech? Have you both identified the same thesis statement? Do you have agreement on the main points and subpoints of the speech? If you do not have agreement, is it because of lack of clarity on the part of the speaker, or do you or your classmate lack understanding of the organizational process?
9. Your authors advocate the extemporaneous mode of delivery. Explain this method of delivery and contrast it with other possible modes of presentation.
10. What guidelines can you suggest to the speaker who must respond to questions from the audience?

Courtesy of The Bettmann Archive

6

Understanding Audiences

OBJECTIVES

By the time you finish reading this chapter, you should be able to:

1. Differentiate between and among *pedestrian, passive, selected,* and *organized* audiences.

2. Characterize the following types of message receivers: *intended, unintended, irrelevant,* and *interested third party.*

3. Differentiate between audience *analysis* and audience *adaptation.*

4. List a number of group membership variables (demographics) that are of interest to the speaker.

5. Explain how a speaker can use group membership variables (demographics) to predict expected audience interest, knowledge level, involvement, and attitude.

6. Describe an information-based theory of attitudes, listing component parts of an attitude and explaining how the parts operate in combination.

7. Explain the process the speaker uses to adapt (form strategies) to the interests and attitudes of the audience in general and to individual subgroupings of the audience in specific.

The effective speaker recognizes that a message must be audience-centered. This means that the many choices made by the speaker are effective only to the extent that they appropriately acknowledge the interests, beliefs, and attitudes of the intended audience. *Audience analysis* is in part the process by which the speaker gathers such potentially useful information. Audience analysis and subsequent adaptation are complex processes that permeate all phases of speech-making. As Paul Holtzman observes, "Audience analysis is *not* an isolated step in preparing to speak; it is a part of every step."[1] It is the process through which the speaker attempts to discover how audience members view *their* world. To analyze an audience is to identify the interests and knowledge levels of the listeners, the beliefs that the members consider to be salient and important, and the attitudes that they are likely to hold. Within this chapter, we consider the many complexities associated with a speaker's attempt to understand his or her audience. Specifically, we examine types of audiences and detail the

---

[1]Paul D. Holtzman, *The Psychology of the Speakers' Audiences* (Glenview, Ill.: Scott, Foresman, 1970), p. 14.

processes of audience analysis and adaptation, explaining how the speaker gathers information about the audience and makes strategic choices based on that information.

The Nature of an Audience

Earlier chapters of this text make many references to "the audience," but really have not been very specific about the meaning of the term. It is time for us to be more exact. Many adjectives are applied to audiences. We hear them referred to as warm or cold, friendly or hostile, interested or restless, and attentive and inattentive. These adjectives do little in terms of providing us with any real understanding.

The classical categorization of audiences was suggested by Henry L. Hollingworth. He devised a system for distinguishing among audiences on three dimensions: the orientation of the audience to the speaker or the speaker's cause, the degree of preexisting structure present, and what we will later explain as the salience of the speaker's task. According to Hollingworth, audiences can be classified as *pedestrian, discussion group* or *passive, selected, concerted,* and *organized.*[2]

The Pedestrian Audience

This type of audience typically has no preexisting feelings about the focus of attention (the speaker) or about the subject matter of the speaker's address. It is the type of audience that we find in department stores listening to a demonstration of a new microwave oven or a power tool. The audience is frequently relatively heterogeneous (although they share an immediate interest); they depend on physical proximity for membership. By this we mean that the composition of such an audience is determined by the individuals who happened to be in the location of the event at the time of its occurrence. Usually the members of such an audience do not know one another and have had little or no prior contact; consequently, no preexisting organization or division of labor exists for them.

The Discussion Group or Passive Audience

This second type of audience is considered to be partially oriented. Its members will have some prior involvement with the speaker, with his or her cause, or with some organization responsible for bringing the speaker and audience together. The members of the passive audience are usually "captive," compelled for various reasons to attend the event. During a regular school day you undoubtedly serve as a member of a number of passive audiences. The classroom lecture audience, Rotarians

[2]Henry L. Hollingworth, *The Psychology of the Audience* (New York: American Book Co., 1935), p. 17.

or Kiwanians listening to an invited guest speaker, and the attendees of a banquet listening to an after-dinner speech all exemplify the *passive audience*. Compared to the pedestrian audience, these audiences are more homogeneous and are likely, because of conventions associated with organizational affiliations, to have more internal structure.

Selected Audience

Have you ever been invited to a speaking event because of some special interest you had previously displayed? If so, you have served as a member of a *selected audience*. Perhaps you had visited your school's financial aid office, inquiring about potential sources of financial assistance, and later found yourself invited to a lecture sponsored by that office on "Funding Your College Degree: Some Alternatives." Recently, a friend received a letter informing him that because of his excellent credit rating and standing in the community, he was invited to attend a lecture on investment opportunities. Had he accepted the invitation, he would have been a member of a selected audience. He chose not to attend, sacrificing the free gift promised to all attendees. As you can see, the selected audience is quite homogeneous. Frequently, the individuals within this type of audience are selected because they share a combination of characteristics that might make them amenable or vulnerable to a speaker's influence attempts.

Concerted Audience

See if you can identify what the audiences in the following circumstances have in common.

1. A group of farmers meet to hear an attorney discuss what options they have with respect to stopping a high- voltage power line from being built across their properties.
2. Thirty people pay $300 each to attend a one-day training session where a speaker will explain "How to Make Your Small Business Succeed."
3. The dean of students addresses an audience composed of students who favor some changes in dormitory rules, changes that the dean opposes.
4. The President of the United States addresses a meeting of the National Conference on Dislocated Workers.

All four of these audiences are examples of what Hollingworth would call the *concerted audience*. Each has an active purpose that revolves around a mutual interest. The audiences have a high degree of involvement in a shared cause and are committed to some kind of task accomplishment or issue resolution. They are, then, because of the shared involvement, quite homogeneous—at least with respect to a particular topic.

The Organized Audience

Audiences with high preexisting internal structures typify the *organized audience.* Military and quasi-military units, athletic teams, and certain parliamentary bodies stand as exemplars of this type of audience. In such audiences, internal superior-subordinate relationships are firmly established, as are lines of authority and communication channels. In such bodies, the speaker typically, by virtue of his or her position within the group, exerts considerable influence or control. Drill sergeants' addresses to their troops, the coach's halftime speech, and a dean's "state of the college address" to the faculty represent this type of audience.

Salience of Speaker Purpose

Before we leave Hollingworth's classification of audiences, we should note another of his concepts—the responsibilities or duties of the speaker. He views these in terms of a linear progression (see Figure 6-1) that orders attention, interest, impression, conviction, and direction. In

FIGURE 6-1 A representation of dominant or salient speaker responsibility in conjunction with audience type.

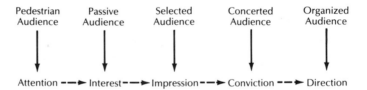

other words, Hollingworth suggests that the salient focus of a speaker who wishes to move an audience to action will be a function of the type of audience present. With a pedestrian audience, the speaker will have to begin by securing attention, then capture interest, make an impression, persuade, and finally call for action. For the passive audience, initial attention is not a primary problem. Instead, the speaker must concentrate on developing interest and subsequently must move through the progression. So it is with the remaining audience types, each one requiring a higher-level responsibility as the salient starting point of the speaker until one reaches the organized audience level, where the speaker has only to give the audience instruction as to what is expected of them.

Here we should note that Hollingworth's classification schema is not composed of rigid and mutually exclusive categories. Audiences can be dynamic, in that an audience that begins as one type might be transformed by the speaker, the speaker's message, or by environmental events into yet another type. For example, a group of individuals congregates in a shopping mall for a microcomputer demonstration and is invited to reassemble for a more complete demonstration at a later time. Those who reappear no longer compose a pedestrian audience but are now a part of an audience that is *selected* in character.

Relevant and Irrelevant Receivers _____

While Hollingworth's classification of audiences is useful, it is important to consider a second method of classification. This second system reminds us that not all audience members will be equally pertinent with respect to whether or not the speaker achieves his or her intended purpose. Wallace Fotheringham identifies four classes of individuals, differing in relevancy, who collectively compose audiences: *intended receivers, unintended receivers, irrelevant receivers,* and *interested third parties.*[3]

Intended Receivers

Intended receivers are those in whom the source of influence (speaker) seeks to develop effects that are instrumental to his or her goal. Thus, a political candidate primarily attempts to influence registered as opposed to unregistered voters. Porsche salespersons direct their appeals to those with considerable financial resources, and college recruiters focus on high school seniors. The intended audience is composed of those whom the speaker *can affect* and those whom the speaker *desires to affect.* As Fotheringham observes, a speaker's intended audience need not be actually physically present at his or her address. Perhaps at some time or other you have made a comment such as, "For gosh sake, don't tell Bob about this unless you want the whole world to know." If you have made such a statement, you understand an important concept about audiences: they are not just passive receivers of messages but also act as diffusers of messages. A few years ago, one of your authors purchased a new automobile. As he was about to take possession of his purchase, the salesman, sensing a high level of satisfaction in the purchaser, gave him a business card, saying, "If you have any friends interested in a new car, I'd appreciate it if you'd give them my card." While the salesman's immediate strategy was to affect a single individual, he also recognized that his intended audience went beyond that individual. People do talk to others about speeches. Consider the following rather common conversation. "Mary, did you hear the President's speech last night?" "No, I didn't, Jane. What did he have to say?" At this point,

---

[3]Wallace C. Fotheringham, *Perspectives on Persuasion* (Boston: Allyn and Bacon, 1966), pp. 11-19.

Jane would probably go on to give her version or reaction to the speech. Our point here is that intended receivers are those that the speaker desires to affect, but these people need not be physically present for the speech.

Unintended Receivers

Though intended receivers are of primary interest to the speaker, he or she must not overlook the possibility that some individuals for whom the message is *not* intended eventually may become recipients of that message. Fotheringham classifies such recipients as *unintended receivers* and indicates that when they become message receivers, unfavorable results may be created—at least from the speaker's perspective. As the size of an audience increases, so does the likelihood that unintended receivers will be exposed to a message. At an interpersonal level (one-to-one) we might say to a friend, "Don't tell John, but I am going to the party Saturday night." If the intended receiver (your friend) is at all trustworthy, the chances of John (the unintended receiver) learning of your plans are minimal. Consider the case, however, of the politician addressing a national political convention. The immediate audience, all party faithfuls, will be highly homogeneous. All present will have strong allegiances and loyalty to their party and the principles for which it stands. The situation seems ideal for the speaker. It appears as the perfect opportunity for the speech *to reinforce,* a time to "rally the troops," to inspire them to action. Such would be the case if it were not for the presence of a particular "member" of the audience—the television camera. Because of its presence, a difficult situation arises for the speaker, who now must decide what adjustments are necessary to accommodate the demands of the immediate and homogeneous audience as well as the demands of the larger and more heterogeneous audience seated at home before their television screens. Should the speaker concentrate only on the immediate audience, ignoring the television viewers, this larger audience becomes *de facto* unintended receivers and most probably unfavorable recipients of the message. The effective speaker, then, is always cognizant of the possibility that techniques, strategies, and arguments that produce favorable outcomes with one particular audience may produce effects that detract from his or her cause within another group.

Irrelevant Receivers

A third type of audience member can be classified as the *irrelevant receiver*—"those in whom effects are unimportant to the persuader's [speaker's] goal."[4] Two types of irrelevant receivers might be present within an audience. Erving Goffman labels the first type as the

[4]Fotheringham, p. 11.

nonperson.[5] In a primary election campaign, a political candidate might consider members of the opposing party as *nonpersons,* because they could not help his cause in the immediate election. Or, in the days just before an election, the political candidate might concentrate only on the voters who are either undecided or already favorable, ignoring those committed to the opposition. Children frequently serve as nonpersons, with parents talking about them in their presence as if they were not there.

The second type of nonperson is the *shill*—a person whose role is "to furnish favorable but artificial responses to messages."[6] Some would suggest that Ed McMahon occasionally acts as a shill for Johnny Carson, laughing to stimulate a like response in the audience. Commonly, a speaker "plants" questioners in the audience; these people are designated to ask certain questions once the speaker has concluded his or her presentation. Using shills as questioners might be done for several purposes. They can serve as a simple mechanism to encourage the remainder of the audience to participate in the questioning process—to "get the ball rolling," so to speak. Or the questions may be planted for the purpose of giving the speaker an opportunity to address issues that might best be initiated by someone else. For example, a candidate has been accused by his opponent of practicing unethical campaign tactics. The accused thinks that he should address this untrue charge but is fearful that if he makes it a major part of his speech, it will take on the character of an apologia, with his thesis perceived as "I am not a crook." Consequently, the speaker arranges for a friendly audience member to ask, at the conclusion of the address, "How do you respond to your opponent's charges that you are an unethical campaigner?"

Interested Third Parties

A fourth type of potential audience member is what Fotheringham terms the *interested third party*—audience members who are "members of organizations able to secure audiences of their own and professionally engaged in communicating to those audiences."[7] The most obvious interested third party is, of course, "the press" and, where appropriate, speakers go to great length to ensure that media representatives receive and understand their message. It is not uncommon for politicians to send advance copies of their major addresses to media representatives, who then will have the time to study the speeches and subsequently report on them immediately following the speaker's presentation. It seems as if it has become the custom of our principal television networks to follow each major televised political speech with a program devoted to

[5]Erving Goffman, *The Presentation of the Self in Everyday Life* (Garden City, N.Y.: Doubleday, 1959), p. 151.
[6]Fotheringham, p. 11.
[7]Fotheringham, p. 16.

analyzing the address. Not infrequently, those analyses are lengthier than the speech they are analyzing. Advance copy makes this instant analysis possible.

There are still other interested third parties who serve as potential message recipients. Professors, university administrators, club officers, political office holders, and so on, all have audiences of their own to whom they might disseminate a speaker's message. The source of influence is well advised to identify relevant third parties and to make certain that these individuals receive appropriate messages.

Analyzing the Audience-Occasion

Every conscientious speaker strives to present a speech in the most efficacious manner, the manner that will lead to the accomplishment of the speaker's general purpose. If the speaker is attempting to create or add to the information base of the audience, he or she will choose those techniques most likely to produce understanding and information retention. Should the speaker expect to effect changes in attitudes or behaviors, he or she must select those arguments and evidence that the audience, not the speaker, finds most compelling and persuasive. Likewise, the speaker who perceives the general purpose as to reinforce existing audience attitudes, values, beliefs, or behaviors will make appropriate choices only to the extent that his or her analysis of such preexisting audience characteristics is accurate. In this last section of Chapter 6, we focus on how speakers gather information about their potential audience and how strategies are formulated from such information. The chapter closes with what we term *situational constraints*.

Achieving Desired Response

Analyzing an audience for purposes of predicting interests and attitudes, and then formulating approaches that will most effectively achieve an intended effect is a highly complex task, a task that seriously would challenge the most capable statistician armed with sophisticated computers. In fact, when researchers undertake such tasks, their success is quite limited. Fortunately, perhaps, the human mind has the ability to operate in ways not yet available to the computer. We can solve problems in a satisfactory manner with very limited and sometimes incomplete data, and can choose strategies that effectively will add to the information base of an audience. We can also change, modify, or reinforce existing attitudes, as appropriate.

The speaker who truly wishes to accomplish an intended purpose must engage in two operations: *analysis* and *adaptation*. When one analyzes an audience, one must first attempt to discover characteristics that can be associated with or used to predict the audience's present nature (interest and knowledge levels, attitudes, etc.). This is called the process of *audience analysis.* Once the nature of the audience is ascertained, the speaker next attempts to select, from the alternative approaches available, those strategies to which the audience, given its composition, will be most receptive. This later activity is called *audience adaptation.*

Gathering Information—Audience Data. By now we hope you are convinced of the importance of audience analysis, of knowing who your listeners are and using that knowledge as you plan your presentation. But how do we learn the probable interest and attitudinal predispositions that an audience is likely to have with regard to general and specific purposes? One way of discovering such information is to ask the audience members directly. Marketing firms do just that, surveying potential target audiences to learn everything from the colors that individuals most favorably associate with laundry detergent to the characteristics they expect to find in candidates for the Presidency. Usually, however, it is not practical for the public speaker to administer long preference and attitude questionnaires to an audience prior to a speech.

A source of audience information that many speakers overlook is the individual who issues the invitation to speak. Should the program chairperson of a club or organization ask you to address a group, you should query that person about expected interest and knowledge levels, as well as about audience involvement in the topic area and potential attitudinal positions that might be present. Appropriate questioning can pay dividends. For example, suppose that a chemical engineer is invited to speak to a local women's club; the topic is the environmental impact of burning high-sulfur coal. This situation is ripe for the engineer to make some serious errors in audience analysis. Our engineer might decide that she has been asked to address the group primarily because she is a woman who has distinguished herself in what some might regard as a man's world, and given the occupations and educational background of the audience, she might assume that (1) initial interest in the topic will be low; (2) general knowledge with respect to the topic will be minimal; (3) the audience will have little involvement in the topic; and (4) attitudes toward burning high-sulfur coal will be neutral. Given such assumptions, the speaker would probably prepare a simple and straightforward presentation, concentrating on generating audience interest and involvement. But think of how wrong the speaker *could be.* What if this women's club is just considering a year's worth of programs on the environment? What if they are involved in raising funds to donate to various organizations studying the adverse effects of acid rain? What if this organization has protested the construction of a coal-generated electrical power plant in the local community? Given these conditions, a different approach would be in order. The speaker can acquire such background information if he or she takes the trouble to ask the right questions. Do not overlook the individual who extends your invitation to speak. That person, as well as other audience members whom you might know, can provide useful insights.

Even when individuals who will be members of your intended audience can provide valuable data about expected audience perceptions, you must keep in mind that they are offering their own, sometimes unique, impressions. The speaker will always want to test such impressions against his or her personal assessment of the situation. In addition, there are many times when program chairpersons or future audience members will not be of great assistance to the speaker. In all cases, the speaker will want to address the following question and the designated subquestions as a first step in audience analysis.

What is the composition of my intended audience?

A. What age levels will be present in the audience? Which age level is dominant?

B. How many males and how many females will be present?

C. What races will be represented and to what degree?

D. What education levels are present in the audience and to what degree?

E. What occupational and avocational interests will be represented and to what degree?

F. What socioeconomic levels are present in the audience and to what degree?

G. What political affiliations are represented and to what degree?

H. To what social organizations do the audience members belong and to what degree?

I. What religious affiliations are represented and to what degree?

J. From what cultural backgrounds do the audience members come and in what numbers?

K. To what information sources are the audience members exposed and to what degree?[8]

Reflected within each subquestion is the suggestion that we think statistically about audiences, that we consider both averages and variabilities. For example, two audiences may have the same average age (40) but require entirely different approaches because the first audience is composed of individuals ranging from 15 to 75 years of age, whereas the other has less variability on this characteristic, with all audience members being 35 to 45 years of age.

Making Predictions. Although some speakers might find it intrinsically interesting to know that the average age of an audience is 40, that they are predominantly male, and that they represent three racial groups, such information becomes of value to the speaker only to the extent that it can be used to predict audience perceptions and predispositions. Once the speaker has obtained a demographic breakdown of the audience, it is useful to ask the following:

[8]Our questions have been generated from a set of listener groups identified by Paul D. Holtzman, *Speakers' Audiences*, pp. 75-77.

Given my topic, what audience-composition variable, or combination of variables, will predict their interest, knowledge, or involvement level?

A. Will it be age?
B. Will it be sex?
C. Will it be religion?
D. Will it be age and sex?
E. Will it be age and religion?
F. Will it be sex and religion?
G. Will it be age, sex, and religion?

To illustrate how this process might operate, consider the case of a speaker who plans to talk about birth-control techniques and who is interested in predicting the degree of interest that the intended audience would be likely to have in such a topic. To make such a prediction, the speaker would first investigate the demographic characteristics of the audience for those variables likely to be associated with an interest in the subject. Suppose our speaker decides that of the potential variables, the ones most closely associated with an interest in the specified topic are sex, age, religion, and socioeconomic status. Specifically, our speaker might decide the following:

1. Females will be more interested in birth-control techniques than males.
2. Females of childbearing age will be more interested in the topic than those who are not of that age.
3. The age range of males who are interested in the topic will be greater than the age range of females.
4. Members of religious denominations that condone birth-control techniques will be more interested than those who are members of nonapproving denominations.
5. Individuals of higher socioeconomic status will be more interested than those of lower status.

At this point, the speaker has created a kind of interest profile. It appears, if the speaker's assessment is correct, that those most interested in the topic would be high socioeconomic-level females of childbearing age who are capable of reproduction and who are members of religious denominations that condone birth control. The speaker next has only to match the characteristics of the intended audience with this interest profile. To the degree that the two match, interest in the topic is likely to be present. Naturally, this prediction reflects an inexact science, dependent for its success on the speaker's ability to furnish accurate generalizations regarding various demographic classifications.

Just as it is advantageous for the speaker to know the interest, knowledge level, and degree of involvement to be expected, it is of equal importance to anticipate the attitude the audience is likely to hold with respect to the speaker as a person. In Chapter 7, we demonstrate that for many purposes speakers who are perceived by their audience as competent and trustworthy are more effective than speakers who lack such characteristics. Speakers who are perceived as both competent and trustworthy typically are considered to have high *source credibility*. Speaker credibility is what is called a *perceptual variable*. That is, the credibility of a speaker resides not in the speaker but in the perceptions of the audience. Thus, source or speaker credibility can be considered an audience attitude; like other attitudes, it can be modified, changed, or reinforced. First, however, it must be assessed. Here again, we suggest a predictive process centering on the following question:

Given my topic, what audience composition variable or combination of variables will predict the audience's attitude toward me?

A. What variable or combination of variables will predict perceptions of my competence?
   1. Will it be age?
   2. Will it be educational level?
   3. Will it be vocational or avocational affiliations?
B. What variable or combination of variables will predict perceptions of my trustworthiness?
   1. Will it be age?
   2. Will it be political affiliation?
   3. Will it be educational level?

Thus, a government economist making predictions about the economy might reason that he or she will be perceived as most credible by middle-aged, moderately educated audience members who are members of the same political party as the speaker. To the extent that these assumptions are correct and to the extent that the audience actually matches such a profile, the speaker will have high credibility. Here we should caution, however, that factors other than demographic characteristics may well come into play. Previous contact or association and the outcome of that association are certainly among such factors, as is the economist's history as a prognosticator. In other words, the reputation that the speaker brings to the event will affect initial audience attitude.

Finally, the speaker must anticipate the attitude that the audience is likely to hold with respect to the specific purpose (thesis statement). Making an accurate prediction is a difficult and complex process requiring an understanding of what constitutes an attitude. Many theorists propose what is termed an information-based theory of attitudes.[9] By this, they suggest that the basis of an attitude is a set of

---

[9]Our discussion follows the view of Martin Fishbein and Icek Ajzen, *Belief, Attitude, Intention and Behavior: An Introduction to Theory and Research* (Reading, Mass.: Addison-Wesley, 1975).

beliefs that an individual might hold with respect to an attitude object—a person, concept, proposition, and so on. Let us consider the case of the speaker who advocates donating blood to the Red Cross. Trevor Murray, a member of the potential audience, has the following beliefs about donating blood:

1. Donating blood saves lives.
2. Donating blood reduces an individual's medical expenses.
3. Donating blood is painful.
4. Donating blood takes a lot of time.
5. Donating blood makes the donor susceptible to disease.
6. Donating blood can produce blood clots in the donor.

Most people will have between five and nine beliefs about an attitude object. Trevor is no exception. If we examine each of his six beliefs, we discover that a belief stands as the pairing of an attitude object with a specific attribute. Not all beliefs are held to the same degree of certainty. Trevor will be more confident of the connection of the attitude object and the attribute in some beliefs than he is in others. If we were to obtain a measure of how probable Trevor considers each of the connections specified in the six beliefs (on a scale ranging from 0.00 for "impossible" to 1.00 for "absolutely certain"), the following probabilities might result:

Belief	*Probability*
1.	.90
2.	.80
3.	.95
4.	.70
5.	.60
6.	.40

Beliefs and the probabilities associated with them stand as one component of an attitude. The second component is an evaluative judgment of the attribute with which the attitude object is paired within each salient belief. For example, we might ask Trevor to consider each attribute and to supply an evaluation of it on a scale ranging from *good* to *bad*. Trevor's evaluations might look as follows:

Attribute	*Evaluation*
1. saves lives	good **(+3)** +2 +1 0 -1 -2 -3 bad
2. reduces individual's medical expenses	good **(+3)** +2 +1 0 -1 -2 -3 bad
3. is painful	good +3 +2 +1 0 -1 -2 **(-3)** bad
4. takes a lot of time	good +3 +2 +1 0 **(-1)** -2 -3 bad

	Attribute	*Evaluation*
5.	makes the donor susceptible to disease	good +3 +2 +1 0 -1 -2 (-3) bad
6.	can produce blood clots in the donor	good +3 +2 +1 0 -1 -2 (-3) bad

Martin Fishbein and Icek Ajzen suggest that an individual's attitude can be expressed algebraically as follows:

$$A_o = \sum_{i=1}^{n} b_i e_i$$

where A_o denotes an attitude toward an object, person, proposition, policy, or idea, b represents the strength of belief that attribute i is related to the attitude object; and e is the individual's evaluative response to the i distribution of attributes.[10] To put it another way, we might say that an attitude is the sum of the cross-products of one's estimation of the extent to which an object possesses a given attribute and one's evaluative response to that attribute. Table 6-1 displays Trevor Murray's attitude toward donating blood.

TABLE 6-1   A Conceptualization of Trevor Murray's Attitude Toward Donating Blood

	Probability (b_i)	Evaluative (e_i) Response	$b_i e_i$
b_i	.90	+3	+2.70
b_2	.80	+3	+2.40
b_3	.95	−3	−2.85
b_4	.70	−1	− .70
b_5	.60	−3	−1.80
b_6	.40	−3	−1.20
		$\sum_{i=1}^{n} b_i e_i$	−1.45

[10]Fishbein and Ajzen, p. 29.

It would be desirable for the speaker to have available information like that displayed in Table 6-1 for each member of the audience. However, this is usually not possible. Instead, the speaker must estimate or predict such information, primarily from the demographic characteristics of the audience. Here the speaker might ask a question such as the following:

What audience-composition variable or combination of variables will predict the attitude toward my topic (thesis)?

> A. What audience-composition variable or combination of variables will predict their salient beliefs?
>   1. Age?
>   2. Sex?
>   3. Educational level?
> B. What audience-composition variable or combination of variables will predict their evaluation of salient beliefs?
>   1. Age?
>   2. Sex?
>   3. Educational level?

Imagine that the speaker who advocates giving blood begins the process of assessing or predicting expected audience attitude. He or she examines the listing of demographic variables and decides that age, sex, education, and socioeconomic level are likely to be associated with donating blood. The speaker formulates the following generalizations:

1. Middle-aged people will have the most favorable attitudes toward donating blood.
2. Males will have more favorable attitudes than females.
3. People with higher levels of education will have more favorable attitudes than those with less education.
4. People at the higher socioeconomic levels will have more favorable attitudes than those at the lower levels.

Once again, the speaker has created a *profile* of an individual who has a positive or negative attitude. Specifically, if the speaker's generalizations are correct—and they may not be—an individual with a positive attitude would be male, middle-aged, well-educated, and from a high socioeconomic level. To the extent that the audience matches the profile, a positive attitude can be expected.

We must emphasize that predicting attitudes can produce error. The method we propose here is a way of thinking about audiences. It is effective only to the extent that a speaker can identify those audience characteristics *likely* to be associated with what is to be predicted. Although error is possible, this method frequently stands as the only means available for the speaker to predict interest, involvement, knowledge level, and attitude.

Formulating Strategies

Thus far, we have described a method of analyzing an audience, of learning about their expected perceptions. Once this is learned, the speaker must then formulate strategies for best accomplishing his or her general and specific purposes. This *strategy-formation* phase of speech-making is called *audience adaptation*. In general, the speaker who formulates strategy addresses a question and subquestions such as the following:

Given my general and specific purposes, how can I best accomplish them?

A. Are there potential content choices that will be better than others?
   1. For audiences in general?
      a. Will some arguments be better than others?
      b. Will some evidence be better than other evidence?
      c. Will some forms of reasoning be better than other forms?
   2. For audiences having particular characteristics?
      a. Will some arguments be better than others?
      b. Will some evidence be better than other evidence?
      c. Will some forms of reasoning be better than other forms?
B. Are there potential organizational choices that will be better than others?
   1. For audiences in general?
      a. Should I place my strongest argument first, last, or in the middle of my speech?
      b. Should I use climactic or anticlimactic order?
      c. Should I present a one- or two-sided argument?
      d. What degree of structure do I need to be understood?
   2. For audiences having particular characteristics?
      a. Should I place my strongest argument first, last, or in the middle of my speech?
      b. Should I use climactic or anticlimactic order?
      c. Should I present a one- or two-sided argument?
      d. What degree of structure do I need to be understood?
C. Are there some language choices that will be better than others?
   1. For audiences in general?
      a. What level of language difficulty is appropriate?
      b. What level of language intensity is appropriate?
   2. For audiences having particular characteristics?
      a. What level of language difficulty is appropriate?
      b. What level of language intensity is appropriate?
D. Are there some delivery choices that will be better than others?
   1. For audiences in general?
      a. What mode of delivery is most effective?
      b. What degree of fluency is necessary?

   2. For audiences having particular characteristics?
      a. What mode of delivery is most effective?
      b. What degree of fluency is necessary?

Much of the remainder of this text is devoted to providing advice on these questions. We discuss evidence and reasoning, language, organization, and delivery in considerable detail, devoting an entire chapter to each. We attempt to provide you with explanations of each area in which a speaker exercises choices; we also specify the effects produced by a variety of those choices. Where differential effects might be produced in different kinds of auditors (i.e., males or females, informed or uninformed, young or old, etc.), we so indicate.

Situational Constraints

In many ways, it is accurate to say that the composition of the audience—with regard to their interests, knowledge levels, attitudes, and so on—constrains the speaker's choices. These factors restrict the speaker and oblige him or her to behave in some ways and not in others, to take some approaches and not others, or to discuss some ideas and not others. But there are other factors that also have an impact on a speaker's choices, that further restrict the speaker. We identify these as the *situational constraints* that are present in the specific public-speaking context. To locate such constraining influences, the speaker is advised to address such questions as the following:

   1. Do the physical arrangements, including the size of the room, the amplifying system, and other factors, pose any problem?
   2. Is the gathering formal or informal?
   3. What agenda (singing, speeches, announcements) precedes or follows the speech?
   4. Will the hour of the day or day for the meeting affect audience reception?
   5. Are there are holidays (local, national, religious) that should be acknowledged?
   6. Is my speech part of a larger ceremonial event that should be acknowledged?
   7. What are the time limits for the speech and the meeting of which my speech is a part?

Any instructor who has taught an 8:00 A.M. class can assure you that different instructional techniques are needed at that time than at 2:00 P.M. Likewise, the speaker who knows that the audience will be composed of a few people at an informal gathering prepares a very different speech than what he or she might present to an audience of 300 people gathered for a formal affair of some type.

Summary _____

1. Audiences can be classified as *pedestrian, passive, selected, concerted,* and *organized.* Within each of these classifications, the speaker has different initial goals—*attention, interest, impression, conviction,* and *direction,* respectively.
2. Not all members of an audience will be of equal interest to the speaker. Potential receivers of a message can be categorized as *intended* (those the speaker wishes to affect), *unintended* (those for whom a message is not intended; these listeners may produce unfavorable results for the speaker should they become message recipients), *irrelevant* (those in whom effects are unimportant), and *interested third parties* (audience members who can pass on the speaker's message to audiences of their own).
3. *Audience analysis* is a process of discovering characteristics that can be associated with or used to predict the nature of the audience.
4. *Audience adaptation* is the process in which the speaker attempts to select, from potential approaches, those strategies to which the audience, given its composition, will be most receptive.
5. Many sources of audience data are available to the speaker, but frequently the speaker is on his or her own and must infer audience interest, knowledge, involvement, and attitude from demographic or group-membership characteristics of the audience.
6. Information-based attitude theory suggests that an attitude is the sum of the cross-products of probability of belief and evaluation of a set of beliefs.
7. When one practices strategies of audience adaptation, one attempts to consider the nature of an audience (in terms of interest, knowledge, involvement, attitude, and so on) and the specific composition (group memberships). One then makes choices that will best accomplish the general and specific purposes of the speech.

Questions and Exercises _____

1. Explain this assertion: "Audience analysis is *not* an isolated step in preparing to speak; it is a part of every step."
2. Describe and provide an example of each of the following audience types: pedestrian, discussion group or passive, selected, concerted, and organized.
3. What relationship does Hollingworth observe between salience of speaker focus and audience type? Explain the linear progression that orders attention, interest, impression, conviction, and direction and that associates the progression with audience type.
4. Audience members can be classified on a dimension of relevance. The names given to the various audience members so classified are

intended receivers, unintended receivers, irrelevant receivers, and interested third parties. Define each of these classifications and detail a speaking situation in which one or more of these receiver types might be present.

5. Differentiate between what your text refers to as *nonpersons* and *shills*. Why are these types of audience members termed "irrelevant receivers"?

6. While the press might well be the most obvious interested third party, what other individuals or groups might fit this classification?

7. Explain the distinction between *audience analysis* and *audience adaptation*.

8. List at least three sources from which a public speaker might gather information about his or her intended audience.

9. Your authors suggest a method of audience analysis based on making predictions or drawing inferences from discovered information. Explain in detail how this process should operate.

Basic Principles of Speechmaking

Courtesy of Dr. Benjamin Spock

7

The Speaker as a Source of Influence

By the time you finish reading this chapter, you should be able to:

1. Differentiate between the source and the sender of a message.
2. Define source credibility and enumerate its components, providing descriptions of each component or dimension.
3. Illustrate how the components or dimensions of credibility can be regarded as independent of one another.
4. Explain why source credibility is considered a perceptual variable.
5. Explain how the credibility accorded a speaker can vary with different audiences and messages.
6. Compare the Aristotelian concept of *ethos* with contemporary views of source credibility.
7. Describe credibility as a process variable with reference to initial, transactional, and terminal credibility.
8. List and define five sources of data that audiences have available with regard to a speaker.
9. Contrast symptomatic and symbolic nonverbal behaviors.
10. Explain how audiences arrive at judgments of a speaker's credibility, distinguishing between observable and nonobservable characteristics.
11. Explain how the personal involvement of the audience appears to mitigate the effects of speaker credibility.
12. Describe two situational characteristics that are determinants of the ideal or most effective speaker.

Communication can be considered as the study of "who says what to whom in what channel with what effect."[1] This chapter is about *who.* More specifically, it is about how certain audience perceptions of a speaker can be determinants of whether a speaker achieves an intended effect. Not all speakers are equally believable or equally effective at gaining understanding or compliance. In this chapter, we first examine the many components of an audience's attitude toward a source or

[1]Harold D. Lasswell, "The Structure and Function of Communication in Society," in *Mass Communication,* ed. Wilbur Schramm (Urbana, Ill.: University of Illinois Press, 1960), p. 117.

speaker. We focus on such characteristics as competence, trustworthiness, similarity, and attraction. Second, we examine the process by which an audience forms an image or attitude toward a speaker. Third, we discuss some of the effects that differential perception can produce. Finally, the chapter closes with a discussion of some situational characteristics that serve to define the ideal public speaker.

Source (Speaker) Credibility

In 1949, Franklyn Haiman conducted what has since become a classic experiment.[2] He prepared a fifteen-minute persuasive speech that argued for compulsory health insurance. The speech was recorded and played to three different but equivalent audiences. The first group was told that the speaker was Eugene Dennis, who was then Secretary-General of the Communist Party of America. The second audience was told that the speaker was Dr. Thomas Parran, Surgeon General of the United States. Haiman led the third audience to believe that the speaker was an anonymous Northwestern University sophomore. When the researcher compared audience opinion before and after the persuasive speech, it was clear that when the speech was attributed to the Surgeon General, significantly more changes of opinion occurred than when it was attributed to either the Communist Party administrator or the anonymous college student. These latter two "speakers" produced no changes of opinion.

What Haiman demonstrated was, of course, that different individuals might produce differential results—even when they were presenting the same message. This study and others like it have sparked a great deal of interest in determining which characteristics contribute to the speaker's effectiveness, why some speakers are believable and others are not, and why one individual's influence attempts bring compliance and another's attempts do not.

In short, there are certain characteristics of individuals that make us judge some sources to be competent, trustworthy, *or otherwise acceptable*. We consider these speakers to be high in *credibility*.

Source (Speaker) Credibility Defined

To define the term *source credibility*, we must first agree on what constitutes a message *source*. We mean, simply, the *originator of a message*. In many situations, but not in all, the source is also the *encoder* or *sender* of the message. In the public-speaking situation, the source and the sender are typically the same person. A common and current practice is for entire speech staffs to collaborate on the addresses

[2]Franklyn S. Haiman, "An Experimental Study of the Effects of Ethos in Public Speaking," *Speech Monographs, 16*: 190-202 (1949).

of some politicians and business executives. In your role as a public speaker, however, you alone will be both the source—*the originator of your message*—and the sender. For the remainder of the present chapter, therefore, we consider *source credibility* and *speaker credibility* to be identical concepts.

We must also define the concept of *speaker credibility*. A speaker does not possess *speaker credibility* in the same manner that one possesses a new house, a new dress, or a new automobile. The credibility of a speaker resides, instead, within the perceptions of the audience. Speaker credibility is a judgment or evaluation that the audience members formulate regarding the speaker. It is best defined as *the audience's general attitude or feeling of favorableness to unfavorableness toward the sender (originator) of a message (speech)*.

Source Credibility as a Perceptual Variable

Speaker credibility falls within a class of variables that we term *perceptual*. A speaker may come to the presentation thoroughly prepared and with nothing but the best of intentions toward the audience, but unless they perceive him or her as competent and well intentioned, it is likely that the speaker will be less than effective. What your audience perceives will be related to their past training and experience, their prior attitudes toward the speaker and the topic, and their value system. To put it another way, what an audience perceives will be a function of their perspective—their physical and psychological position in both time and space.

Credibility: Its Components

Our attitude toward a speaker (the speaker's credibility) is multi-dimensional. This means that there are multiple components of the attitude, involving *separate* and *potentially unrelated* areas of judgment. Aristotle suggested that speaker credibility, which he called *ethos,* is composed of three separate characteristics: intelligence, character, and good will.[3] In his view, the ideal source would be perceived as sagacious, of noble character, and acting in the best interest of the audience. As we evaluate a speaker, we can observe each of these components or dimensions separately. Our evaluations of the dimensions can lead to different conclusions. For example, we might say to a friend, "Well, that guy really didn't know what he was talking about, but he did seem like a nice fellow who meant well," indicating a low evaluation of the speaker's competence (intelligence) and a high evaluation of the speaker's character and good will. Conversely, we might say of a speaker, "He certainly knows his subject matter, but I'd never buy a used car from

---

[3]Aristotle, *Rhetoric*, 2.1.1378a, trans. Lane Cooper (New York: Appleton-Century-Crofts, 1932), pp. 91-92.

him"—a positive evaluation of competence and a less than satisfactory perception of character and perhaps intent.

It is not known exactly what components are involved in arriving at an assessment of credibility. As the study of source or speaker credibility continues and our understanding of the variable increases, new dimensions continue to emerge. For our present purposes, we will address five aspects of an audience's attitude toward a speaker.[4] The five areas are *competence, trustworthiness, dynamism and extroversion, sociability and liking,* and *composure.*

Competence. An individual in need of an operation would rarely advertise among surgeons for competitive bids, attempting to secure the lowest possible fee. Usually, patients are only secondarily concerned with money in such matters. One may seek comparisons, but the goal is to find the most capable surgeon, not the most inexpensive one. So it is with the communication process in general and the persuasive process in particular. We expect those who would influence us to be competent, informed, knowledgeable, trained, and intelligent. Of all the dimensions of speaker credibility, competence is ranked as the most important. We expect speakers to know what they are talking about and to be expert, through training, study, or experience, on those issues that they bring before us.

Trustworthiness. It is frequently not sufficient for the speaker just to be competent. There are many instances in which to be effective the speaker also must have the trust of the audience. Frequently, the most trustworthy sources are those who advocate a position that is contrary to their self-interests. Consider the case of an executive in the liquor industry who campaigns for moderation in drinking or the habitual criminal who calls for mandatory and increased prison sentences. Under the majority of circumstances, trustworthiness stands as the sine qua non for all who would be effective communicators. Quintilian, the Roman teacher and rhetorical theorist of the first century A.D., advanced what we might call the *good man theory* of persuasion. In his view, an individual could not lay claim to the title of "orator" unless he was first of all a good man. To Quintilian, the orator was the good man (or, we add, woman) speaking effectively.

Dynamism and Extroversion. Would you rather listen to a speaker who is assertive, active, animated, and enthusiastic, or one who is shy, passive, static, and apathetic? Chances are that you, and most other people, prefer the speaker who possesses the former rather than the latter characteristics. Do not expect your audience to be excited about your topic unless you first display your own excitement, your own enthusiasm, and your own sense of involvement. The dynamic speaker is energetic, vigorous, and forceful. He or she does not stand rooted in

_____

[4]To formulate our conception of the dimensions of source credibility, we have drawn on factor-analytical studies and bodies of social psychological research on interpersonal attraction and person perception.

one spot, clutching the podium in some form of a death grip. The dynamic speaker instead displays involvement through bodily movement, gestures, and facial expressions that convey a sense of enthusiasm.

Sociability and Liking. Most of us would rather engage in communicative activity with people whom we like and who like us. We avoid those individuals who are hostile, unfriendly, or otherwise not social. Would you rather take a class from a professor who is competent and trustworthy or one who is competent, trustworthy, *and* likeable? What makes us like another individual or perceive that person as sociable? The answer to this latter question is complex. Psychologist Elliot Aronson posits some interesting answers.[5] He suggests that we like those people whose attitudes and interests are much like our own, those who offer us genuine praise and perform "no-strings-attached" favors, those who have special competencies and such admirable qualities as loyalty, kindness, and reasonableness. He also claims that we like those people who like us in return. It is not by accident that television advertisers employ attractive and accomplished athletes and theatrical figures to endorse their products. Each year, millions of dollars are spent associating friendly, pleasant, attractive, and affable individuals with products ranging from motor oils to brassieres. We expect information sources to exhibit friendliness and a *genuine* liking for us. If we do not perceive these qualities, the outcome of communicative activity is affected negatively.

Composure. Public speaking frequently occurs in stressful contexts. Nevertheless, our preferred information source is relaxed, poised, calm, and controlled. The composed speaker displays mastery of the situation and gives every appearance of enjoying his or her time before the audience. Most of us identify with the speaker's situation, and because we recognize the potential difficulties of the speaker's circumstances, we are likely to empathize with him or her, vicariously feeling the speaker's successes and failures, delighting when things go well, and feeling uncomfortable when the presentation falters. In addition, nonfluencies—umms, ahhs, and ohs—can reveal that the speaker is less than comfortable before the audience. These deficiencies detract from the speaker's perceived credibility. We also observe that audience perceptions of composure may be generalized to other perceptions about the speaker. What feeling do you have about the lecturer whose hands shake and legs quiver, who is white in the face, who is continuously short of breath, and whose voice cracks and seems at a bit too high a pitch? Certainly you will perceive such a speaker as lacking in composure, but under many circumstances you might also use that perception to infer that someone who is that uncomfortable before an audience might have good cause for feeling apparent anxiety. Is the speaker really prepared? Does he or she know the subject matter? Is the speaker unsure of his or her position? Is he or she telling the truth? These are just a few of the questions that lack of composure or control might elicit from an audience.

[5]Elliot Aronson, *The Social Animal* (San Francisco: W. H. Freeman, 1980), pp. 237-270.

Credibility's Situational Nature

Credibility is not possessed by the speaker, but is accorded to the speaker by the audience. Both the composition of the audience and the topic of the message may affect the degree of credibility accorded to the speaker.

Audience Composition. A speaker's credibility does not transfer from one audience to another. Is Ronald Reagan a credible source? What about Chicago mayor Harold Washington, Phil Donahue, Margaret Thatcher, Betty Friedan, Gloria Steinem, or Jesse Jackson? If we were to survey a cross-section of Americans and ask them to rate the credibility of these people, it is quite likely that we would find considerable variability in the responses. More than likely, certain groups of people would consider the individuals to hold high credibility, but at the same time there will be a considerable number of Americans who would consider some of the individuals on our list as low-credibility sources. We suspect that there are numerous Americans who still regard Richard Nixon as an unimpeachable source. Thus, it becomes clear that groups with different values and attitudes can accord differing degrees of credibility to the same source. Similarly, audiences who possess differing levels of expertise might accord differing levels of credibility to the same source.

Topic of the Message. When a dentist tells us that we would benefit from flossing our teeth, we generally believe him or her and adopt the practice, at least temporarily. But when the same dentist tells us that we would benefit from voting for his or her favorite politician, we are likely to perceive him or her as less credible on the dimension of competence. When an expert steps outside his or her area of expertise to address a topic, our perceptions of competence can potentially diminish. Whereas a former drug addict might be perceived as highly credible when discussing the dangers of drug abuse, chances are that the same source will be less credible when advising us on our choice of investments.

The credibility accorded a speaker by an audience will be related to the topic addressed and to the composition of the audience. With some topics, the audience is likely to regard the speaker as competent and trustworthy, but with a topic outside the speaker's area of expertise, the listeners may regard the person as lacking in competence, though still trustworthy. Of course, other less favorable perceptions also are possible.

Credibility as Process

Thus far, we have suggested that credibility is a perceptual, multi-dimensional concept and that it potentially can vary as a function of the composition of the audience and the topic of the speaker. Here it is useful to consider an additional Aristotelian conception: credibility can be either *assumed* or *demonstrated*. In Aristotle's view, our perceptions of a speaker will be based in part on the reputation that he or she brings to the public-speaking event and in part on the behaviors (verbal and nonverbal) that the speaker exhibits while delivering the address. Into every speaking event speakers bring their past history, their record of accomplishment, their prior successes and failures. Even before the speaker utters the first word of a speech, the audience members have made initial judgments of that speaker. These judgments may result from prior knowledge that they have of the speaker's activities or from observations made as the speaker sits on the stage awaiting the moment of the address.

Contemporary researchers and theorists have distinguished among what they term *initial, transactional,* and *terminal* credibility. *Initial credibility* may be compared to what Aristotle called *assumed ethos*: it is the attitude that an audience holds toward a speaker at the beginning of the presentation. Similarly, the contemporary term *transactional credibility* is equivalent to the concept of *assumed ethos.* The concept means that credibility is not static, but is in process. Audience perceptions of a speaker's credibility can continuously fluctuate as a result of the speaker's behaviors.

At the conclusion of a speaking event, listeners develop a final impression of the speaker, an attitude resulting from prior knowledge of the speaker and observations of the person in action. This final impression of the speaker's competence, trustworthiness, dynamism, sociability, and composure is termed the speaker's *terminal credibility.*

The Audience Forms an Image _____

Think of the many ways that an audience might perceive a speaker: high on competence, high on trustworthiness; low on competence, high on trustworthiness; high on competence, low on trustworthiness; high on competence, high on trustworthiness, and similar to the audience; high on competence, high on trustworthiness, but dissimilar from the audience; and so on. What combination of perceptions, then, is characteristic of the most credible and maximally effective speaker? In order to address this question—and there is no simple answer—we must consider the process by which an audience formulates an image of a speaker and determines his or her acceptability or believability as a source of information.

The Data Base

It is our position throughout this text (see Chapter 6) that most of our attitudes are information-based. We have defined *credibility* as a special kind of attitude that individuals of the audience hold toward a speaker. Because credibility is an attitude, it, too, should be based upon information. Gary Cronkhite and Jo R. Liska provide a useful system for categorizing the kinds of information the audience has available, to various degrees within each category, about a speaker. These categories, which they collectively refer to as composing a *social array,* are *reputed* characteristics, *nonverbal* characteristics, *verbal* characteristics, characteristics of *social interaction,* and self-reported characteristics.[6]

Reputed Characteristics. As we have already indicated, part of the information that an audience has about a speaker comes from other people's observations. They may report to us that a speaker is fat or thin, good looking or unattractive, honest or dishonest, dynamic or dull. Here it is useful to note Aristotle's caution that an impression of a speaker "should be created by the speech itself, and not left to depend upon an antecedent impression that the speaker is this or that kind of man."[7] Nonetheless, *reputed characteristics* remain as one category of information in the data base that the audience utilizes in forming an attitude.

Nonverbal Characteristics. The nonverbal behaviors of a speaker compose a second category of information available to an audience. Here Cronkhite and Liska make a useful distinction between *symptomatic* and *symbolic* behaviors.[8] Symptomatic behaviors are those nonverbal speaker responses related to the speaker's biological conditions: pupil dilation or contraction, respiration, sweating, flushed face, and so on. Symptomatic nonverbal behaviors are typically not willed directly by the speaker. Few people have control over their perspiration, breathing rates, or blushing. These symptomatic behaviors can, however, be observed by an audience, and as a speaker progresses through a presentation the listeners may note that the speaker seems to (1) be short of breath at times; (2) perspire to a seemingly unwarranted degree; and (3) blush frequently.

A second class of nonverbal speaker behaviors is symbolic, that is, the actions are part of what Cronkhite and Liska refer to as "a rule-governed symbol system shared by the communicants."[9] Put another way, we might suggest that many nonverbal behaviors are communicative; they are coded replacements for verbal expressions. If both the speaker and the audience know the code, they are likely to share common meanings for the nonverbal behaviors. To illustrate how various nonverbal codes might be utilized to derive information, examine the following list of observations that might be made about a speaker:

1. The speaker gestures frequently.
2. The speaker's face is very expressive.
3. The speaker is physically attractive, well groomed, and immaculately dressed.
4. The speaker shook hands warmly with everyone on the speaker's platform and put his arm around a number of these people.
5. There was considerable inflection in the speaker's voice.

[6]Gary Cronkhite and Jo R. Liska, "The Judgment of Communicant Acceptability," in *Persuasion: New Directions in Theory and Research,* ed. Michael E. Roloff and Gerald R. Miller (Beverly Hills, Calif.: Sage, 1980), pp. 101-139.

[7]Aristotle, *Rhetoric,* 1.2.1356a, pp. 8-9.

[8]Cronkhite and Liska, pp. 108-109.

[9]Cronkhite and Liska, p. 109.

6. The speaker began on time and concluded in the announced time of 20 minutes.
7. The speaker frequently walked out from behind the podium and approached the audience.

These observations represent nonverbal communicative behavior. They became part of the information base from which the audience forms an image of the speaker.

Verbal Characteristics. Verbal characteristics form a third source of information that an audience has about a speaker. Listeners will note the extent to which the speaker abides by the rules and normative standards associated with our language.

Audiences can note when words are mispronounced or pronounced with accents associated with different sections of our country or with foreign countries. One would not have to listen very long to Jimmy Carter or Ted Kennedy to associate them with the South and Northeast, respectively. Their regional dialects are readily apparent within their pronunciation. A speaker's sentence structure—the way he or she strings words together to form phrases and sentences—embodies a second type of verbally-based data that the speaker provides. With every sentence, information is revealed about language sophistication. The verbal component of a speaker's presentation is a valuable source of information about the person.

Characteristics of Social Interaction. Also observable by an audience are characteristics that relate to social interaction. As Cronkhite and Liska observe, these include such aspects as "the total amount of communication in which communicants are observed to participate, the ratio of communication produced to that received, the number of others with whom they communicate, the types of others from whom messages are received, and the types of messages sent to and received from various types of others."[10] A moment's reflection will suggest that these characteristics of social interaction do have message value.

Self-reported Characteristics. A final category of available observable information about a speaker includes those characteristics that a speaker self-reports. "I am not a crook" certainly falls within this category, as do assertions of competence, friendliness, admiration, and so forth. Notice here that when a speaker says he or she is honest, the honesty is not directly observable. What is observable is that the speaker *claims* to be honest. Few speakers would be so blatant as to claim such characteristics as competence or trustworthiness for themselves. Self-reporting these characteristics is frequently counterproductive. But a speaker does self-disclose many personal qualities, primarily through reporting past behaviors, attitudes toward a wide array of issues, and opinions held with respect to the audience.

[10]Cronkhite and Liska, p. 112.

Inferred Characteristics: Factors of Credibility?

It is important to note that information within Cronkhite and Liska's *social array* is either directly observable by the audience or that it may easily be checked for authenticity. Such observable data become the raw data from which audiences attribute more abstract qualities to the speaker—qualities such as competence, trustworthiness, dynamism, sociability, composure, and perhaps other components of credibility that have yet to be discovered.

To illustrate how this process works, let us examine how an audience might come to regard a speaker as *trustworthy*. First, our speaker, Juan Bermudez, is introduced to us as a man of high integrity; testimony from several respected individuals is introduced to support this claim (reputed characteristics). Second, as Juan speaks, he looks us directly in the eyes; he seems free of tension; his nonverbal and verbal behaviors are consistent in the messages they convey; he smiles easily and naturally (nonverbal characteristics). Third, the evidence Juan reports comes from sources we judge to be credible, and the substance of the evidence is consistent with what we consider to be the facts. Juan's language is noninflammatory, even though it appears he could sway his audience with emotional language (verbal characteristics). Fourth, it is apparent from what Juan says that he communicates frequently with important officials with regard to highly sensitive matters (self-reported characteristics of social interaction). Finally, Juan reveals several of his past experiences that suggest his integrity, and what he says seems consistent with other observations we have made of him (self-report). In addition, when we take all of our observations of this speaker into consideration, we recognize a high degree of internal consistency and judge that Juan is a trustworthy source of information.

We could go on to show how we might form a judgment of competence, dynamism, sociability, or composure, but we are sure that we have made our point. From generally observable data, audiences infer that speakers possess abstract qualities to greater or lesser degrees. These abstract qualities—perceptions of the audience—become the substance of the audience's attitude toward the speaker. More specifically, they can be regarded as the components or dimensions of speaker credibility.

The "Ideal" Source

As we noted at the beginning of this chapter, many possible combinations of perceptions of a speaker are possible. We also indicated that it is not easy to determine the exact combination of perceptions that will produce the most credible and maximally effective speaker. Examining some relevant research may shed some light on the issue, however.

Competence. In an attempt to determine if the expertise of a source alone could account for persuasiveness, Stephen Bachner and C. A. Insko presented a written communication, supposedly a reading comprehension test, to a number of equivalent groups of subjects. The communication concerned the number of hours of sleep per night required for people to function properly. The message was attributed to either a Nobel prize-winning physiologist (a high-expertise source) or a YMCA director (a low-expertise source). The two sources, who were assumed to be approximately equal in trustworthiness because neither would have anything to gain by misleading the subjects, advocated from eight to zero hours of sleep per night. The researchers found that the extreme positions advocated by the physiologist produced a greater number of attitude changes. By contrast, when the low-expertise source advocated these extreme positions, less and less attitude change was observed.[11] Such results suggest that expertise may be most important when a speaker advocates a position that varies from the audience's initial position. The more extreme the advocated position, the more important the need for speaker expertise.

Our results are qualified, however, when we distinguish between two types of persuasive situations. The first situation is one in which an audience has low personal involvement or minimal knowledge about the issue under consideration. In such circumstances, credibility seems to have maximum effect, particularly when the speaker advocates a position contrary to the prior attitudes of the audience. As Richard E. Petty and John T. Cacioppo observe, "when people do not have much prior knowledge about an issue... or when involvement is low, messages from sources of high credibility are accepted without much thought."[12] In other words, when the message will not have great personal impact on individuals, these people are likely to disregard the arguments of the message and be swayed by the competence and/or trustworthiness of the source alone. However, in a case in which the audience has high topic involvement or prior knowledge, the situation is quite different. From their review of pertinent literature, Petty and Cacioppo conclude that within such a situation audiences will not be easily swayed by the credibility of the speaker alone but will look more closely at the speaker's message and the arguments and evidence used to support it. When arguments are strong and well supported, the high-credibility source will have an advantage over the low-credibility source presenting the same arguments. When arguments are mediocre, no advantage will exist.[13]

Trustworthiness. Numerous studies have demonstrated that speakers who advocate a position not in their own best interest are highly persuasive. Thus, a representative of the liquor industry calling for moderation in alcohol consumption, a local apartment-house owner who urges his community's involvement in the construction of a large-scale subsidized housing project, and a politician running for reelection and

[11]Stephen Bachner and C. A. Insko, "Communicator Discrepancy, Source Credibility, and Opinion Change," *Journal of Personality and Social Psychology,* 4: 614-621 (1966).

[12]Richard E. Petty and John T. Cacioppo, *Attitudes and Persuasion: Classic and Contemporary Approaches* (Dubuque, Iowa: William C. Brown, 1981), p. 236.

[13]Petty and Cacioppo, p. 237.

advocating a substantial increase in personal income taxes all could be quite persuasive because their expressed positions are at variance with what might produce obvious personal gain.

Trustworthiness of a message source also has been operationalized with respect to the source's *intent to persuade.* In general, a source whose apparent intent is to persuade has been presumed to be less trustworthy than one who simply intends to inform. Results in this area are somewhat mixed: some investigators find that persuasive intent inhibits attitude change, and others find no effect. Here again, Petty and Cacioppo advance the hypothesis that the effect depends upon the degree of personal involvement the subjects have in the issue under deliberation. To test their hypothesis, they prepared a message advocating that university seniors be required to pass a comprehensive examination in their major field before they would be allowed to graduate. Half of the university students who composed their sample were told that they were to hear a tape designed to persuade students of the desirability of changing certain college requirements (persuasive intent present). The other half were informed that they were going to evaluate radio editorials (no persuasive intent). In addition, one subgroup was told that the examinations might be instituted at their school by the end of the year (high involvement). A second group was instructed that the examinations would be instituted at their school within ten years (moderate involvement), and a third group was informed that the examinations were to be instituted at other schools (low involvement).[14] Results clearly indicated that attitude change was inhibited by forewarning in the personally involved conditions. That is, those who were forewarned that the change in university policy might apply to them directly were least amenable to the message. Apparently, forewarning of intent to persuade can decrease attitude change, at least with respect to issues that entail personal involvement.

Sociability and Liking. Under many circumstances, we are influenced not by the competence or trustworthiness of the message source but apparently by our *liking* for the individual. Earlier, we suggested that we develop *liking* for others who are co-oriented with us and who share our beliefs, attitudes, and values; who reward us through genuine praise and favors; who possess special competencies; and who like us in return. Here it may be useful to elaborate on some effects of liking another person.

Given a free-choice situation in which individuals can choose to communicate with any of a number of potential receivers, people select those persons who are most like themselves. Communication is best achieved between individuals who share similar experiences, attitudes,

[14]Richard E. Petty and John T. Cacioppo, "Effects of Forewarning of Persuasive Intent and Involvement on Cognitive Responses and Persuasion," *Personality and Social Psychology Bulletin, 5*: 173-176 (1979).

and beliefs.[15] As Elliot Aronson observes, "Literally dozens of tightly controlled experiments. . . have shown over and over again that, if all you know about a person are his or her opinions on several issues, the more similar those opinions are to yours, the more you like the person."[16] Under some circumstances, we also can note that the speaker who shares characteristics with the audience may be the most persuasive.[17]

The implication here for the public speaker becomes quite clear. Where similarities exist between a speaker and the audience, the speaker well may benefit by making note of those areas of common ground, by pointing to shared life experiences or to mutually held attitudes, beliefs, and values. This is particularly so when the areas of common ground have a bearing on the topic under consideration.

A second cause of *liking* is speaker praise of an audience. It has long been argued that those who would be effective sources of influence should praise their intended target. One analysis of Dale Carnegie's famous book, *How to Win Friends and Influence People,* suggests that "Carnegie's advice is deceptively simple: If you want someone to like you, be pleasant, pretend that you like him, feign an interest in things that he's interested in, 'dole out praise lavishly,' and be agreeable."[18]

Is Carnegie correct? Are such tactics effective for the public speaker? We suspect that under most circumstances they are not. All too often we hear a speaker say, "You're a great audience" or "I'm so happy to have the opportunity to speak to such an intelligent and informed group." In general, we probably dismiss such comments as ritualistic if not insincere remarks. We suggest that when you offer praise to an audience, do so with caution. We suspect that praise can be highly effective if (1) the praise is warranted and (2) the audience perceives the speaker as having no ulterior motive for bestowing it. The circumstances of the public-speaking event are usually such that the speaker typically cannot satisfy these criteria, at least not easily. Consequently, before you undertake to lavish praise upon your audience, reflect on the potential outcomes that might be produced and proceed with care.

The physical attractiveness of the speaker also has a bearing on his or her appeal. Numerous scientific investigations illustrate the link between liking and speaker influence,[19] but let us look at one in particular. A woman who was considered attractive posed as a graduate student in psychology and interviewed a number of college males. At the close of the interview, she gave half the males negative evaluations of their role

[15]See Everett M. Rogers and Dilip K. Bhowonik, "Homophily-Heterophily: Relational Concepts for Communication Research," in *Speech Communication Behavior,* ed. Larry L. Barker and Robert J. Kibler (Englewood Cliffs, N.J.: Prentice-Hall, 1971), pp. 206-225.

[16]Aronson, p. 256.

[17]E. Burnstein, E. Statland, and A. Zander, "Similarity to a Model and Self-Evaluation," *Journal of Abnormal and Social Psychology, 62*: 257-264 (1961).

[18]Aronson, p. 239, referring to Dale Carnegie, *How to Win Friends and Influence People* (New York: Simon and Schuster, 1952).

[19]See, for example, Judson Mills and Elliot Aronson, "Opinion Change as a Function of Communicator's Attractiveness and Desire to Influence," *Journal of Personality and Social Psychology, 1*: 173-177 (1965).

in the interview and the other half positive evaluations. In a second condition, the interviewer provided the same types of evaluation but was made to look physically unattractive (she wore a frizzy wig and ill-fitting clothing). The investigators discovered that when the interviewer was less attractive, the subjects did not seem to be differentially affected by the type of evaluation they received. When the interviewer was considered attractive, however, the subjects liked the woman a great deal when she provided positive evaluations and disliked her (more than in any other condition) when she provided a negative evaluation.[20] For the persuasive speaker, the advice is simple enough: try to present yourself as personally attractive. Although certain aspects of appearance are beyond our control, we are able to adjust our dress and personal grooming.

A Point of View _____

We have not yet answered the question, "What qualities characterize the ideal public speaker?" At least two situational characteristics are determinants of the ideal or most effective public speaker: the audience's reason for participating in the communicative event with the speaker and their degree of involvement in the issue(s) under deliberation.

Reason for Participation

Audiences choose to expose themselves to a public speaker for one of two primary reasons. They participate in a public-speaking event either *to gain information* of present or future value or *to be entertained*. It is unlikely that an individual would choose to attend a public speech in order to be persuaded. This suggests to us that we might have very different expectations for a speaker when we are seeking information than when we only wish to be entertained. Because most of us wish to base our decisions and actions on reliable and valid information, we prefer competent and trustworthy sources when we seek information. In such a circumstance, Cronkhite suggests that the ideal source would be one who possesses the following characteristics:

1. Was in a position to observe the facts he or she reports.
2. Has the physical, intellectual, psychological, and emotional capabilities to make the observation, along with sensitivity toward the facts.
3. Is motivated to perceive and report accurately, having nothing to gain by deception.

[20]Harold Segall and Elliot Aronson, "Liking for an Evaluator as a Function of Her Physical Attractiveness and Nature of the Evaluation," *Journal of Experimental Social Psychology, 5*: 93-100 (1969).

4. Has a history of reporting accurately on this and other topics.
5. Is accountable for the proffered testimony.[21]

An inspection of such criteria should certainly suggest the importance of the competence, trustworthiness and, perhaps, co-orientation of the speaker when the audience enters the public-speaking situation for the purposes of adding to their information base.

At other times, when the audience simply desires *to be entertained,* the definition of the ideal public speaker is likely to change. Under such circumstances, it is possible that competence and trustworthiness may not perform such prominent roles. In these cases, the audience may be more influenced by their liking for the speaker, their perceptions of the speaker's dynamism, physical attractiveness, and degree of composure.

Degree of Involvement

It appears that the credibility of a source has greatest impact when the audience is less personally involved in the issue. When the matter at hand has little to do with the personal dealings of audience members, factors of credibility can effect considerable attitude change. Apparently, under such conditions individuals are willing to accept the word of the high-credibility source. But on matters that personally affect the audience, it seems as if speaker credibility is of somewhat less importance. Here the audience looks beyond the individual and examines the quality of the message. The listeners weigh the strength of argument and the evidence used for support. With high-involvement issues, the most effective source is the competent and trustworthy source who also has strong and well-supported arguments.

A Concluding Note

We began this chapter by observing how communication can be defined as the study of "who says what to whom with what effect." Throughout the chapter, we have emphasized that *who* presents a message does make a difference. Evidence strongly suggests overall that credible sources are more effective than those who are less credible. We are not aware of any reliable evidence showing the opposite position. We conclude by suggesting that it is to the speaker's benefit if the audience perceives him or her as high in competence, trustworthy, likeable, dynamic, and composed. As we have just observed in conjunction with high-involvement topics, achieving such a perception will not always be an advantage for the speaker, but it seldom, if ever, will be a disadvantage. During our discussion, we have suggested how a speaker might produce favorable perceptions within the audience. We emphasize, however, that if you wish to be perceived as a credible speaker, the best guarantee of producing this perception is to *be a credible speaker*—to be

[21]Adapted from Gary L. Cronkhite, "Scales Measuring General Evaluation with Minimal Distortion," *Public Opinion Quarterly, 41*: 65-73 (1977).

competent in the field, to have the best interests of your audience at heart, to genuinely like those with whom you communicate, and to present your ideas dynamically and with composure. On a short-term basis, people can be fooled (as P. T. Barnum was so well aware!). Over the long haul, however, the *truly credible* speaker will have the advantage.

Summary

1. A source of a message is the originator of a message. Typically, and particularly in the public-speaking situation, the source and the sender of a message are the same person. However, this is not always the case.
2. Source or speaker credibility is the audience's general attitude or feeling of favorableness to unfavorableness toward the sender of a message.
3. The credibility of a speaker is not inherent within the speaker but resides within the perceptions of the speaker's audience.
4. Speaker credibility is a multidimensional variable. It is composed of audience evaluations of a speaker's competence, trustworthiness, dynamism or extroversion, sociability and liking, composure, and, perhaps, additional yet-to-be-recognized components.
5. The dimensions of credibility are potentially independent of one another; a source may score from high to low on any combination of dimensions.
6. The degree of credibility accorded a speaker is variable, depending on the audience addressed and the topic under consideration.
7. Within a given presentation, three stages of credibility are present: *initial* premessage credibility; *transactional* credibility, produced by the message content and speaker behaviors; and *terminal* credibility, resulting from the interaction of initial and transactional credibility.
8. Audiences formulate or infer judgments of a speaker from *reputed, nonverbal, verbal, social-interaction,* and *self-reported* characteristics.
9. Nonverbal characteristics of a speaker are either *symptomatic* (associated with biological functioning) or *symbolic* (following a rule-governed symbol system shared by the communicants).
10. From observable and verifiable speaker characteristics, audiences formulate more abstract judgments. These abstractions form clusters of judgment that define the dimensions of speaker credibility.
11. It is clear that in some circumstances speaker credibility is responsible for attitudinal change, particularly when the issue under consideration is not highly involving for the audience.
12. Competence alone, trustworthiness alone, and even liking seem to be capable of effecting attitude change, especially when the audience has a low degree of personal involvement in the topic.

13. It appears that what constitutes the ideal or most effective speaker is dependent on at least two situational characteristics: the audience's reason for participating in the communicative event with the speaker and the degree of involvement that the audience has in the topic.

14. It is generally to the speaker's benefit if the audience perceives him or her as high in competence, trustworthy, likeable, dynamic, and composed. Achieving such a perception will not always be an advantage, but seldom, if ever, will it be a disadvantage.

Questions and Exercises _____

1. Describe a speaking situation in which the source and sender of the message are not the same person.

2. Your text indicates that source credibility is a "perceptual" variable. Explain why the variable is so classified.

3. Since the time of Aristotle, source credibility (*ethos*) has been viewed as a multidimensional variable. Enumerate five dimensions (components) of credibility and explain what is involved within each of the dimensions.

4. The dimensions of credibility are generally viewed as potentially independent of one another. Explain this position and illustrate it by pointing to specific public speakers with whom your classmates are also familiar.

5. Make a list of five speakers you consider to be high in credibility. Compare your list with those of your classmates. What differences of opinion do you note? How do you account for these differences?

6. Reexamine the list you made in item 5. Can you make such a list without a consideration of the topic on which an individual might be speaking? How does this notion relate to what your text refers to as the "situational" nature of speaker credibility?

7. Differentiate among initial, transactional, and terminal credibility. Relate these concepts to the Aristotelian conception of *demonstrated* and *assumed ethos.*

8. Identify the components of the data base from which an audience forms an image of a speaker and explain how an attitude toward a speaker is formulated from this data base or "social array."

9. Nonverbal speaker behaviors can be classified as either *symptomatic* or *symbolic*. Provide examples of each type of behavior and explain why we tend to think of one of these types as more revealing of a speaker's "true" self.

10. Speaker credibility is an important communication variable, but it seems to have its greatest effect under special circumstances. Identify these circumstances and offer your explanation as to why these circumstances impact on the importance of speaker credibility.

11. Offer your definition of the ideal speaker and be prepared to justify your response.

Courtesy Carter Presidential Materials Project

8

Organizing Effectively

OBJECTIVES

By the time you finish reading this chapter, you should be able to:

1. Discuss the process of organization and how it helps you and your audience.
2. Identify and provide examples of temporal orders, causal orders, spatial orders, classification orders, and topical orders.
3. Use various outlining techniques.
4. Explain and use the rules of formal outlining for your speeches.

Organization is one of the most important features of message construction. With rare exceptions, the materials presented in well-organized messages are better remembered and more influential than when those materials are presented in poorly organized messages.[1]

Organization may be defined as the process of developing and expressing ideas in patterns that both you and the audience understand and remember. To be well organized is to follow a pattern, to recognize that you are following it, and to communicate the pattern and the fact that you are following it to your audience. The result is that the audience better retains the message content. Information or materials that are remembered enable the audience to comprehend the ideas that support your thesis. That leads to greater acceptance of your thesis. This chapter explains how you can achieve the goal of a well-organized speech. The first section explains the nature of each of five patterns and how to recognize them. The second section discusses outlining. The third section explains how organization and outlining aid you in developing your speech.

SELECT A PATTERN
FAMILIAR TO YOU.

LET YOUR AUDIENCE KNOW THE
PATTERN YOU ARE FOLLOWING.

AUDIENCE MEMORY, UNDERSTANDING, AND
SUPPORTIVE THOUGHTS WILL INCREASE.

AUDIENCE ACCEPTANCE OF YOUR THESIS
WILL INCREASE.

[1]Robert N. Bostrom, *Persuasion* (Englewood Cliffs, N.J.: Prentice-Hall, 1983), pp. 173-176.

The Five Basic Types of Organizational Patterns _____

There are numerous patterns of organization. We have selected five of the most useful types. They are the following: (1) temporal or chronological orders, (2) causal orders, (3) spatial orders, (4) classification orders, and (5) topical orders. When you tell friends about your trip to the Grand Canyon, you may recount your experience in *temporal order*—the order in which the events occurred. If you see a crowd of students surrounding a speaker on your campus (the *effect*), you may ask another student for an explanation (the *cause*). If a stranger asks for directions to a building on your campus, you reply with a series of lefts, rights, just beyonds, or perhaps norths and souths—the order in which your campus is arranged in *space*. If you wish to buy a can of chocolate syrup at a supermarket, then you will want to know whether the grocer classifies it as a baking supply, a topping, or a candy. Finally, you may order a number of your routine activities on a *topical* basis. Among other meanings, Webster suggests that this term refers to "topics of the day or place."[2] If you analyze the President's budget proposals in terms of their economic, social, and political effects, you are employing topical order.

Temporal Orders

The first, and perhaps the most common way of developing and expressing thoughts, is in chronological (temporal) order. You report an interesting event by following the order in which the event occurred, from beginning to end. Sometimes, however, you start with the end and work your way back to the beginning. If you report on how you dented the car, you may start by mentioning the accident, and then work your way backward to discover how you could avoid such an accident in the future. When the speaker announces, "We must review where we have been; we must locate our present position; we must then decide where we go from here," the audience can discern chronological order in these references to the past, present, and future. A speech on "Climbing a Mountain" could be arranged in the following chronological sequence:

I. Climbing Mount Whitney
   A. The month before the climb was spent gathering gear and practicing together.
   B. The initial phase of the climb was scenic but uneventful.
   C. From 7000 feet on, the hours were filled with narrow scrapes and exhaustion.
   D. Reaching the summit made the effort worth it.

[2]*Webster's New Collegiate Dictionary* (Springfield, Mass.: G. and C. Merriman Co., 1975), p. 1231.

Causal Orders

Causal organizational patterns are close relatives of time patterns. This is because effects follow causes in chronological sequence. However, the distinctive feature of causal patterns is that they focus on *why* events occur. We frequently ask *why*. The Japanese, Russians, and Norwegians hunt whales to the point of extinction. Why do they do that? Some students and adults drink to the point at which they become ill and have to spend the following day or days recovering. What causes them to do that? Scholars have identified four common causal patterns to explain *why* events occur.

Problem-solution order for speeches is the most widely found causal order. As its name implies, the pattern divides the speech into two sections: a discussion of an issue identified as a problem and a second part that deals with how to resolve that problem. The *problem* section of speeches describes the situation and identifies its causes. The *solution* section explains a proposal or plan that removes the causes and discusses benefits gained from the solution. Generally, a problem-solution pattern leads to seeking answers to these questions:

I. What is the problem?
   A. How can the problem be described? (What are its effects, signs, or symptoms?)
   B. What is producing or causing the problem?
II. What is the solution?
   A. What plan or program will remove the causes?
   B. What benefits may be expected if the plan or program is adopted?

For example, if you decide to speak on "Smoking," you might develop a problem-solution outline like the following:

I. Those who smoke risk early and painful death.
   A. Smokers risk cancer and heart disease.
   B. Cigarette tars produce cancer; nicotine produces heart disease.
II. Stopping smoking produces health and happiness.
   A. Attending a "Stop Smoking Clinic" frequently ends the smoking habit.
   B. Stopping smoking decreases the risks of death and suffering and increases enjoyment of most activities.

A variation of the problem-solution order is Alan H. Monroe's Motivated Sequence,[3] which recommends that all speeches follow a

---

[3]Alan H. Monroe, *Principles of Speech*, 4th brief ed. (Chicago: Scott, Foresman and Co., 1958), pp. 201-212.

pattern of five psycho-causal stages. First, the speaker gains the attention of the audience. Attention results when the speaker presents materials that refer to the new or unique (the novel), things that are close at hand (proximity), disputes, arguments, or controversies (conflict), and major, pressing, immediate concerns of the audience (the vital).[4] Second, the speaker explains to the audience why they need the information, beliefs, or objects promoted in the speech. Monroe called this step *need*. Third, the speaker presents materials that satisfy the need—he calls this the *satisfaction* step. Fourth, the speaker supplies materials to help the audience picture or visualize themselves enjoying the benefits of the information, beliefs, or objects presented in the satisfaction step. This step is the *visualization* step. Finally, in the fifth step, the *action* step, the speaker offers materials that "close the sale" of the information, beliefs, or objects. These materials have the highest degree of motivational impact; they move the audience to decision or action. Building speeches around attention, need, satisfaction, visualization, and action is effective in some situations. However, the exercise of forcing all speeches into this format has little to recommend it. Speakers, audiences, and topics differ widely in the ease with which the Motivated Sequence can be adapted to their abilities and needs.

Cause to effect is the third causal order. Sometimes the audience is aware of a cause but wants increased information about its effects. In these cases, the speech summarizes the causes succinctly but discusses the effects at length. If your school proposes an increase in tuition, your classmates know the cause and prefer to hear about the effects of that increase. If you title your speech "The Effects of the Tuition Increase on Student Reenrollment Plans," your outline might look like this:

Cause: I. Tuition increases have been approved by the Trustees for next year for undergraduates.

Effects: II. Financial and psychological pressures of the increase will adversely affect students.
 A. Ten percent of undergraduates feel they will have to drop out of school for the time being.
 B. Half of the undergraduates think they will need to seek part-time work or expand the hours at their current jobs.
 C. Almost all of those receiving support from parents expect increased pressures for good grades.

Sometimes you face an opposite situation, in which the audience knows the effects but may want information about the causes. In this

[4]Monroe, p. 197.

type of situation, you should employ the fourth causal pattern: effect to cause. If you speak on inflation, you might briefly recount its effects and discuss its causes at length. Your outline might look like this:

Effect: **I.** Inflation rates continue to have adverse effects upon the poor, the middle class, and, to some degree, the rich.

Causes: **II.** Spending money that we do not have produces inflation.
- **A.** Federal deficit spending generates disproportional inflationary pressure.
- **B.** Consumer credit-buying generates even greater pressure than the Federal deficit.
- **C.** Business credit-buying generates the greatest pressure.
- **D.** Wage rates rising faster than productivity rates make the other pressures worse.

Spatial Orders

Spatial orders deal with the relationships between events and objects as they occupy space. When you enter a building to find the office of a faculty member, the building directory is separated into floors. When you set out from Athens, Ohio, to travel to Myrtle Beach, South Carolina, the map you follow is arranged in spatial order. If you give directions to a stranger, you organize them according to space: east to west, left to right; up this hill, down that hill, around the curve; the second street after the third stoplight. If you give a speech entitled "American Housing Will Be Radically Different by 2050," a section of the speech, if not the entire speech, might be arranged spatially. The outline might resemble the following:

I. The costs of energy will ensure that houses of the future are circular or close to circular to enclose as much space as possible with the least external area exposed.
- **A.** At the center of the circle, a cylinder will contain the main supporting beams and all utilities.
- **B.** The central cylinder will be surrounded by a larger cylinder divided into pie-shaped slices containing storage space, bath, and laundry facilities. One of the slices may contain a chimney if a fireplace or heating stove is to be used.
- **C.** The outer perimeter will contain the living space, divided to suit the needs of the occupants.

Classification Orders

The fourth type of pattern is called classification order. In this pattern, material is divided into categories. A familiar referent for this kind of organization is the classification of animals in biology into phyla, subphyla, genus, and species. For a speech on "Kinds of Mental Illness," a general outline following classification order might look like this:

I. Professional psychologists and psychiatrists classify mental illness in two ways:
 A. The process-reactive classification is concerned with whether the onset of the disease is sudden (reactive) or has developed over a long period of time (process).
   1. Reactive illness is frequently produced by some external situation, such as the death of a close relative.
   2. Process illnesses cannot be traced to an immediate situation, but generally develop from internal psycho-physical conditions.
 B. The neurosis-psychosis classification has to do with the basic nature of the mental illness.
   1. Neuroses usually affect some specific area of the individual's behaviors and are represented by hysterias and phobias.
   2. Psychosis usually affects most or all of the individual's behaviors and are represented by paranoia and schizophrenia.

Topical Orders

Finally, some patterns are determined by the peculiar nature of the subject matter. Most of these orders—called *topical*—could also take other forms. You might, for example, give a talk on the two most significant books you have read or the three most important events in your life. These subjects could follow chronological order, but somehow that type of organization would miss the point. In a talk about the best place on earth to visit, you could divide your speech into the subjects of scenery, people, and food. The number of such topical patterns is endless. If you consider using one of these patterns, be sure to ask yourself whether your organization will be easily recognized by the audience.

The two most common organizing principles for creating topical orders are *importance or priority principles* and what we will call *arbitrary principles*. Speeches on subjects such as life philosophy typically use topical patterns based upon priority. These types of speeches might discuss health first, family and friends second, and career third. Another example—a speech on the three principal energy sources for America's future—would discuss solar, synthetic, and hydrogen sources.

Topical orders based on arbitrary principles occur mainly when a speaker cannot find another satisfactory pattern. Good speakers seldom face the need for an arbitrary pattern. One comparatively rare situation in which arbitrary order may be helpful is when a speaker must speak impromptu. In such situations, one author suggests such arbitrary orders as "The Right Way, the Wrong Way. . . Mentally, Morally, Physically. . . Socially, Economically, Politically. . . Theoretically, Practically. . . Employer, Employee, and the General Public. . . ."[5]

Picturing the Results of Organization: The Outline _____

An outline presents a picture of the organizational relationships in a way that is quickly comprehended. Traditional outlines are composed of symbols and blank space—minimal elements that demonstrate the patterns of relationships existing among your ideas.

Rules of Outlining

The rules for outlining are fairly simple.

1. Select a consistent symbol system.
2. Use a pattern of indentation and spacing to emphasize the symbol system you have selected.
3. Use complete sentences in your final outline. (In the experience of your authors, the use of complete sentences in outlining helps assure fine organization, a high quality of language usage, thought, and adequate numbers and varieties of supporting devices. A sentence outline more than any other device enables you to recognize flaws in your preparation.)

The following paragraph presents the conventions of outlining. Table 8-1 then illustrates how these conventions actually appear in outlines.

The major ideas are identified with Roman numerals, starting with I and proceeding to II, III, IV, V, and so on. The first level of subordination is indicated by capital letters—A, B, C, D, E, and so on. The next level is indicated with sequenced Arabic numerals—1, 2, 3, 4, 5, and so on. This is followed by lower-case English alphabet letters—a, b, c, d, e, and so on. The process then begins to use parentheses. The level after the lower-case English alphabet letters repeats the Arabic numerals in parentheses—(1), (2), (3), (4), (5), and so on. These are then followed by the

[5]James M. Lewis, "Spur-of-the-Moment Speeches," *Today's Speech, 6*(3): 9-10 (1958).

TABLE 8-1   A Sample Outline Illustrating Formal Outlining Procedures

Thesis or purpose sentence: Humans prefer peace.

I. The idea that humans are inherently aggressive or warlike is a myth.
   A. The "humans are warlike" myth is perpetuated by historians who emphasize war.
     1. Most Americans have studied history in a way that emphasizes war.
       a. Most of us can readily name the major wars in which we have engaged.
         (1) From our early history, you remember the War of Independence, or the Revolutionary War, as well as the War of 1812.
           (a) Some of the events you best remember about our revolutionary period are battles and related events.
             (I) You probably recall the Battle of Bunker Hill and that it was really fought on Breed's Hill.
             (II) You may recall Valley Forge or Washington crossing the Delaware River.
           (b) What you remember about the period around the War of 1812 is:
             (I) The sacking of Washington by the British.
             (II) Andrew Jackson's victory in the Battle of New Orleans.
         (2) Most of what you know about the middle period of our history has to do with events that took place during the Civil War, especially the violent events.
         (3) We are all so familiar with wars in contemporary history, World Wars I and II, the Korean War, and the Vietnamese War, that examples of battles need not be mentioned.
           (a) Pause for a few seconds and think of what you recall about each of these wars. It will be battles and heroes of battles in most cases.
         (4) You may also remember our minor wars.
            (a) From the Mexican-American War, you may not remember its date of 1846 to 1848, but you "Remember the Alamo."
           (b) You may not remember that the Spanish-American War was fought at the turn of the century, but you "Remember the Maine."
     2. Most Americans have learned social studies and humanities in time periods that are marked off by war.
       a. For example, consider titles like J. O. Urmson's *Philosophical Analysis Between the Two World Wars*.
       b. Our best-loved movies and novels frequently are set in wartime.
   B. The "humans are warlike" myth is perpetuated by the news media.
     1. Newspapers and news magazines devote most of their resources toward reporting any war or dispute they can find.
     2. Television news reporters literally lust after the opportunity to report guerilla warfare, close to home if possible, but in obscure places otherwise.
       a. El Salvador and Honduras are currently receiving heavy coverage.
       b. If the situation quiets in Central America, then undoubtedly television will turn again to the horn of Africa or the guerilla war in Northwest Africa.

TABLE 8-1 *(continued)*

   II. An accurate picture of American history indicates much longer periods of peace than war.
      A. There are two figures to consider to determine the ratio of peace to war in America:
         1. If you count the approximately 153 years during the colonial period when we were not at war with Britain, then you get one figure.
         2. If you don't count those 153 years, you get another figure.
      B. If you count the 153, America has existed for approximately 363 years and been at peace approximately 97 percent of the time.
         1. All our wars involved approximately 25 years of our history.
         2. But our memory of the major contributions to peace does not exist in an organized fashion so that it seems we have been forever at war.
      C. If you don't count the 153, America has existed approximately 210 years and has been at peace 88 percent of the time.
         1. Again, all our wars have involved approximately 25 years of our history.
         2. If you prefer to measure our existence as a nation from the Declaration of Independence, then we still have a remarkable record of peace—our war years constitute only 12 percent of our total history.
      D. Other peoples have even better peace records than ours.
         1. Some people, such as the Hopi, have never fought a war.
         2. Some peoples of Africa and Asia who have fought from time to time have remained at peace for centuries.

---

lower-case English alphabet letters in parentheses—(a), (b), (c), (d), (e), and so on. If you need to go below that, one way of doing so is to use the Roman numerals again in parentheses—(I), (II), (III), (IV), (V), and so on—followed by the English capitals in parentheses—(A), (B), (C), (D), (E), and so on. Below that, small English letters from near the end of the alphabet are used in alphabetical order—t, u, v, w, x, y, z. If your outline is still more detailed, you can make up your own procedure. It is usually neater in outlining to indent each level of subordination so that the left margins as well as the letters indicate the level. Table 8-1 makes use of nearly all these levels. Note, however, that outlines for speeches usually do not go below the first three or four levels of emphasis or subordination.

The Process of Organizing and Outlining _____

     Organizing a message is a process that involves selecting a topic and jotting down a preliminary outline composed of a tentative thesis and a list of subordinate ideas. Use that preliminary list to guide your reading and discussions about the topic. As you read and talk with others about your speech to come, you will discover that some (and perhaps all) of the thoughts you listed must be discarded or replaced by different ideas. You will also discover that the subordinate topics are complex and that they must be divided into further levels of subordination. You may change the order of your major points or discover that an idea you had associated with one major point really fits better with another.

Your research may alter your thinking and your outlining to the point at which you feel that you have developed an entirely new topic. This can make you feel frustrated and discouraged. Take comfort, however, in the fact that there are few people who pick a topic, spend a few hours in the library, write an outline that meets the instructor's requirements, and give an excellent speech. The process of constant revision and change in organization is a necessary part of preparing a speech.

Because of unexpected frustrations resulting from the interaction between organization, research, and thought, many students quit preparing for their speeches too soon. Your authors study the speech preparation behaviors of several hundred students each year. It is common to discover that many of them develop excellent plans for preparing their speeches. They set aside reasonable lengths of time for each of the tasks in preparing (though not as much rehearsal time as they should), and they proceed to do what they have planned to do— until they find themselves confused and frustrated by the interaction between organization, research, and thought. They become discouraged and assume that they have made a bad choice of topic or that they are not worthy of the topic they have chosen. In most cases, the confusion and frustration will end if these students simply spend the rest of the time they had planned to spend on research, thought, and outline revision. They are close to an excellent performance, but they talk themselves out of completing the work necessary to do it.

A contributing cause for stopping short in the preparation process is a frequently held belief that written documents are ends in themselves rather than tools for achieving an end. When something is written down in the form of an outline, it ought to be permanent—or so many students think. You will do much better to think of outlining (at least in the preliminary stages of preparation) as a tool. Whatever the final requirements for the outline you will turn in, you do not have to meet those requirements until relatively late in the preparation process. In the meantime, you may develop your ideas through trial outlines in various forms, notes of all kinds on paper or cards, or even a chalkboard, along with talking aloud about your topic and jotting down what you have said. All these things can be shuffled and tried out again in different forms. If you keep at the process long enough, then everything will come together and you will discover that the quality of your presentations will improve and that writing the outline to meet your class requirements will be relatively simple.

The process of organizing and outlining works better for some students if they use forms that help them picture relationships in the initial stages of speech preparation. In fact, some of the ways of picturing organization can make effective visual aids for speeches. Pictures that have a strong visual component help you to think clearly about your topic. Compare the example of a traditional outline on the topic of "Canadian Vacations" in Table 8-2 with the visually oriented ways of expressing similar ideas in Figures 8-1 through 8-4.

TABLE 8-2   Picturing Ideas with a Traditional Outline

I. Canada is an excellent place to vacation.
    A. Canada is widely acclaimed among people who love sports.
        1. Excellent fishing abounds.
        2. Hunting is excellent.
    B. Canada offers vacation activities for those who prefer culture to sports.
        1. The Stratford Shakespeare Festival is widely known.
        2. The major cities are centers of art and culture.
            a. Montreal provides an atmosphere and activities that are typically French.
            b. Toronto provides historical sights, museums, and other events typical of large metropolitan areas.
    C. Canada offers spectacular parks and scenery.
        1. The Maritime provinces offer seashores full of marine life.
        2. The eastern highlands and western mountains are among the most beautiful and accessible of such lands.

FIGURE 8-1   Picturing Ideas with Brackets

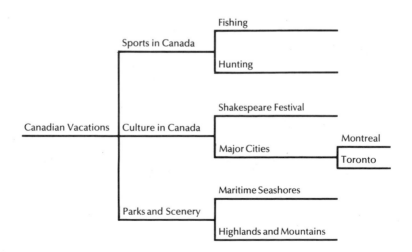

FIGURE 8-2 Picturing Ideas with Circles

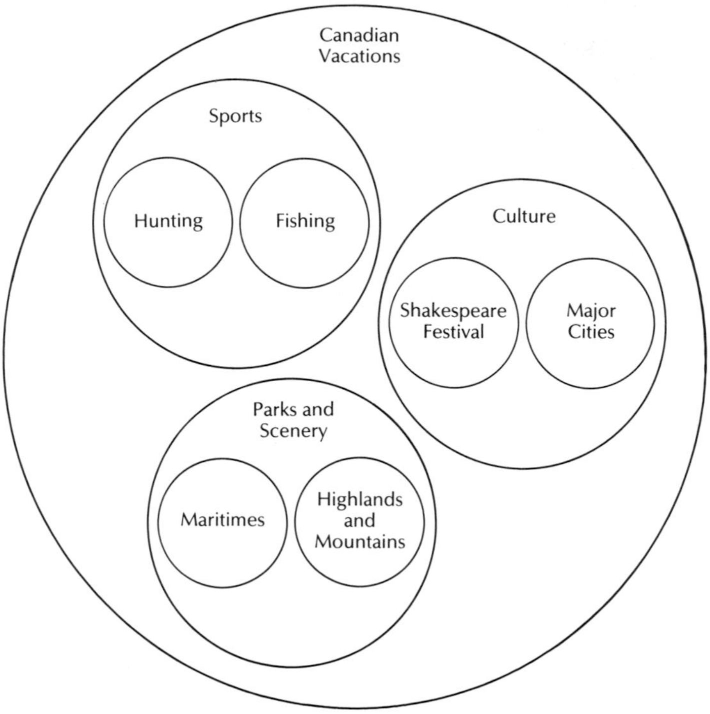

Canadian
Vacations
Sports
Hunting
Fishing
Culture
Shakespeare
Festival
Major
Cities
Parks and
Scenery
Maritimes
Highlands
and
Mountains

FIGURE 8-3 Picturing Ideas with an Arrow and Bracket Template

Fishing
Hunting
Sports
Canadian
Vacations
Culture
in
Canada
Shakespeare
Festival
Major
Cities
Montreal
Toronto
Parks and
Scenery
Maritime
Seashores
Highlands and
Mountains

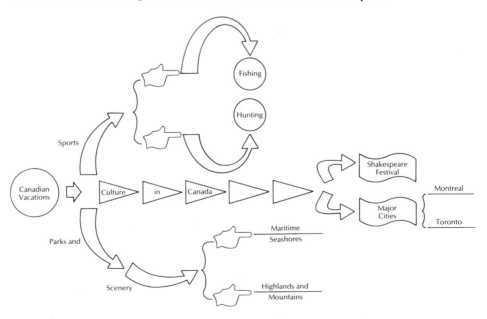

FIGURE 8-4   Picturing Ideas with a Computer-Flow Diagram Template

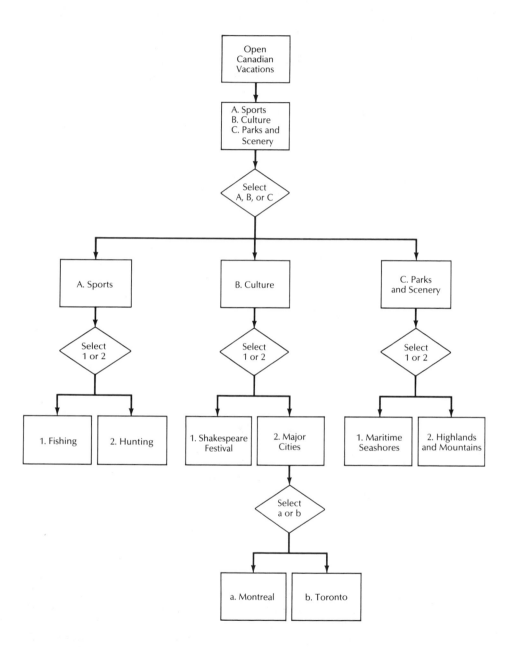

Summary

1. Organization is essentially presentation of ideas in patterned form that aids both the speaker and the audience.
2. There are five basic organizational patterns, based on time (temporal orders), based on why things happen (causal orders), based on locations (spatial orders), based on logical subdivisions (classification orders), and based on topical principles.
3. The rules of formal outlining are clear and simple. They serve as a useful check for you and your instructor in determining whether your preparation for a speech is adequate.
4. Useful outlines may take the form most generally associated with outlines, but outlines may also be constructed in a number of other forms.

Questions and Exercises

1. Discuss the cues speakers provide to let the audience know the organizational pattern they are following. List as many such cues as you can. Compare your list with lists composed by classmates, and add cues until the class comes up with a fairly complete list.
2. With one or more classmates, divide the list composed in Question 1 into three categories: (a) cues that are overused to signal organizational patterns, (b) cues that are most often used with positive effects, and (c) cues that would be effective but that are seldom used. In reviewing your next speech, try to eliminate most of the (a) category, substituting cues from categories (b) and (c).
3. Discuss how listeners use the organizational cues that they receive. What kinds of thoughts are generated by the cues? How do these thinking processes facilitate recall and acceptance of the speaker's message?
4. Identify a speech topic about which you and several of your friends in class know quite a bit. Attempt to develop a sensible outline for the topic, using each of the orders discussed in the chapter—causal, spatial, classification, and topical. Try to carry the outline down to the third level of subordination—that is, use Roman numerals, capital letters from the English alphabet, and Arabic numbers.
5. Select a detailed outline such as the one given as Table 8-1. In the margin of a copy of that outline, identify the overall organizational pattern in the speech and the pattern used in each of the subordinate sections.
6. Using as a basis the alternative methods of outlining represented in Figures 8-1 through 8-4, attempt to develop new and creative ways for expressing the relationship between the parts of speeches you have given or that have been given by classmates during this term.

7. For each of the five general types of organizational patterns in this chapter, write a brief outline that typifies that pattern. Compare your work with that of your classmates and attempt to reconcile differences in viewpoints.

8. With your classmates or friends, attempt to make a list of the rules of outlining without looking at the rules presented in this book. When you and your friends or classmates are sure that you know the rules well, one of you should select a topic with which everyone is familiar, and as a group you should try to compose a brief outline that meets all the rules.

9. Conduct an experiment with your classmates. Make up a brief set of instructions about where you will meet after class. For some classmates, organize the instructions and make the organization as clear as possible. For other classmates, present the instructions in a haphazard manner. Record the questions each group asks before they feel they are able to follow your instructions. How do the questions asked by each group differ? After answering the questions of both groups, do you see any advantage in making instructions as clear as possible?

Russ Busby, B.G.E.A.

9

Beginning and Concluding Effectively

By the time you finish reading this chapter, you should be able to:

1. Explain why introductions and conclusions are important to an effective speech.
2. Identify the effects of good introductions and conclusions on audience response.
3. Identify the effects of poor introductions and conclusions on audience response.
4. Explain the role of addressing the audience in the introduction.
5. Give examples of ways of establishing audience attention.
6. Explain the importance of announcing your thesis and the response you wish.
7. Explain how to construct an initial summary or preview of a speech.
8. Explain the importance of providing a transition between the introduction and the rest of the speech.
9. Identify the two functions of a conclusion.
10. Explain how to construct a final summary for your speeches and the way in which that summary differs from the initial summary.
11. Explain the importance of producing a sense of closure for the audience and the techniques that may be used to achieve it.

There are two reasons for careful planning of introductions and conclusions. First, planning is vital because a good speech can be made ineffective by a weak introduction or conclusion. By contrast, an excellent introduction and conclusion can remedy weaknesses in the body of the speech. Second, in the planning of introductions and conclusions, more than in any other part of speech planning, the speaker tends to focus directly on audience needs and interests. As we discuss ways of producing effective introductions and conclusions, you should keep in mind that much of what we say applies throughout the speech. The techniques we discuss in this chapter, with slight or no modification, may be used in the entire speech as you focus planning upon audience response.

Despite emphasis on the importance of introductions and conclusions, some speakers fail to prepare them adequately. A student who comes to the front of the room and begins his or her speech with a deep sigh and then says, "I guess I'll talk about what I did last summer. It really wasn't very interesting, but, ya' know, I've got to talk about something so I'm going to tell you about my job and this real bad sunburn I got" is not likely to succeed. Even if the job was chauffeur for Robert Redford and the bad sunburn came from a day on the set of a movie when the stunts were being filmed, the poor introduction may cause negative audience response. The student who ends an otherwise good speech with "I guess that's about all I have to say—well, maybe one more thing—my aunt isn't really as strange as you may think after this speech—but maybe you—ahh, skip it—that's it" will reduce audience recollections of the quality of the performance. To help you plan effective introductions and conclusions and to help you avoid poor ones, we will discuss three topics in this chapter. First, we will discuss *the importance of introductions and conclusions.* Second, we will discuss *how to construct an effective introduction.* Finally, we will discuss *how to construct an effective conclusion.*

A good introduction has five goals, and a good conclusion has two. You may wonder how speakers reserve any time for the body of the presentation. Professor N. Edd Miller, Chair of the Communication Department at Northern Kentucky University, studied the percentages of time devoted to introductions and conclusions, and reported that the average speaker spends about 10 percent of speaking time on introductions and about 5 percent of the time on conclusions. In speeches that aimed to stimulate or inspire, the time spent on introductions was higher, averaging 13 percent.[1] Although Miller's work was done in the 1940s, a comparison of his report with *Vital Speeches of the Day*[2] for 1985 reveals that his categories and time allotments are accurate. If you spend an average amount of time on an introduction in a ten-minute speech, the introduction would take about one minute and your conclusion would last about thirty seconds. Our experience indicates that these figures are about right for most classroom speeches that are five to ten minutes in length. Even when classroom speeches are shortened to five or six minutes, most students still use about one-minute introductions and thirty-second conclusions in their speeches.

Is a minute long enough to accomplish the things a good introduction should accomplish? The answer is "Yes." If the opening words are planned carefully, then time should be no problem. So it is with the conclusion. Thirty seconds is long enough for a carefully planned conclusion for a short speech. But keep in mind that these are average figures. Your subject, your audience, and the way you deal with the subject may lead you to spend a greater or lesser amount of time on introductions and conclusions.

---

[1]N. Edd Miller, "Speech Introductions and Conclusions," *Quarterly Journal of Speech, 32*: 181-183 (1946).

[2]*Vital Speeches of the Day,* vol. 52 (New York: The City News Publishing Company, 1985-1986).

Effective Introductions _____

We will identify five characteristics of a good introduction. The order in which we discuss these characteristics represents the temporal order in which they usually appear in speeches.

1. Plan to address the audience.
2. Plan to gain audience attention.
3. Plan to announce your topic—*always.*
4. Plan to provide a scheme or pattern that will aid audience understanding and retention of the contents of your message.
5. Plan to motivate the audience so that they will want to accept your message.

Plan to Address the Audience

Your authors may be somewhat old-fashioned in recommending this step. More and more speakers begin a speech without this preliminary. Most of them say things like, "I'll be talking about three important concerns this evening. . ." and launch directly into their speech. It is true that there are circumstances in which the importance of the speech or the prestige of the speaker may make such an opening effective. Generally, however, we recommend that you address the audience directly. The traditional "Ladies and gentlemen" may still be used in rare circumstances, but the fact that its form involves male-female stereotypes means that it has limited use, as do other gender-based means of addressing the audience. "Fellow classmates" or "Fellow students" may serve in your classes, as will "Friends." You could also begin with a line such as "Students concerned about substance abuse." As the formality of the speaking situation increases, the necessity to address the audience also increases.

Plan to Gain Audience Attention

The amount of detail you put into a plan to gain audience attention should vary according to the motivation of the audience to listen to your presentation. What techniques can you use to help to establish attention? Professor Miller's study of the lengths of introductions and conclusions also classified the various techniques speakers use in introducing and concluding their remarks.[3] He discovered eleven techniques used by speakers to begin their speeches. We discuss them in the order in which he presented them—from the most frequently used to the least frequently used method. If your speech calls for a standard introduction, you would use one of the techniques discussed near the beginning of this section. If you wanted to be unusual or different, you would employ one of the techniques discussed near the end of the section.

[3]Miller, pp. 181-183.

Three Techniques: Reference to the Subject, Occasion, and Audience. The first three attention-gaining techniques derive from the context in which the speech is given. You have heard speakers employ them many times. If audience interest in the topic is high, then a *direct reference to the topic* may be sufficient to gain their attention. If the audience is gathered for a special purpose, then *reference to that occasion* will gain attention. Finally, *identifying members of the audience by name* is an effective method of warming up the audience.

Quotation. As you read about your topic, you may find sentences or even a poem that makes a point so well that it provides exactly what you need to introduce your topic. At other times, a quotation can be made to fit your topic. If, for example, you were speaking on the possibility of extraterrestrial visits, you might begin with the following quotation: "There are tens, even hundreds of billions of stars in the Universe. Astronomer Carl Sagan points out that close to home, '. . .the Milky Way Galaxy contains 250 billion stars, and even with a million civilizations, less than one star in 200,000 would have a planet inhabited by an advanced civilization.' This means that contact is far less likely than television and the movies imply."[4]

Reference to Current Events. Newsworthy events provide excellent introductory material. If some event related to your topic is fresh in the minds of the audience, a reference to it should establish attention. If you decide to speak on "Farm Subsidies—The Price We Pay to Avoid Food Shortages," you might begin with "On this morning's 'Today Show,' they announced that farmers in the Midwest will receive four hundred million dollars in drought relief. You've all heard similar announcements—relief for farmers due to floods, relief to buy up surpluses, relief for crop failures, and so on. Why this commitment of tax money to help farmers with problems? I'd like to explain why our desire to avoid food shortages leads to extensive farm subsidy."

Historical References. Another effective way to introduce a speech is to refer to historical events with which the audience is familiar. Even references to fictional events that are a part of our common culture can gain the interest of the listeners. If you were speaking on affirmative action programs to ensure equality of opportunity for women, you might begin by noting that the nineteenth amendment to the Constitution was adopted by Congress on June 4, 1919, and ratified as a part of the Constitution on August 26, 1920. You might go on to point out that for two-thirds of the history of our nation, women were unable to vote.

Anecdotes. An anecdote is a short story or narrative that is usually drawn from your personal experience. Anecdotes are frequently humorous, though they need not be. If you were speaking on the devastation

---

[4]Carl Sagan, *Broca's Brain: Reflections on the Romance of Science* (New York: Ballantine Books, 1979), p. 315.

produced by floods, you might begin by telling about your experience in a flood (or the experience of some friend or relative that you know). You might in this case focus on that individual's feelings of helplessness as the waters began to rise.

Startling Statements. There is a tendency for this technique to be overused, though it can still prove highly effective when the statement really is startling and is truly applicable to a particular audience. It can be contrasted with the "Gee whiz" technique in which the speaker says words to the effect of "Hey! I bet you didn't know. . . ." What makes a statement startling is that it violates our expectations. It is not startling for most of us to hear that there are in excess of 50,000 deaths in automobile accidents in the United States each year. We have heard these figures often. It would be more startling, in a speech on automobile safety, to reveal the costs of automobile accidents in dollars. When lost wages, medical costs, and insurance administration costs are totaled, they come to slightly over forty and one-half billion dollars annually.

Questions. Two kinds of questions frequently are used to begin speeches. We shall call them the *journalistic question* and the *rhetorical question*. Journalistic questions appear at the beginning of speeches and articles; the speaker or writer goes on to provide answers to them. Rhetorical questions have answers so obvious that the audience can supply them by themselves. Rhetorical questions are not really questions at all, because they imply a proposition that the speaker or writer wishes the audience to accept. Like the startling statement, these devices (both the journalistic and rhetorical versions) are overused and are perhaps more appropriately found as transitions in the body of the speech. Nevertheless, on occasion they can be effective. One effective technique is to ask a series of them. For example, in beginning a speech on "Evolution Is Fact, Not Theory," you might ask a series of journalistic questions of this sort: "What is the difference between a fact and a theory in science? What is the essential feature of scientific theories that distinguishes them from such theories as creationism? What is the motive of those who insist on teaching 'scientific' creationism in addition to evolution in biology classes? These are the questions I intend to answer in my speech today." A series of rhetorical questions in a speech on merit pay for teachers might begin, "How will you feel about merit pay when you discover that your child's teacher has consistently been in the bottom ten percent for the last ten years? Do you want your child taught by a teacher who knows that he or she is worse than any of the other teachers? How would you feel if the administration here started issuing three kinds of degrees—meritorious for the upper third of the class, B.A.A. (adequate bachelor's degree) for the middle third, and 'more or less O.K.' for the lower third? I'd like to talk to you today about why, though I favor recognizing teacher merit, it is wise to look carefully at the advantages and disadvantages of this idea."

Humor. The idea that every speech ought to begin with a joke dies hard, but we hope that you will reject it. There are occasions for which a humorous story or anecdote is highly effective. The wide variety of introductory techniques available means, however, that you do not need to use this method often.

Personal Reference. This technique is appropriate when you have relatively high status or legitimacy with respect to a particular audience. The commander addressing the foot soldiers may begin with, "I bring you my personal greeting and my personal appreciation for what you have accomplished." Those who are intimates of high-status persons can also use a second-level personal reference such as, "When I talked with the President yesterday, he remarked that he wished he could be here with you and that I was to include his personal greetings along with my own." The personal reference may also refer to a special experience of the individual. Recently, a student referred to her experience as a tour guide at Disney World in a speech about the inner workings of the Magic Kingdom.

Announcing the Topic to Your Audience

Announcing your topic helps the audience:
—Set aside thoughts about other matters.
—Focus on the subject of your speech.
Announcing the response you seek helps the audience:
—Understand what you expect of them.
—Become more likely to respond as you wish.

After you establish the attention of the listeners, you should make sure that the audience has grasped your topic and the response you wish them to make to it. Announcement of the topic provides the audience with information they need for receiving the substance of your message in the body of the speech. It gets them ready for your preview of the major ideas you will be covering. It can aid in getting them to set aside thoughts of other matters. You should also announce the response you would like to receive from the audience. They are more likely to respond as you wish if they know the reaction you want. They are less likely to respond as you wish if they have to figure out what you want.

The simplest way of announcing your topic and the response you wish to receive is to tell the audience the thesis sentence of the speech. "My thesis is that you should appreciate the impressive facts about the size and behavior of blue whales." A string of topic and response announcements beginning with "My thesis is. . ." may soon sound redundant in speech classes, but the method frequently works quite well elsewhere. You can work out less obvious ways to ensure that your audience knows your topic and the response you expect.

Summarize or Preview the Major Ideas

A Summary or Preview:
  —Should appear in all of your speeches.
  —May be direct and simple.
  —Should include all of the major points of your speech.
  —May be based on your organization pattern or mnemonic devices.
  —Should also be used before each section of your speech.

Always for the beginning speaker—and almost always for the experienced one—the initial summary is the most important feature of the introduction. If your attempt to get attention causes yawns, if your announcement of topic and response gets garbled, or if any other feature of the beginning is ineffective, a well-planned preview of the speech may save all that follows. Without it, the audience is left guessing about when you have begun to develop your first major idea and when you have finished with idea development and are ready for the conclusion. Without the preview, there is no guide to your progress through the speech. Audience attention may flag. Without the initial summary, many beginning speakers may even become lost themselves. They do not yet have the skill to use transitions and internal summaries to keep themselves on track.

Initial summaries or previews range from the direct and simple to the indirect and elaborate. For the beginning speaker, the direct, simple, and obvious summary is best. If you have three major reasons that support your thesis, you should immediately declare, "I have three major ideas that I will present to support my thesis." Follow this by reciting the reasons exactly as they appear on your outline.

Beyond the minimal summary, there are a number of effective ways to preview the body of the speech. One method is based upon the organizational pattern you have selected. You might say, "I'll develop this speech first by considering the effects of the problem and second by looking at its causes." Sometimes initial summaries employ memory (mnemonic devices) such as the ABC's of something, for example, foot care for joggers. A—Always warm up adequately, B—Buy the best shoes, and C—Correct your running style. This device is probably overused, but similar kinds can be created where appropriate. A related technique is to employ a device such as alliteration so that all the main points begin with words that start with the same letter. An example would state, "The ways of finding someone to marry are these: availability, attitude, and amour."

In writing initial summaries or previews, keep in mind the short time limits that are usually found in speech classes. However, if the speech is to last thirty or more minutes, it is probably wise to use a more detailed initial summary-preview that explains how each of the major points will be supported.

Finally, we urge you to note that the techniques used for the summary-preview may be applied throughout the speech. As you begin each major point, it is wise to tell the audience, for example, "As we discuss what can go wrong with the car's electrical system, I'll focus on three major trouble spots: the battery, the distributor, and the spark plug wires." Such previews within the body of the speech serve to focus the attention of the listeners.

Provide a Smooth Transition Between the Introduction and the Body of the Speech

Smooth and effective transitions from the introduction to the body of the speech need to be planned almost as carefully as your initial summary-preview. All too often, carefully organized materials sound choppy and are hard to follow. A transition serves to connect ideas. Sometimes a single word like "next" can be a sufficient connector, but between the introduction and the body one or more sentences are usually required. A transitional sentence will (1) mention the preceding idea,

---

Transitions:
  —Mention the preceding idea.
  —Mention the relationship.
  —Mention the idea to follow.

---

(2) mention a word or phrase expressing a relationship, and (3) mention the succeeding idea. Thus, the basic transitional sentence between the introduction and conclusion would imply or say, "I have finished my introductory materials (the preceding idea) and I'm moving now to the first major point in the body of my speech (the succeeding idea)." It is better to use this generic transitional sentence than not to have one at all. In time, you will be able to compose less cumbersome transitional sentences.

The transition from introduction to body encompasses an audience-centered concept worth using throughout the speech. Carefully planned transitions should appear not only between the introduction and the body, but also between each of the major points of the speech and between the final major point and the conclusion. Additional transitions are necessary at all points where they will help the audience to understand the relationship between the points of the speech.

Effective Conclusions _____

There are two things that an effective conclusion should accomplish. First, an effective conclusion provides a summary or review of the principal ideas presented in the speech. Second, it produces a sense of closure or completeness for the audience.

Final Summary—Review

As with the initial summary in the introduction, virtually no speech should lack a final summary that shares the characteristics of the initial one. Specifically, the purpose and the audience response should be restated, as should the major points in the speech that support the thesis. For example, a minimal summary in the conclusion of your speech might say, "We began with three reasons for the elimination of final exams, and we end with those same three reasons: (1) final exams encourage cramming instead of reflection, (2) final exams weigh too heavily in determining grades, and (3) final exams distract teachers and students alike during the last week of the term." You will, of course,

---

The Final Review or Summary Should:
—Reflect your major points.
—Reinforce the support presented for those points.

---

want your final summary to differ in language from the initial summary. After all, the initial summary serves as a guide to the materials you are about to present. When you state your final summary, the audience should have a wealth of detail and supporting materials that you have incorporated into the body of your speech. It is wisest for you to construct a final summary that not only reflects your major points, but that also reinforces the support for those points. Rather than just repeating the major points in a speech advocating elimination of final exams, you might more effectively say, "I've suggested that this institution abolish final examinations. I hope you'll agree with me and agree that the studies I have cited show that crammed material is forgotten material! That illness during exam week coupled with the undue weight of finals lowers grade points excessively! That the pressure of finals stops new learning in most courses during the final week of the term!" The variety of summary techniques available to you is virtually endless. If you cannot discover one that you think will be particularly effective for your speech, then be sure you employ at least a minimal summary of your thesis and main points.

Closure

Closure is a term used by Gestalt psychologists to refer to the need or tendency to complete that which is incomplete.[5] If you see a triangle with only two sides drawn in, you will most likely still recognize that the figure is a triangle. If you are asked to complete the drawing, like most people you will simply add a straight line. When you give a speech, the

[5]Benjamin B. Wolman, ed., *Dictionary of Behavioral Science* (New York: Van Nostrand Reinhold Co., 1973), p. 65.

audience will tend to complete it for you—to produce their own sense of closure—if you fail to provide for it yourself. Unfortunately, audiences are generally poor at guessing the conclusions to speeches.[6] The speech will be more of a success if its conclusion provides a sense of completion. How can this be achieved?

Closure for Your Ideas Comes From:
—Converted introductory techniques.
—Challenge.
—Visualizing the future.
—Inspirational appeals.

Almost all of Miller's techniques for introductions may be applied to conclusions. For example, you might refer to your subject again, by providing a statement such as, "Now that I've told you about some of the strange ways human decorate their bodies, I want you to remember my thesis the next time you choose a shade of lipstick or a tie of one color rather than another: our ways of decorating ourselves are no more 'civilized' than those of other cultures." You could refer to the audience again by announcing, "I began by pointing out that several of you knew a great deal about this subject. So let me close by reminding all of you that if you have further questions about scuba diving, I will be glad to talk with you after class." So it is with the other techniques used in the introduction: they can be employed after or in conjunction with your final summary to produce a sense of closure.

Miller's study also discovered additional techniques that speakers sometimes use after or in conjunction with the final summary. We shall discuss three of them.

Challenge. With this technique, the speaker issues a challenge to the audience to try the advice presented in the speech. An example is the following: "We have seen what a few dollars can do for these unfortunate people. I challenge each of you to call the Red Cross tomorrow and make your pledge." If you were talking to your class about how to make final examinations less traumatic, you might end with, "I dare you to try all three steps I have suggested for preparing for final exams. In fact, I dare you to try any one of them. You will be as surprised as I was last quarter when I almost enjoyed my finals."

Visualizing the Future. This technique paints a word picture of how a situation will appear if the speaker's proposal is accepted. If you were speaking on the importance of physical exercise, you might conclude with, "With the fifteen minutes a day I have proposed, in two or three days you will notice that food tastes better, though you will eat

[6]Carl I. Hovland and Wallace Mandel, "An Experimental Comparison of Conclusion-Drawing by the Communicator and by the Audience," *Journal of Abnormal and Social Psychology, 47*: 581-588 (1952).

slightly less. Despite some soreness and stiffness in your muscles, within a week you will notice that you feel better generally. After studying, you will have more energy left to do the things you most enjoy. Within a month, you will notice that your clothes fit better and that you are firm where flab used to abound."

Inspirational Appeals. Inspirational appeals make use of connections between your topic and some higher purpose or value important to receivers. Suppose you are speaking to raise funds for research to discover the causes and cures of heart disease. You might conclude by saying, "Anyone who has visited the heart unit of a large children's hospital has viewed a 50-bed ward filled with apparently normal babies. But you know that all of them are likely to die soon. Each of us, in viewing that scene, would be overcome with joy, rather than grief, if we thought that giving up the cost of a daily bottle of pop for a year would save those children. We would do it gladly, and the pride in this act would restore our joy whenever we would think of it. Your donation to support such research, joined with the donations of others, will help to do exactly that. It will help those children and thousands like them to live!"

At this point, you should be fully aware of the importance of introductions and conclusions. You should recognize that an excellent introduction can enhance audience perceptions of the quality of your speech, whereas a poor introduction will produce the opposite effect. You should also recognize that the kind of audience-centered thinking that goes into constructing introductions and conclusions can be applied throughout the speechmaking process. You should know that an effective introduction addresses the audience, may employ any of eleven techniques to gain audience attention, usually identifies the thesis of the speech and the response desired, and provides an initial summary and a smooth transition into the body of the speech. You should know that the conclusion leaves the audience with a final summary of the materials you have covered, as well as with a sense of closure. As one leading authority, Professor Bert E. Bradley of Auburn University, writes in the third edition of his book, *Fundamentals of Communication,* "If the introduction creates a poor image, the listeners may become prejudiced toward the ideas to be presented in the body of the speech. If the conclusion leaves a bad final impression, it may nullify the impact of the ideas presented earlier."[7]

[7]Bert E. Bradley, *Fundamentals of Speech Communication: The Credibility of Ideas,* 3rd ed. (Dubuque, Iowa: Wm. C. Brown, 1981), p. 159.

Summary

1. Effective introductions and conclusions help to ensure an effective speech. Poor introductions and conclusions obviate otherwise well-organized and well-supported materials in the body.
2. The emphasis on audience analysis that most people give to planning introductions and conclusions should be used in planning the entire speech.
3. Many speakers spend about 10 percent of their speeches on introductions and about 5 percent of the time on conclusions. Even if you generally follow this pattern, you may wish to retain an introduction of one minute and a conclusion of one-half minute for a short speech of four or five minutes.
4. A direct address to the audience provides a clear verbal cue that the speech is beginning.
5. There are many ways to establish audience attention. Among them are the following: refer to the subject, to the audience, and to the occasion; use quotations; refer to current events; use historical references, anecdotes, startling statements, questions, or humor; provide a personal reference.
6. In most situations, make sure that your introduction clarifies both your thesis and the response you wish the audience to have.
7. An effective introduction should contain a summary of the major ideas you will present in the body of the speech. For longer speeches, a more detailed summary will help the audience follow and respond appropriately to the speech.
8. Your speech should contain a clear transition between the introduction and conclusion.
9. The conclusion of your speech should summarize your major ideas and remind the audience of how those ideas support your thesis and warrant the response you seek.
10. In addition, the conclusion of your speech should produce a sense of closure for the audience. Most of the techniques used for establishing attention in the introduction can be converted for this purpose. You may also use challenges, visualizations of the future, and inspirational appeals.

Questions and Exercises

1. Discuss each of the functions of the introduction to a speech. Take your own or a classmate's speech topic as an example, and decide on several ways of accomplishing each of those purposes.
2. Discuss each of the functions of the conclusion of a speech. Take your own or a classmate's speech topic as an example, and decide on several ways of accomplishing each of those purposes.

3. Discuss the importance of effective introductions and conclusions. The chapter suggests that sometimes introductions and conclusions can compensate for weaknesses elsewhere in your presentation. Do you agree? Do you think your instructor should give a low grade to a speech that has an excellent introduction and conclusion but that has other weaknesses (even if the class did not notice those weaknesses)?

4. Identify the most effective introduction to an oral presentation you have ever heard. Be prepared to explain why it was so effective. Did it follow the rules for effective introductions given in this chapter?

5. Identify the most effective conclusion to an oral presentation you have ever heard. Be prepared to explain why it was so effective. Did it follow the rules for effective conclusions given in this chapter?

6. Make a list of the things that catch your attention during an hour in which you are interacting with other people. Compare it with a list of what catches your attention during an hour of watching television.

7. Consult an anthology of speeches or the semi-monthly *Vital Speeches of the Day.*[8] Look at the introductions to five or ten speeches, and make a list of the attention-getting techniques employed by each of the speakers. How does your list of techniques compare with the list suggested in this chapter?

8. Taking a detailed outline of one of your own speeches or of a classmate's speech, analyze the transitions used. Find out how many were used and where they appeared. Were enough transitions used to enable listeners to follow what was said? Where could transitions have been added to improve the listeners' understanding?

[8]*Vital Speeches of the Day* (New York: City News Publishing Company, 1985).

10

Using Evidence Effectively

By the time you finish reading this chapter, you should be able to:

1. Define and test evidence derived from facts, opinions, and statistics.
2. Introduce evidence into your speeches.
3. Understand the nature of evidence.
4. Identify five kinds of evidence and their uses in public speaking.
5. Analyze and critically examine the evidence you use, as well as the evidence used by others.

If you make an assertion that someone doubts, you may be asked, "What evidence do you have for that?" Listeners want to know what facts, opinions, or statistics you can cite to back up what you say. In speeches, it is customary to anticipate such questions and to make sure that a point others might doubt is supported with materials from another source. This chapter explains the nature and use of evidence in speeches. We will discuss two general areas. First, we will give you a basic understanding of the types of evidence students frequently use in their speeches. You will learn how to evaluate these types and how you can introduce them into your speeches smoothly and effectively to support your points. Second, we will explore the nature of evidence in greater depth. In that exploration, we will formally define *evidence* and explain the implications of that definition. We will discuss the kinds of materials that are used as evidence and the uses you may make of them to increase the effectiveness of your presentations. Finally, we will discuss how you may analyze evidence to make sure that your own and that of others will lead to sounder conclusions.

Types of Evidence

Speakers support their points by citing facts, opinions, or statistics. Facts come from a variety of sources, such as encyclopedias, government and United Nations documents, *The Guinness Book of World Records, The Book of Lists,* newspapers, magazines, and journals. Facts may be regarded as reports of actual events or summaries of those events. They generally appear in answers to questions that start with the words *Who? What? Where? When?* and *Why?*

Opinions, by comparison, are someone's interpretation of events. The individual interpreting may be an expert or a layperson. He or she may be evaluating facts that have been heard from others or facts that have been observed firsthand. He or she may even be interpreting the opinions of others. It is not the case, however, that one opinion is as good as another when it comes to supporting a point in a speech. In your speeches, more often than not you will want to limit your opinion evidence to quotations from expert sources. Opinions of experts—people who are authorities in an area—will be more convincing than opinions of laypersons.

Statistics are numerical summaries of facts and sometimes of opinions. They come in many forms, but most frequently they appear as the arithmetic mean, the median, the mode, or as comparisons of "averages." Almost as frequently cited as statistics are percentages (such as the percentage of Independents who voted for the Democratic candidate in the last election, or the percentage of Democrats who voted for Reagan and against Mondale in the 1984 presidential election).

Tests of Evidence _____

Tests of Factual Evidence

When you present facts to support your points, it is important that they be recent, reliable, and that they clearly and directly support the point you are making.

Recency. If you investigate almost any significant problem, you will discover that new and relevant facts continually develop. The number of Americans living in poverty varies from year to year. So does the enrollment at most colleges and universities. On topics of current interest, the most recent facts are the most useful. Even on matters of ancient history, new facts come to light. For virtually all speech topics, you will want to make sure that you have checked the most recent factual sources available.

Reliability. Facts are reliable to the extent that independent observers report or summarize the events in similar fashion. Consequently, before accepting one report as factual, it is usually wise for you to look for confirmation from another independent source. If you hear it on "ABC World News," does *Time* report the same fact? A surprising number of so-called facts turn out to be questionable.

Relevancy. Facts should be related to the point you are making. That seems obvious, but too often the desire to include as many facts as possible in a speech leads students to include information that is simply irrelevant to the point being made.

The classic example of the irrelevant use of facts occurred in debates about lowering the voting age during the 1960s. "Old enough to fight, old enough to vote," was the cry. Soldiering skills, however, are quite different from skills needed for wise voting. Today, the same arguments are being raised in debates about maintaining the drinking age for people in their late teens.

Tests of Opinion Evidence

It is important that opinions be based on facts, that the person giving the opinion have the expertise necessary to interpret the facts, and that other expert authorities support the interpretation.

Factual Base. Opinions based on other opinions are not usually valid. The columnist who predominantly gives an opinion of the opinions of other columnists may not be a reliable source of evidence. Speakers who express opinions as evidence should first gather and check out facts.

Expertise. If a speaker uses opinion evidence to interpret facts, his or her degree of expertise becomes important. What qualifications does the source have that make his or her interpretation authoritative? Is his or her interpretation likely to be correct?

Support from Other Experts. One expert opinion by itself, even if factually based, is not necessarily valid. Other authorities with similar factual bases and similar expertise should express similar opinions. When an apparent authority's opinion stands alone or contradicts the opinions of most other authorities, you should probably not accept it. It is rare for one person's opinion to be correct when different experts rule otherwise.

Tests of Statistical Evidence

It is virtually impossible to give a brief explanation about evaluating statistical evidence. There are many forms of statistics, and as computers become commonplace, there are more and more tools producing numerical summaries that purport to support one viewpoint or another. The best way to learn about statistics is to take a college course in the subject. Nevertheless, there are at this point four tests that can prevent you from being misled by statistics and from using statistics that might mislead others.

Understand the Base. First, make sure you understand the base for the statistic. Statistics are summaries of numerical representations of facts. At some point, someone has taken measurements. Frequently, these measurements are derived from answers to questions, markings on scales, or blanks filled in by people. What were the questions? What scales did the people mark? What blanks did they fill in? What checks were conducted to make sure their responses were accurate?

Understand the Sample. Second, because it is costly to have everyone fill out a questionnaire or fill in a form, statistics usually involve a sample from the group about which you want to generalize. It is important to know the characteristics of that sample. If it is composed entirely of college students, then they are brighter, healthier, and more knowledgeable than people in general. It is risky to draw conclusions about all people on the basis of a college-student sample. Many other samples used to compute statistics are similarly biased. But if you know the nature of the measurements taken and the nature of the sample from which they were drawn, you know the basis of the statistic. You are then prepared to make a preliminary evaluation of whether the statistic is worth using.

Understand the Computation. Third, make sure you understand how the statistic is computed. This does not mean that you need to know the mathematical formulas or computer program employed. You do, however, need to have a general understanding about what is being done with the numbers. You should know how means, medians, and modes are computed. Statistics called *t's* and analysis of variance are computed by a method similar to the way the mean is computed, with the purpose of providing comparisons between two or more means. Multivariate analyses have the same purpose, but they remove the effects of some relationships between measurements. Correlational techniques indicate how two or more measures vary with respect to each other. If the explanation of the way the statistic is computed makes no sense to you, even in a general way, then you might ask a faculty member to explain it to you. If you cannot understand it after that, do not use the statistic. The most serious error in using statistics is to assume that because the explanation is beyond your understanding, it is a better statistic.

Understand the Application of the Statistic. Fourth, recognize that statistics usually apply to large groups rather than to individuals. It is generally true that 100 people with high SAT or ACT scores will perform better in college than 100 people with low SAT or ACT scores. But this information does not mean that you will not flunk out if you have a high score. It also does not mean that you will not graduate cum laude if you have a low score. It only means that out of 100 individuals who score high, more will do better than the 100 who score low. However, only the foolish will judge an individual on the basis of such a statistic.

Introducing Evidence in Your Speeches _____

Once you gather facts, opinions, and statistics to support your points, you face the problem of introducing evidence into your speech. Your speaking time is limited. It is important that you work in the evidence efficiently and with maximum effect.

Consider Effects. Think about the effects you want the evidence to have on the audience. Do you want your listeners to remember that the idea you are supporting is also supported by others? Do you want them to remember the information contained in the evidence? Many footnotes in books and articles are examples of authors demonstrating to the reader that the idea presented is supported by others. If you were giving a speech on limiting nuclear weapons, you could announce in your introduction, "Most of my thinking about nuclear arms comes from my reading of two books." You would then mention the authors, titles, and publication dates of the books. This way, you would let your audience know that the facts and statistics in your speech are based on authoritative information. Later in the same speech, you may want the audience to remember statistics about the frequency of nuclear accidents. You might say, "You may be unaware of how often we have accidents with nuclear materials," and go on to back up this statement by stating, *"The New York Times* for May 17, 1981, reports, 'The Pentagon yesterday released details on 32 nuclear accidents that killed 56 persons in the last 30 years.' "[1] If you want the audience simply to remember that your points are supported by evidence, tell them the sources of your information. If, however, you want them to remember *specific* information from your evidence, go further, and emphasize the particular details you want them to retain.

Words to Say and Words to Avoid. When you present evidence in your speeches, there are certain words to stress and other words to avoid. For example, in a speech titled "Who Are the Vandals?" you might introduce an authoritative quotation by saying the following:

> I'd like to establish that overcrowding or the reduction of personal space may be at the heart of much vandalism. Philip Zimbardo, a widely known social psychologist, in an article called "Anonymity and Destruction in the Real World," points out that "where social conditions of life destroy individual identity by making people feel anonymous, then what will follow is. . . assaultive aggression, senseless acts of destruction, motiveless murders, great expenditure of energy and effort directed toward sheltering traditional forms and institutionalized structures. . . ."[2]

In this example, you have mentioned (1) the source, (2) the qualifications of the source, (3) the title of the article in which the information is found, and (4) the date. You could even add more detailed information, as we have done in the footnote. The more controversial or doubtful the point, the more important it is to give full bibliographic information in introducing the evidence. If everybody in your audience knew who Philip Zimbardo was, then you might not need to present his qualifications.

Note also that when you quote an authority, you do not need to use the words *quote* and *unquote* every time you cite a piece of evidence. It is only when the exact beginning and the exact end of a quotation are of concern that you need to use these words.

[1]"Details on 32 Nuclear Accidents with 56 Fatalities Are Released," *New York Times,* May 17, 1981, p. 17.

[2]Philip Z. Zimbardo, "Anonymity and Destruction in the Real World," in *Social Conflict: Readings in Rule Structures and Conflict Relationships,* compiled by Philip Brickman (Lexington, Mass.: D. C. Heath and Company, 1974), p. 59.

As you begin to gather evidence for your speeches, some problems may arise. Two reliable authorities may provide contradictory opinions, or two facts may seem to contradict each other. Suppose you decide to investigate a complex matter for one of your speeches. "America's Welfare System" is an example. In your research on the welfare system, you will discover apparent contradictions. You will want to resolve those discrepancies. In such situations, you will find it helpful to know more about the nature of evidence, the kinds of materials used as evidence, and methods for analyzing evidence that will help you select the best evidence to support your points. Those matters are discussed in the remainder of this chapter.

Nature of Evidence

Paul D. Brandes, Professor of Communication at the University of North Carolina, defines evidence as "that material that the audience perceives as relatively free from speaker bias."[3] Gerald Miller, Professor of Communication at Michigan State University, and Thomas R. Nilsen, Professor Emeritus at Northwestern University, claim that "evidence consists of those data that are intended to induce a sense of belief in the proposition which the data purportedly support."[4] These definitions make two important points about the nature of evidence. Brandes's definition focuses on audience perceptions of the independence of the speaker and the evidence: he emphasizes that evidence must come from some source other than the speaker's imagination. Miller and Nilsen emphasize that even material that is relatively independent of the speaker may not count as evidence unless the audience accepts the data as support for the speaker's point, the evidence is not valid for that audience. In other words, evidence must meet two general tests: it must be independent and it must convince your audience.

Kinds of Evidence

What kinds of materials do audiences perceive as relatively free from speaker bias? What kinds of materials convince audiences? If you think about televised or actual trials, you will recall most of the kinds. *Documents* are frequently used. The judge or lawyers read the applicable laws to the jury from books or other reports. The prosecution may introduce letters written by the defendant or the defendant's friends. The defense may submit police reports of the arrest or interrogation of the defendant. The lawyers may quote famous jurists, Shakespeare, the

[3]Paul D. Brandes, "Evidence," in *Argumentation and Debate: Principles and Practices,* rev. ed., ed. James H. McBath (New York: Holt, Rinehart and Winston, Inc., 1963), pp. 145-146.

[4]Gerald R. Miller and Thomas R. Nilsen, *Perspectives on Argumentation* (Chicago: Scott, Foresman & Co., 1966), p. 25.

Bible, or poetry in their summations. In addition to being exposed to documentary evidence, the jury may be taken to the site of the crime, may be shown the weapon or weapons employed, or may view the holes made by the weapons in the garments of the victim. These items of evidence might be called *objects* or *artifacts*. There will, of course, be numerous *witnesses*. Most will be laypersons who observed the crime or events relevant to it. Some will be people who know the defendant and who are called to attest to his or her character. Some may be expert witnesses, people who are considered capable of testifying about interpretations of other evidence. A ballistics expert may be called to link a bullet to a gun, or a psychiatrist may be called to evaluate the mental state of the defendant. It is possible that other exhibits will be introduced, including charts, maps, diagrams, and models of the site. *Representations* is a serviceable name for this kind of evidence. Finally, photographs, audio tape recordings of conversations, videotaped depositions, and other facsimiles may be presented. We shall call them *reproductions*.

Your speeches may employ any or all of these five kinds of evidence, although the use of witnesses will be rare. Certainly, you will employ documents as evidence. You will use these more than any other form, because they are readily accessible in the library. It is relatively easy to gather documents, copy them, and carry them to your classroom for use in your speeches. One problem faced by both speakers and writers is the tendency to overuse documents while excluding other forms. Audiences are comparatively unimpressed by documents, for they know, as do you, that to find this sort of evidence is comparatively easy.

Objects or artifacts frequently provide convincing evidence to support your points. If you talk about adding variety to diets, try distributing small bites of exotic foods from other countries to your listeners. This act could be more convincing than a series of quotations from nutritional experts might be. Suppose you wished to talk about the ways other cultures view the world. Exhibiting a painting or sculpture from another culture might help you explain those views better than simply quoting a renowned anthropologist. If you wish to argue for or against a ban on leg-hold traps, you might bring a trap to class to show how it operates. That demonstration may produce greater acceptance of your point than quoting an expert's opinion would do.

Witnesses who support your view are obviously effective in gaining audience acceptance. Unfortunately, time seldom enables you to use a witness for the short speeches given in class. The costs in time and money of bringing a witness to a presentation are considerable. But if these considerations are minimal, witnesses serve to add their knowledge and credibility to your own. Furthermore, in terms of the independence criterion, witnesses are particularly effective. Witnesses can be questioned. They can supply firsthand observations of an event that you did not witness yourself; they can add their expertise and their ability to interpret events to your own; and they can add alternative explanations to aid the audience's understanding. In short, where they are available and appropriate, they can serve as one of the most effective forms of evidence to support and clarify your points.

Melvin Belli, one of the most successful civil damage lawyers in America, makes a strong case for the effectiveness of representations.[5] Getting a jury to understand how a faulty piece of equipment or the error of a surgeon caused an injury is a complex matter. So is getting juries to understand how that injury impairs the functioning of an individual. Belli claims, correctly we think, that use of representations as evidence is largely responsible for his success. Charts, maps, diagrams, working models, and other representations produce levels of belief and understanding that exceed those of the same information expressed verbally. If you want your listeners to comprehend one or more problems of the Middle East, then a map showing the locations of the countries involved will enhance their understanding. If you want the audience to accept the idea that limits should be placed on the number of nuclear weapons, then a chart showing the per-capita tonnage of explosive force will help. To the passenger, airliners appear to bob and weave as they approach a landing at an airport. Explaining why that happens will be far easier with a model of a plane and a diagram of the airport's runways.

Reproductions of actions or events convince by enabling the audience to become eyewitnesses (or earwitnesses, in the case of audio recordings). If you wish to convince the audience that advertising is deliberately misleading, then running a thirty-second spot on video equipment could make your speech more convincing. A brief replay of a segment of one of Richard Nixon's speeches may help you explain why he is vilified by so many. Audio tapes of music may help you convince the audience to listen to or accept a specific kind of music. A vivid slide of handicapped children should be convincing in a speech designed to raise funds for their benefit.

The potential effectiveness of evidence in the form of objects or artifacts, witnesses, representations, and reproductions is great; however, the convenience of documentary evidence means that you and other speakers will probably use it extensively while using the other forms sparingly. When time is tight, documents permit you to expose much more evidence. The other forms take more time to gather, plan for, prepare, and use. The equipment required for the other forms may malfunction and destroy the effectiveness of your message unless its use is thoroughly rehearsed. Nevertheless, you should consider using these forms to supplement and complement documentary evidence whenever that is feasible.

[5]Melvin M. Belli with Robert Blair Kaiser, *Melvin Belli: My Life on Trial* (New York: William Morrow & Co., Inc., 1976), pp. 92-93.

Assuring the Quality of Evidence

There are five steps to take to ensure that your evidence will produce audience understanding and belief.

Direct Observation. The first, and perhaps the most important characteristic of quality evidence, is whether the source made direct observations. The firsthand account of an event is almost always more reliable than second- or thirdhand accounts. You have all played the party game in which one person whispers a story to another, and the second person to another, and so on. The tale at the end of the chain is repeated aloud and compared with the original story. Each person who retells the story modifies it—inadvertently—so that the final telling bears little resemblance to the original. Oral or written reports of events observed firsthand by a person are almost always more accurate than secondhand reports will be. In the courtroom, firsthand evidence is preferred. In most situations, secondhand (hearsay) evidence cannot be presented if firsthand evidence is available.

Despite the importance of firsthand observations to the quality of evidence, there are two potential problems with them: (1) they may be biased, and (2) they may not exist. The problem of bias in a source of evidence is reduced when additional tests are applied. There are also cases for which firsthand reports are not available. These may range from unwitnessed crimes to events so large and disorganized (such as riots) that it is impossible to observe the overall event. Sometimes you must settle for a secondhand interpretation or a summary based on firsthand reports.

Corroboration. Fortunately for us, there is competition in the media that bring us most of our information. You need to know if evidence is corroborated by other sources. Two independently written firsthand reports that agree in important features can increase belief in the accuracy and absence of bias in both. Even if you deal with weekly summaries of the news such as appear in *Time, Newsweek,* and *U.S. News and World Report,* the odds for accuracy and lack of bias in a report are increased if all three report essentially the same story.

Evaluate Expertise. In many cases, the ability to interpret observations correctly is critical to the quality of a report. You might witness a high-speed accident on a freeway and report what you saw with as much objectivity and detail as you could muster. But a professional race-car driver witnessing the same accident could probably report with greater accuracy. You could describe the movements of the cars. The professional driver would be able to provide a more detailed description. He or she could also provide insight as to whether the movements resulted from locked brakes, blown tires, or poor driving skills. You would observe the same events, but the expertise of the professional driver would make his or her interpretations more accurate than yours.

There are three items to consider in determining the expertise of a source. In our society, credentials serve as a fairly reliable sign. Earned or honorary degrees from colleges and universities, special awards and honors connected to the area of expertise, and extensive or influential publications in that area are the credentials you should look for. Special experiences of the source constitute the second item to check in determining expertise. The source who has only read about the area is probably less qualified in the field. The individual who lived a number of years in China is likely to be more expert on China than an otherwise qualified individual who visited there occasionally. If possible, you should investigate the accuracy record or the track record of the source.

As Robert P. Newman and Dale R. Newman, writing at the University of Pittsburgh, have stated,

> The more accurate the description and prediction record of a source, the higher the credibility of his testimony in general. We believe accuracy record to be the single most important index of credibility.[6]

Qualify. The fourth way of assuring the quality of evidence is to take note of the degree to which the source qualifies his or her conclusions. Few conclusions that appear in evidence are *absolutely* certain; there are usually exceptional cases. Sources of evidence who are reliable and accurate are aware of these exceptions, and these experts qualify their conclusions accordingly. Consumer's Union carefully tests and rates cars against each other, ranking them from best to worst. Despite their care in testing, they point out that some aspects to be considered in purchasing a car are beyond their testing procedures. Price is one, as is the responsibility of choosing a reputable dealership. The most highly rated car is of little use if it is sitting in a remote dealership waiting for a common part that the dealer does not keep in stock. The admission of qualifications leads consumers to have considerable faith in the accuracy and reliability of reports that appear in *Consumer Reports*.

Like Consumer's Union, most reliable and accurate sources qualify their conclusions. By using words and phrases such as "frequently," "on the whole," and "in situations like the one under discussion," they let you know that exceptions exist. It is, however, important to apply other evidence tests in conjunction with qualification. Some inaccurate and unreliable sources purposely disguise their bias by carefully qualifying their distortions. A popular technique among bigots is to qualify their statements with, "Some of my best friends are _____, but. . . ." Even though careful qualification is occasionally a sign to be wary, usually careful qualification is a sign of reliable evidence.

Use Common Sense. The final method of assuring the quality of evidence is to make use of common sense. *Common sense* will lead you to ask a question that derives from the verifiability criterion you may have studied in philosophy. That question is "What would I be able to see or do if this evidence were true?" If a source claims that food stamps are being abused by many people, then those living in the heart of

[6]Robert P. Newman and Dale R. Newman, *Evidence* (Boston: Houghton Mifflin Company, 1969), p. 82.

Appalachia, where poverty and food stamps abound, would expect to observe that abuse. Food-stamp users in supermarket checkout lines would wear fresh designer clothes and drive off in new automobiles or pick-up trucks. Your authors live in Appalachia. We have never observed these things, despite the fact that we observe two or three food-stamp families in supermarket checkout lines every week. Consequently, our common sense tells us that food-stamp abuse, if it is occurring, occurs subtly in Appalachia or is rarer than the authority implies. Passively reflecting on personal experience to make a common-sense evaluation of evidence is fine, but you can also actively seek common-sense verification.

Active use of common sense involves asking questions of people who have valid information. Consulting a faculty member who is expert in an area is an active use of common sense. Telephoning your Congressperson or a spokesperson for an industry often leads to positive results. When you doubt a published assertion, make use of your common sense to check it out. Ask yourself what you would have seen or heard if the assertion were true. If that is insufficient, use your common sense to contact someone who is likely to know the truth.

Summary

1. Students usually support the points in their speeches with evidence of fact, evidence of opinion, or statistical evidence.
2. Factual evidence should be recent, reliable, and relevant.
3. Opinion evidence should have a factual base, come from experts, and be backed by other experts.
4. Before you accept statistical evidence, you should understand its base, understand the sample, understand how the statistic was computed, and understand the application of the statistic.
5. There are five kinds of evidence: (1) witnesses, (2) documents, (3) reproductions, (4) representations, and (5) objects or artifacts.
6. Witnesses are people who appear in person and who can presumably be questioned by the audience.
7. Documents refer to most printed or written materials—the kind of materials usually found in libraries.
8. Reproductions refer to audio, video, or other such techniques (including photographs).
9. Representations refer to charts, maps, diagrams, and the like.
10. Actual objects or artifacts refer to objects such as the murder weapon, the garments of the victim, and so on.
11. Generally, effective use of evidence increases audience acceptance of your thesis or proposition.
12. Although there are other considerations, evidence based on first-hand observations usually exceeds hearsay evidence in quality.

13. The greater the discrepancy between evidence and expectation, the greater the need for corroboration to assure quality.
14. Expert evidence is usually preferable because of contextual factors available to the expert in his or her observations of events.
15. The track record of expert sources is the most important criterion to consider in evaluating their reports.
16. Unqualified conclusions indicate that you should evaluate evidence more carefully than usual.
17. Evidence that violates common-sense expectations should be viewed with considerable suspicion.

Questions and Exercises

1. Look through a current magazine or newspaper editorial page. Find one or two examples of evidence that rely upon facts, opinions, or statistics. Be prepared to present the examples you have found to your class.
2. Either find new examples of factual, opinion, or statistical evidence, or use the ones found in Question 1. Subject each kind of evidence to the basic tests of that kind of evidence given in the early part of the chapter. Be prepared to defend the evidence you have found as adequate, good, inadequate, or weak, in terms of the tests.
3. Prepare an abbreviated speech composed of a simple declarative sentence and one or two pieces of evidence designed to show that the sentence is true. Follow the rules that indicate how to introduce evidence smoothly and effectively.
4. Read through a fairly detailed account of a trial, such as the Claus von Bulow murder trial. Usually, *The New York Times* is a good source for accounts of such trials. (Your local newspaper is probably a good source for detailed accounts of local trials.) Note the forms of evidence used by the prosecution and defense in criminal trials or by the plaintiff and defendant in civil cases. Write a brief synopsis of each of the kinds of evidence used. Which seems to be most influential in leading to the verdict reached in the trial? Why?
5. Select a controversial issue such as a nuclear freeze, dangers of nuclear reactors for power generation, capital punishment, and so on. Flip a coin with a classmate for sides, and go to the library for a specified period of time—perhaps an hour or two. Find and copy all the evidence for your side that you can locate in that period. Each of you should then present your evidence to the class in a ten- or twelve-minute summary. Both your partner and the class should then try to reconcile the contradictions in the evidence. Why do these contradictions occur?
6. Each year, radio, television, newspapers, news magazines, and organizations make predictions about matters for the coming year. In addition, Jeane Dixon and a number of other people who claim

special ability in this area publish their prognostications. Get a copy of the predictions of someone like Dixon and a copy of the predictions of the reporters for a news organization. Bring them to class for a discussion of whose predictions turned out to be most accurate.

7. Interview friends and acquaintances about an incident that one has witnessed firsthand and that the other has only heard and read about. Do the interviews at different times, take notes, and be prepared to explain to the class the differences between the information provided by the eyewitness and that of the secondary source.

8. Discuss with your classmates the times when you and they have accepted something as true from a single, uncorroborated source. What kind of faulty conclusion did each of you reach? Have you adopted a policy of seeking corroboration before acting in all cases as a result? If not, what is your policy? Do you think you should follow a more stringent policy in selecting evidence for your speeches? a less stringent policy?

9. Review recent speech topics you and your classmates have used. Pick five you know most about. Prepare a list of the people or organizations that you think have the greatest degree of expertise in those five fields. Review the sources of evidence used by your classmates in their speeches. How does the evidence actually used compare with your view about who is really expert? If the lists differ, why do they differ?

10. Identify at least one informational item in a newspaper, in a news magazine, or on radio or television news that you do not quite understand or that you doubt to be true. Devise a common-sense method of finding out the truth about that item. What should you be able to observe if it is true? if it is false? With whom could you talk to find out? You might even try telephoning them.

Courtesy of Peter Falk

Effective Reasoning

OBJECTIVES

By the time you finish reading this chapter, you should be able to:

1. Name and explain the six points of the Toulmin system of analyzing arguments and diagram your own arguments and those of others according to this system.
2. Name, define, and explain each of four forms of reasoning.
3. Explain the tests of each form and apply them to your own arguments and the arguments of others.

Discussions of reasoning in public speeches usually identify four basic types of reasoning: analogy, example or generalization, sign, and cause. Traditional definitions of inductive reasoning place analogy and example in the inductive category, because both move from specifics to generalizations. The traditional definition of deduction places sign and cause in the deductive category, because both start with generalizations about the nature of associations and draw conclusions about specific cases. Modern definitions of induction and deduction focus on the degree of certainty of the conclusion of a piece of reasoning. When the certainty is absolute, then the reasoning is called *deductive. Inductive* reasoning occurs when there is a degree of probability associated with the conclusion—when the conclusion is less than certain. Whether it is inductive or deductive, reasoning involves discovering links between ideas.

The ways in which the ideas are linked enable you to draw conclusions from the ideas. Sound reasoning results from clear and concise statements of the ideas, the links between them, and how those links lead to conclusions. This chapter discusses the Toulmin diagrammatic system of describing the links between ideas and goes on to describe the nature of those links in terms of analogy, example, sign, and cause. Stephen Toulmin, British psychologist and author specializing in reasoning and ethics of science, presents a systematic way of naming the elements of reasoning and diagramming the links between the elements.[1] He suggests that any piece of reasoning must contain three major parts and that careful reasoning often contains three supplemental parts. The major parts *always* appear. All three supplemental parts might appear,

[1]Stephen Toulmin, Richard Rieke, and Allan Janik, *An Introduction to Reasoning* (New York: Macmillan Publishing Co., Inc., 1979), pp. 26-27.

but one may appear without the other two or two might appear without the other one.

The Toulmin System

Toulmin suggests that the three major elements of any argument are claims, grounds, and warrants. *Claims* are the propositions or statements that you wish to prove. Examples of the kinds of claims that may appear in student speeches are these: "Cults use unethical techniques to gain and hold members" or "Pornography involving children should be prohibited by law." A claim may also be called a *conclusion*.

Grounds are those statements or propositions that contain information or data upon which the claim is based. A statement such as "Those who attend cult retreats are frequently deprived of sleep, adequate food, warmth, and are subjected to intense peer pressure" might serve as partial grounds for documenting the unethical practices of cults. A story of the abuse of children to force them to appear in pornographic films would provide grounds for severely penalizing the makers of such films. Other commonly used words for *grounds* are *data, facts,* and *evidence.*

The *warrant* is the principle or rule that justifies making the claim on the basis of the grounds provided. It is a scheme or rule of thinking that justifies moving from the grounds to the claim. The warrant linking the claim and grounds about cults might be "Influence attempts that prevent people from thinking clearly are unethical." The warrant linking the claim and grounds in the case of pornography might state, "Any activity that involves sexual abuse of minor children should be severely punished." Although it may be used in a technical sense to refer to other kinds of propositions, the word *premise* is frequently equivalent to *warrant.* The relationship between claims, grounds, and warrants is depicted in Figure 11-1.

There are three supplemental parts to the system. Warrants, for example, may be subject to two factors that weaken their ability to link grounds and claims. First, you might ask, "Don't advertising and many

FIGURE 11-1 Primary Elements of Toulmin's System

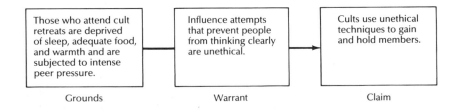

Those who attend cult retreats are deprived of sleep, adequate food, and warmth and are subjected to intense peer pressure.	Influence attempts that prevent people from thinking clearly are unethical.	Cults use unethical techniques to gain and hold members.
Grounds	Warrant	Claim

other influence attempts try to get us to do something without thinking clearly?" Here, you are really asking about the kinds of *backing* available for the warrant. You might back your warrant about cults with the following statement: "Unlike most influence attempts, cults make their pitch under retreat conditions that foster dependence and debilitation." *Backing* is information about the degree of validity or reliability of warrants. Second, you might ask, "How many cults really engage in the kind of practices described? How certain is the warrant?" It should be obvious that warrants that are less than 100 percent certain lead to claims that are less than 100 percent certain. The term used to refer to the restrictions placed on conclusions because of uncertainty is *modal qualifier*. Thus, in the Toulmin system, if the association between cults and dependency and debilitation is less than 100 percent, you would have to qualify the warrant and subsequent claims. You would need to say, "In most cases, influence attempts that prevent people from thinking clearly are unethical."

Even with the restrictions that result from backing and modal qualifiers, one other element must be considered. This element, called *possible rebuttals,* identifies circumstances that might operate to reduce the soundness of the argument. Consider this possible rebuttal to the cult argument: "People who are converted to cult membership are simply psychologically weak." You must be prepared to deal with that argument if it is raised. Thus, you would need to be prepared to argue that studies of those who have become cult members show that these people had earlier shown no greater number of psychological problems than people in the population in general. To see how all six elements look when they are incorporated into one picture, study Figure 11-2.

The Toulmin system helps you picture an argument and the relationships among its various parts. In instances of weak arguments, this is sometimes enough. When you present an argument based on a faulty warrant, inadequate grounds, or an ambiguous claim, a mental picture may enable you to recognize the weaknesses in your argument. If a mental picture fails to reveal interrelationships adequately, then diagramming should enable you to identify obvious weaknesses. There are, however, arguments for which the detection of weakness requires more than Toulmin's diagramming techniques. Potential errors are often more subtle than they are in the examples just presented.

Kinds of Reasoning

When you deal with the complexities of analogy, example, sign, or cause, you would like to be able to recognize which of those four forms you are employing and whether the relationship you are trying to establish is sound. Consequently, the following discussion of reasoning

Figure 11-2 Primary and Secondary Elements of Toulmin's System

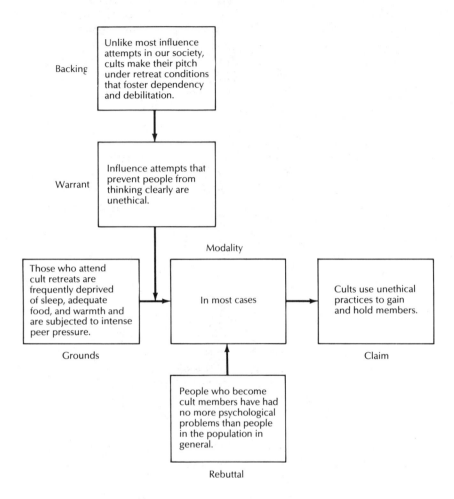

has these parts: (1) each form is named and defined; (2) its general characteristics are explained; (3) special instances or techniques of its applications are examined; and (4) the various tests or rules for employing that form of reasoning correctly are discussed.

Literal Analogy: Definition and Explanation. Analogy can be defined as the form of reasoning that says that if two or more things are alike in important respects, they will be alike in other respects. If several of your friends who are intellectually similar to you (i.e., they have similar grades in the same classes and have similar study habits) experience difficulty in a required math class, you may reason by analogy that you, too, will have difficulty. If a friend has a problem with the bursar, you can expect difficulty too. If this friend praises the worth of a class, you expect it to be a good class. Analogy is useful, but it is a less rigorous kind of reasoning than the other forms are. Your expectations may not always occur: the bursar may not give you trouble, and you may find the class dull.

You may well ask, at this point, "If it is unreliable, why don't we reduce our use of it and turn to more reliable forms?" The answer is that many times analogical reasoning is the best you can do. If properly used, analogy approaches the reliability of other forms, particularly if it is based on comparisons of numbers of instances. If the physician examines you and decides that you have influenza, he or she will be basing that decision on analogical reasoning. Two things will differ between his or her application of analogy and yours. You observe the similarity of your symptoms to those of a friend. The physician takes your temperature, probes for swollen glands, smells your breath, looks at your eyes, and into your nose and throat. His or her list of important respects in which humans are similar is much longer than yours. In addition to that, the physician has also seen hundreds and perhaps thousands of patients who have had influenza, as well as patients who have had different diseases with similar symptoms. Thus, the physician's analogical reasoning is more reliable than yours is.

Literal Analogy: Tests. It may already be clear to you that there are two major rules for developing reliable analogical relationships. First, you must determine if the things being compared are alike in important respects. This means that you have to know what the important respects are. Second, you will note that the more comparisons you use in the analogy, the more reliable your reasoning will be. When you present an analogy, you should ask the following two questions: (1) Are the things being compared alike in important respects? and (2) Is the analogy based upon many comparisons?

Figurative Analogy: Definition and Explanation. Literal analogy typifies the way in which two things that are like each other can be compared. In some instances of analogy, the things compared are quite unlike each other. People are biologically members of the same species; they are not mechanical contrivances like heating systems. Consider an analogy that says, "My friends all have Honeywell thermostats in their homes and some of those thermostats have been in operation for 20 years with no problems; therefore, I want Honeywell thermostats in my new home." Compare that reasoning with this analogy: "In order to understand how feedback from an audience works, consider how the furnace thermostat in your home works." The first example of analogy is literal; thermostats are members of the same class. The second analogy is figurative; humans and thermostats are members of different classes. Analogies that compare members of the same class are called *literal analogies*. Analogies that compare members of different classes are called *figurative analogies*. Figurative analogies cannot be used to prove anything—they have no probative value. Whenever you use a figurative analogy instead of a literal one, you will discover that the comparison is imperfect.

Figurative Analogy: Tests. Assuming that you make a careful comparison, you must test figurative analogy by asking the following question: "Will the amount of understanding gained from this analogy exceed the amount of misunderstanding it produces?" If the answer is "No," you should not use that figurative analogy.

Reasoning from Example: Definition and Explanation. Reasoning from example involves developing a generalization based upon a sample. There are usually two ways of defining the concept. One definition calls it the form of reasoning that says that what is true of a sample from a class is likely to be true of the entire class. The other definition states that the form draws a generalization from a number of examples. However it is defined, it operates in the following manner. You wish to generalize about a group of people or things, but do not have the time or money to seek out every individual or thing in the group, or even most of them. Instead, you select certain members of the group, a certain number of the things; you question or examine them and use what you find as the basis for generalizing about the entire group. If, for example, you want to know how many people are watching one television network or another at 9 P.M., you select between 1500 and 2000 households, find out what they are watching, and use that as a basis for generalizing about the nation as a whole. How do you make sure your generalizations are reliable and useful? How do you avoid overgeneralizing? The tests that follow provide the answers to these questions.

Reasoning from Example: Tests. From the foregoing discussion, you have probably guessed that the strength of argument from example depends upon two factors: (1) how well the examples or instances represent the class from which they are drawn, and (2) the number of instances or examples used. These tests are usually expressed by questions such as the following:

1. How representative are the instances or examples?
2. How large is the sample?

The first test deals with the degree of bias that might creep into the selection of a sample. If you write for a campus newspaper or work in the news department of a campus radio or television station, you might be asked to find out how students feel about an issue. For example, you might be asked to find out what percentage of the student body plans to vote in an upcoming election. If you talk to 100 students and decide that 85 percent will vote, your generalization will be sound if those 100 students are representative. If they are all political science majors in a department that in its classes stresses the importance of voting, your sample would be biased. The actual percentage of the student body voting in the election might be 65 percent or lower. A sample of political science majors may not predict what English, math, biology, sociology, communication, business, physics, and chemistry majors represented on your campus will do. Biased samples do not provide a sound basis for example arguments.

The second test of example reasoning is to determine if the sample is large enough. Large samples partially offset the need to be concerned about representativeness. With proper statistical procedures, the sample size needed for a given degree of reliability can be calculated. As a rule, a sample of 1 or 2 percent of a population will not yield reliable generalizations, but 5 to 10 percent will yield much more reliable generalizations, and samples greater than 10 percent increase the reliability even more. If, however, appropriate statistical or logical procedures ensure representativeness, small samples can yield reliable generalizations.

In summary, then, arguments from example can be tested by looking at the representativeness and the size of the sample.

Reasoning from Sign: Definition and Explanation. Just as reasoning from example and reasoning from analogy share features, so do causal reasoning and sign reasoning. In both cases, the concern is with the association between two or more events. The degree of association becomes the basis for reasoning that one event can be taken as an indication for the occurrence of another event. The distinguishing feature between cause and sign is that causal reasoning looks beneath the association to determine *why* that association exists. Sign reasoning does not usually attempt to look beneath the fact that the two events are associated. It simply takes one event as an indication of the other event; it asserts that one event is a sign of the other.

The flag at half-mast, which indicates that someone of prominence has died, is a classic example that leads to sign reasoning. The death of someone prominent also serves as a sign that flags will be flown at half-mast. Most cases of sign reasoning are similar to this one, in that two events are, in fact, associated because of underlying causal factors, but there is neither time nor motivation to work out the underlying causal relationships. The association itself—the signs—is sufficient for ordinary purposes.

Sign relationships are of two kinds. The term for sign relationships in which each is a sign of the other is *reciprocal*. Reciprocal sign relationships provide the basis for the strongest sign reasoning. The second kind is exemplified if you conclude that the authors of a medical textbook hold M.D. degrees. Certainly authorship of a medical school textbook is a reasonably strong sign that the writers of that book hold the M.D. There are, however, exceptions. The relationship is not reciprocal, for not everyone who holds the M.D. is a medical textbook author, and not every medical textbook author is an M.D. Nonreciprocal sign relationships obviously are weaker than reciprocal sign relationships.

Reasoning from Sign: Tests. Probably you have already guessed the ways in which you may test sign relationships. First, the two events must be associated frequently enough that you will seldom make a mistake if you make a decision based on that association. If you are to draw valid conclusions from sign relationships, then you must first make sure that there is an association that occurs frequently enough to warrant a decision based on that association.

Second, you should attempt to determine whether the relationship is reciprocal or nonreciprocal. It is quite certain that if you find ice in puddles, the temperature fell below freezing the night before. It is less valid to predict that a person who drinks heavily will develop a bulbous red nose. In the case of the thermometer, whenever it is below 32° Fahrenheit or 0° Celsius, ice forms on puddles, and when ice forms on puddles, the thermometer registers 32° F or 0° C or lower. But although heavy drinking leaves signs on the noses of some drinkers, large, red noses are associated with a number of diseases, and some heavy drinkers simply do not develop red noses. If the relationship is reciprocal, then you can place much more reliance on it than if it is not. If it is not reciprocal (and sometimes even if it is), you need to apply a third test of sign.

In the third test of reasoning from sign you should ask, "Do several signs point to the same conclusion?" The classic example of using sign reasoning to reach conclusions occurs in the detective story. The detective combines numerous clues (signs) to discover who committed the crime.

Causal Reasoning: Definition and Explanation. Causal reasoning yields the highest degree of prediction and control of any of the four forms. It rests on the assumption that there is a regularity in the universe and among humans. This regularity can be discovered and formulated so that if you know one event (the cause) you will be able to predict another event (the effect) that inevitably follows from it. Such reasoning answers the question "Why?" If, for example, Isaac Newton discovers that for every action there is an equal and opposite reaction, then you know why, if you slam a door in anger, it may rebound and strike you in the nose. How do we discover the underlying regularities in physical matters and interpersonal matters that enable us to develop *why* explanations?

For the most part, people use three methods for discovering underlying regularities. First, they observe events over time and notice which events frequently precede other events. Second, they see one event follow another in some cases, but in other cases they see a similar but slightly different preliminary event and note that the second event does not follow. Third, they observe that certain things increase or decrease together, or sometimes that an increase in one is followed by a proportional decrease in the other and vice versa. For example, if you are a surgeon specializing in chest surgery, you may begin to notice that most cancerous lungs that you remove come from males who smoke cigarettes, even though physically, occupationally, and geographically they are highly variable. You may, at conventions and professional meetings, talk with other chest surgeons who have similar experiences with cancerous lungs. You may conclude that smoking is a likely cause of the cancerous lungs you have been removing. This method of discovering underlying regularities has some problems, however. It may be that heavy smokers have an underlying physiological make-up that leads both to smoking and lung cancer. If you wanted to be more certain, then you would employ the second method of discovering underlying regularity. This method requires that you find people who are alike in most respects—including age, diet, occupation, physique, and exercise levels— except that some of them smoke cigarettes and some do not. If it turns out that those people who do not smoke cigarettes seldom contract lung cancer, while those who do smoke cigarettes contract lung cancer frequently, then you may be relatively certain that cigarette smoking causes lung cancer. The final method of finding causes looks at relationships between increases and decreases of the two factors. If, for example, you begin to find that as the number of females who smoke increases, the number of females who contract lung cancer also increases at approximately the same rate, you have further reason to believe that smoking is a cause of lung cancer.

The three methods of discovering causal relationships were three of the four described by the British philosopher John Stuart Mill (1806-1873).[2] The first is called the *Method of Agreement,* because it depends upon situations in which the two factors suspected to be causally linked always appear together (that is, the two situations agree) despite the fact that other factors in the situations are different. Thus, chest surgeons began to notice that heavy smoking almost always preceded the onset of lung cancer, whether male cancer victims were young or old or were truck drivers or college professors. Mill's second method is called the *Method of Difference,* because it depends upon two situations being different in some critical aspect, even though the situations are otherwise alike. If twins, for example, develop similar life styles, but one smokes and the other does not, and the smoking twin develops lung cancer, then it is likely that smoking is the cause. If this same finding is apparent for many pairs of twins, then it becomes a near certainty. If for people in general you can take a large group of smoking Americans and compare them with a similar group of nonsmoking Americans, you will be comparing two groups that are alike, except for their smoking behavior. When the prevalence of lung cancer among the smokers is much higher than it is among nonsmokers, the two groups are similar in most respects but differ (disagree) in whether or not they are smokers. Mill's third method is the *Method of Concomitant Variations.* This means that two things that vary at the same rate or proportional rates are probably causally related. Again, you find the rate of lung cancer among women varying according to the rate at which women are taking up smoking. If

[2]John Stuart Mill, *A System of Logic, Ratiocinative and Inductive,* ed. J. M. Robson (Toronto: University of Toronto Press, 1973), pp. 388-406.

you found that as more women began to smoke, the rate of lung cancer in women failed to rise, then you would have to conclude that smoking is not linked to lung cancer in females.

Mill's methods do not always yield reliable results, particularly when they are applied to human problems. For this reason, you need tests that can be applied to proposed causal relationships that will enable you to make a judgment about the reliability of those relationships.

Causal Reasoning: Tests. For many situations in which causal relationships are proposed, the relationship may hold at one time and not at another. Normally, your electric alarm clock causes you to awaken at 6:00 A.M. on weekdays. If during the night a thunderstorm causes a temporary interruption in electrical service, then you may well oversleep and even be late for your morning class. Before you accept a proposed causal relationship, you need to make sure that no intervening cause has interrupted the usual connection between the cause and the effect. This verification is the first test of causal relationships.

The second test of causal relationships has to do with, oddly enough, whether the proposed cause and effect are related at all. Is there some physical connection between the two events? On the one hand, there is a human propensity to notice that one event frequently follows another; people therefore conclude that the two are connected. Close inspection may reveal they are not connected at all. Many superstitions are based on this kind of faulty causal reasoning. This particular tendency toward faulty causal thinking is so prevalent that it was recognized long ago and given the name of the "fallacy of post hoc ergo propter hoc": after (*post*) this (*hoc*) therefore (*ergo*) because (*propter*) of this (*hoc*). Even if one event follows another with regularity, there is no reason to believe that the first might have caused the second until you have made certain that there is some kind of connection between the two.

The third test of causal reasoning focuses on the ability of some causes to produce multiple effects. The need to apply this test arises most frequently in two situations: when you propose to implement some plan or proposal and when you propose to eliminate some cause in order to eliminate an effect. If you decide to implement increased study hours (the cause) to get better grades (the effect), then you need to consider whether the cause might produce other effects (for example, reducing the number of hours you sleep). If you decide to diet (cause) to reduce your weight (the effect), you need to consider possible side effects of the diet you choose. Many causes produce effects in addition to the one in which you are especially interested. If your increased study hours resulted in better grades but reduced your sleeping time to the point at which you became cross and irritable, causing you to lose friends, then the disadvantages might be more significant than the increase in grade point would justify. If the side effects of the diet you chose led to such a weak physical condition that you were unable to enjoy your improved appearance, then again the disadvantages would outweigh the advantages.

The fourth test of causal reasoning focuses on the fact that some effects are produced by more than one cause. Toward the end of an extremely busy week you may awaken to find that you just do not want to face the day. Why is this so? The probability is that a number of things may have contributed—the late-night cramming before a midterm, the fight with a girl friend or boy friend when you were too busy to go to a movie, the tension associated with the report you had to give in another class, and the heated debate you had at a meeting that left you angry and frustrated. To prevent these causes from operating over the following week will require you to determine the relative contribution of each cause to your depression. If it turns out that inadequate sleep is the primary contributor, you will have a good chance of reducing the end-of-the-week blues. However, if all events contributed equally, then many changes will have to be made to reduce the problem.

Most human problems are produced by multiple causes. Whether it be poverty, war, crime, or soil erosion, a careful analysis will usually reveal that a number of causes are producing the effect. To reduce the problem, you must locate the principal causes and try to remove them.

Summary

1. The Toulmin system of picturing reasoning and evidence involves the concepts of warrant, grounds, claim, qualification, backing, and possible refutations.
2. There are four forms of reasoning: (1) analogy, (2) example, (3) sign, and (4) cause.
3. Analogy compares two things and concludes that if they are essentially alike in some important respects, the second will be like the first in other important respects.
4. In evaluating an analogy, you should focus on the similarities between the objects compared and the number of comparisons available.
5. Reasoning from example involves formulating generalizations based upon sampling the members of a class or inferring generalizations from examples gathered by other methods.
6. Argument from example is evaluated based upon the representativeness of the sample or examples and the size of the sample or the number of examples.
7. Sign reasoning involves asserting that if two events have been closely associated in the past, the presence of one may be taken as an indication of the presence of the other.
8. Evaluation of sign reasoning involves considering the strength of the association between the two events in the past and determining whether that association is reciprocal.

9. Causal reasoning produces prediction and control by discovering why events occur.
10. Underlying regularities can be discovered by employing the method of agreement, the method of difference, and the method of concomitant variations.
11. Causal reasoning may be evaluated by asking whether the usual connection between cause and effect has been interrupted, whether the cause and effect are really related, whether some causes have the ability to produce multiple effects, and whether a given effect is produced by multiple causes.

Questions and Exercises _____

1. Find an example of reasoning in a column or editorial in a newspaper or magazine. Following the diagram used in Figure 11-1, diagram the grounds, warrant, and claim used in the reasoning. Identify any strengths or weaknesses in the argument that are revealed by analyzing the reasoning in this way.
2. Using the same example of reasoning selected in Question 1, produce a new diagram, adding backing, modality, and possible rebuttals. Are any further strengths or weaknesses in the reasoning revealed with the addition of these factors to the diagram? What are they? How did the addition of backing, modal qualifier, and possible rebuttal affect your ability to discover strengths and weaknesses?
3. Jot down all the persuasive attempts that are directed at you for a day or two. What overall reasoning patterns are employed in each of the attempts? Is this day typical in the kinds of attempts at persuasion that are directed at you? What kinds of reasoning patterns should you study most intensely if you wish to be critical of attempts to persuade you?
4. Find examples of figurative and literal analogy that are used in the press or in advertising. Apply the tests of analogy and write a brief criticism of the reasoning based on that application. Be prepared to discuss what you have found.
5. Find samples of example reasoning or generalization that are used in the press or in advertising. Apply the tests of example reasoning and write a brief criticism of the reasoning based on that application. Be prepared to discuss what you have found.
6. Find examples of sign reasoning that are used in the press or in advertising. Apply the tests of sign and write a brief criticism of the reasoning based on that application. Be prepared to discuss what you have found.

7. Find examples of causal reasoning that are used in the press or in advertising. Apply the tests of cause and write a brief criticism of the reasoning based on that application. Be prepared to discuss what you have found.

8. Referring to the detailed speech outline given in Chapter 8, Table 8-1, identify the form of reasoning that is followed overall and in each of the first two levels of subordination—that is, at the capital English alphabet level (A, B, C, etc.) and at the Arabic numeral level (1, 2, 3, etc.).

CHAPTER
12

Using Language Effectively

OBJECTIVES _____

By the time you finish reading this chapter, you should be able to:

1. List the characteristics of effective language.
2. Explain from three different perspectives what it means to say that language is accurate.
3. Describe the relationship existing between and among *symbols, referents,* and *thought.*
4. Distinguish between *denotative* and *connotative* meaning.
5. Define *language intensity,* detail its effects, and list two variables that produce it.
6. Explain the relationship between *economy* of language and economy of listener attention.
7. Define *vividness* and explain how a speaker makes language vivid through employing figures of speech.
8. Provide original examples of *metaphors, similes,* and *personifications.*
9. Define *propriety* and list four ways in which a speaker's language must be appropriate.

Undoubtedly, Archie Bunker has to stand among the greatest of all abusers of the English language. In one episode of the long-running series, Archie's language choices result in a logical contradiction within his argument. "Meathead," of course, cannot resist pointing out his father-in-law's cognitive inconsistency, but Archie is quick to resolve the apparent contradiction by observing, "What I say has nothing to do with what I think." Here Archie is wrong. What you say and how you say it have a great deal to do with what you are thinking and how others think about and respond to your ideas.

Ancient Greek philosophers believed, like Archie, that language and thought were separate entities, that reason was uncontaminated by language. They believed that all men, or at least all "thinkers," shared in the essence of reason. More recent linguistic theorists suggest a very contradictory point of view. They argue that higher levels of thinking are dependent on language and that the structure of one's language affects the manner in which one views the world.[1] Examples abound to

---

[1] See for example, Benjamin L. Whorf, in *Language, Thought, and Reality,* ed. John B. Carroll (Cambridge, Mass.: Technology Press of Massachusetts Institute of Technology, 1956).

illustrate how language shapes our reality. Not long ago your authors were browsing in a men's clothing store. Also in the store was a portly gentleman who was attempting to buy a new suit but could not find one that fit properly. Each of the four or five suits he tried on was too tight. The salesclerk, sensing the man's frustration, shrewdly observed, "Sir, I think a discerning man of your position would be much happier in one of our suits with the *executive cut.*" Sure enough, he purchased not one but two suits of the specified variety. One wonders if the outcome would have been the same had the clerk suggested that the portly man select from those suits specifically tailored for "fat men." Probably not!

The names of things affect how we think and respond to those things. Achieving effective language usage is a very complex phenomenon. Consider, for example, the following three statements of the purpose of this chapter.

1. In the present chapter, the authors elucidate characteristics of efficacious language options available to the discerning and judicious practitioner of orally encoded connected discourse.
2. In this chapter, we describe what constitutes effective language for speechmaking.
3. Ya know, like here, man, we totally and to the max say stay away from the grody and go for awesome language, fer sure and far out.

These three statements reflect basically the same thought but express it in very different ways. Is there one statement that is obviously better than the remaining two? To the conservative grammarian, the choice is simple: the second statement is the clearest. As you read through this chapter, you will discover that deciding on effective language choices is not an easy task. Many variables must be considered before you make your choices. This chapter is about effective language for public speaking. Within this chapter, we will enumerate the characteristics of effective language (accuracy, clarity, economy, vividness, and propriety) and provide some suggestions designed to help improve your style as a public speaker.

Accuracy

Imagine that one of your classmates used this type of language in a speech:

Ya know, like a thousand or so years ago there were a lot of people on this earth. And 500 years ago there were a lot more. Well, ah, today there are two or ah three times as many as then and ya know in the next ten years there will be even more. And if we don't start practicing better birth control or something there is gonna be a lot of problems develop. Okay, now what we should do, ya know, is practice what they call "zero-population-growth" and things like that. . . .

How do you respond to such language? Do you find it vague, non-specific, and lacking in grammatical correctness? If so, you are questioning the accuracy of the speaker's language. Let us now consider three components of language *accuracy*.

Accuracy in Word Choices

Language that is accurate is language that best expresses the speaker's thought. In conversations with others, we sometimes become aware that our language may not represent our thoughts accurately. Consider the following conversation:

> *Andy:* Bob's such a *lazy* person.
>   *Al:* Oh! I'm surprised to hear you say that. It may take him a while but Bob always gets the job done.
> *Andy:* Yes, that's true. What I meant to say was: Bob is such a *procrastinator.*

Assuming that Andy's final comment does not just represent an attempt to accommodate Al's objection, such a conversation illustrates how language can express a thought not actually intended by the speaker.

In the public-speaking situation, the burden to be accurate resides almost exclusively with the speaker. Rarely does a member of the audience interrupt to seek clarification or to determine if a thought expressed by the speaker is the intended thought. Members of the audience typically assume that what a speaker says is what he or she means. Thus, the speaker must consider word choices carefully.

Grammatical Correctness

Accuracy demands *grammatical correctness*. Public speakers are rarely commended for excellence in grammar, but many are ridiculed for using incorrect language. As Cicero observed, "Nobody ever admired an Orator for correct grammar, they only laugh at him if his grammar is bad, and not only think him no orator but not even a human being."[2] Contemporary standards are not so harsh, but grammatical correctness is still of considerable importance. It is, of course, true that a listener can grasp the meaning of such a statement as "I *ain't* got *no* paper" or "*Him* and *me* went to the library." We also know what the speaker means when he or she asks, "*Is* there any *questions?*" Yet, as syndicated columnist James Kilpatrick observes:

[2]Cicero, *De Oratore,* III.14.52, trans. H. A. Rackham (Cambridge, Mass.: The Loeb Classical Library, 1968), p. 41.

My thought is that, just as there is more to eating than merely stuffing one's belly, there is more to communication than merely being "effective." If the purpose of housing is solely to protect one from the rain, the Sun King could have built an A-frame. Instead, he built the palace at Versailles.[3]

Grammatical correctness is generally expected. Why risk a negative response brought about by substandard grammar or usage? Learn the contemporary standards and abide by them. Kilpatrick may be correct when he asserts, "It is up to the collective judgment of society to pronounce that it is bad manners to spit on the floor. It is equally bad manners to spit on the rules of grammar and usage."[4]

Precision

A final component of accuracy is what we label as *precision*. Refer to the speech segment on page   , and note how the speaker's language lacks precision. "A thousand or so years ago," "a lot of people," "a lot more," "two or ah three times as many," "birth control or something," and "things like that," are phrases that reveal lack of precision in language and perhaps thought. To be precise is to delineate clearly. Examine the following paired statements.

1A. He bought a flashy car.
1B. He bought a red Datsun 300 ZX.

2A. I don't like those kind of people.
2B. I don't like people who plagiarize term papers, copy from another's test paper, or steal copies of exams.

3A. He's such a conservative.
3B. It is his disposition to maintain the status quo and to resist innovation or change.

4A. The proposed law is not in the American way.
4B. The proposed law is a violation of the Fourth Amendment to the Constitution.

5A. A tremendous number of Americans died in Vietnam.
5B. In Vietnam, 47,752 Americans died in battle.

If you compare the two sentences in each set, you will notice that the language of the second item of each pair is more specific than that of the first item. When language is vague and abstract, the listeners have a wide array of meanings that they can assign to the language symbols. When a speaker states that "a tremendous number of Americans died in

[3]James Kilpatrick, "To Defy Grammar Is Bad Manners," *The Columbus Dispatch,* June 12, 1983, p. 19.
[4]Kilpatrick, p. 19.

Vietnam," the members of the audience must decide how many people constitute a "tremendous number." Does the speaker mean a thousand? Two million? When the speaker uses precise language, the members of the audience are more likely to grasp the meaning intended by the speaker.

Clarity

Language can be accurate but still lack clarity. James McBurney and Ernest Wrage relate an anecdote that illustrates this point. Their story concerns a plumber who had successfully used hydrochloric acid to open clogged drain pipes. Not sure that such a procedure was safe, the plumber wrote to a government agency, seeking advice. An agency official responded to the plumber's query with the following statement: "The efficacy of hydrochloric acid is indisputable, but the corrosive residue is incompatible with metallic permanence." The plumber supposedly wrote back to the agency and thanked the official for the assurance that it was safe to use the powerful acid. Disturbed by the plumber's response, a second official drafted another statement—"We cannot assume responsibility for the production of toxic and noxious residue with hydrochloric acid and suggest you use an alternative procedure." Again, the plumber wrote back to the agency, indicating his agreement that, indeed, hydrochloric acid worked just fine. At this point, agency scientists deliberated about how to clarify the situation. They finally sent the following statement to the plumber: "Don't use hydrochloric acid. It eats hell out of the pipes."[5]

Undoubtedly, the first two responses to the plumber are technically accurate statements, but they lack clarity—at least with respect to the intended audience. The following statement shares the problem of lack of clarity:

> Consolidated defensive positions and essential preplanned withdrawal facilities are to be provided in order to facilitate maximum potentialization for the repulsion and/or delay of incursive combatants in each of several preidentified categories of location deemed suitable to the implacement and/or debarkation of hostile military contingents.[6]

It is nearly impossible to understand this statement. In fact, the words are Richard Mitchell's tongue-in-cheek paraphrasing of Winston Churchill's famous line: "We shall fight on the beaches, we shall fight on the landing grounds, we shall fight in the fields and in the streets, we shall fight in the hills; we shall never surrender." Mitchell's statement accurately states the proposed British course of action in "their finest

---

[5]*The Chicago Sun,* February 17, 1947, p. 10. Cited by James H. McBurney and Ernest J. Wrage, *The Art of Good Speech* (Englewood Cliffs, N.J.: Prentice-Hall, 1953), pp. 360-361.

[6]Richard Mitchell, *Less Than Words Can Say* (Boston: Little, Brown, 1979), p. 37.

hour," but the simple but powerful clarity of Churchill's words is lost. "Preidentified categories of location" is a poor substitute for the language chosen by England's great orator. There are two useful areas for the speaker who seeks clarity to consider: the nature of meaning and the intensity of language.

Meaning: Its Nature

English is composed of close to a million words, yet even the most verbal language user is familiar with only about 100,000 of them. Stanford Berman reports that the 500 most frequently used words have 14,000 dictionary definitions.[7] It is not surprising, then, that a speaker's intended meaning for a word may not be the meaning the members of the audience assign. During a snowstorm several winters ago, one of your authors decided to purchase a pair of overshoes. Accompanied by the other author, who was wearing the desired type of overshoes, he set out for what he expected to be a simple purchase. Visits to three shoestores produced a negative response to the question, "Do you have any overshoes?" In the fourth store, this author again received the response, "Sorry, we don't stock them." This time, he pointed to his companion's overshoes and asked, "Do you have anything like those?" Here the saleswoman's face took on a look of disgust as she replied, "Of course, but if you wanted Buckle Arctics, why didn't you say so?" It should be clear that there was a difference of opinion about the meaning of the word *overshoe.*

Some language theorists take the position that meanings are in people, not in words; that "words do not mean, only people mean." To understand the implication of such a position, it is useful to consider an approach advocated by theorists Charles K. Ogden and Ivor R. Richards,[8] who visualize the process of meaning in the form of a triangle (see Figure 12-1). At the three points of the triangle, they place the terms *symbol, referent,* and *thought or reference.* By *symbol,* they mean the word that stands for a referent or object. Of note is the broken line between the symbol and its referent; this line indicates that no direct connection exists. According to this view, the connection between a word and the object it symbolizes can be made only through the thought process of a person. Thus, in our previous example the word *overshoe* produced an association or image to the salesclerks that was different than the author's association. Accuracy in meaning was not achieved until the author pointed to the referent and stated the word *overshoe.*

The meanings that the members of the audience assign to language symbols are closely connected with past experiences and associations. The effective public speaker is always aware that words can evoke both

[7]Stanford I. Berman, *Understanding and Being Understood* (San Diego, Calif.: International Communication Institute, 1965), p. 14.

[8]See Charles K. Ogden and Ivor R. Richards, *The Meaning of Meaning* (New York: Harcourt, Brace, & Co., Inc., 1956).

FIGURE 12-1   Ogden and Richards' Meaning Triangle

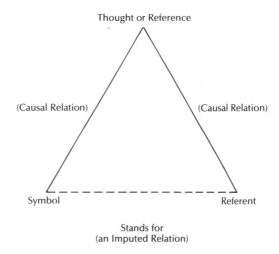

From *The Meaning of Meaning,* by C. K. Ogden and I. A. Richards. Copyright © 1956. Reprinted by permission by Harcourt Brace & Co., Inc.

denotative and *connotative* meanings. The *denotative* meaning of a word is arrived at through societal agreement and is recorded in dictionaries and other words that detail contemporary usage. *Connotative* meanings are personal in nature and are produced by processes that associate the word with some past experience. To illustrate the difference in these two forms of meaning, consider the word *ladder*. A dictionary might define a ladder as a common appliance used for either ascending or descending. This is the denotative meaning. However, for anyone who has ever fallen from a ladder and suffered injury, the word produces numerous associations and evokes images of falling, pain, ambulances, hospitals, doctors, more pain, casts, and so on.

The names of things can have tremendous impact on how individuals respond to those things. The Ford Motor Company, for example, is well aware of the associative power of words and considers very carefully the names of its new automobiles. Tim Moulson, who coordinated the name search for the Ford Tempo, maintains, "A name doesn't sell a car, but a good name gets a car off to a faster start. Car names are more than names; they're features, like power steering. Think of *Thunderbird* and *Lincoln*. The words themselves add value to those cars, because they have a certain cachet attached to them."[9] So important are these associations that individuals have established businesses for the sole purposes of devising product names that will evoke favorable images

[9]Tim Moulson, cited by Robert Garfield, "Name Game: Ford Had a Lot of Better (?) Ideas," *USA Today,* June 8, 1983, p. 3B.

within potential consumers. NameLab, Inc., a San Francisco name-developing firm, was responsible for devising the name *Sentra* for Datsun/Nissan. The firm felt this name evoked the terms " 'sentry' (for protection) and 'central' (for mainstream)."[10]

The public speaker must develop an understanding of the associative power of words and a sensitivity to the various ways members of the audience might respond to language choices. Every audience will have its "snarl words" and its "purr words"[11]—words that have power to produce negative or positive associations. Archie Bunker stands as a prime example of one who ignores our present advice. Habitually, Archie refers to blacks as "coloreds" and uses the phrase "youse people" when he speaks to a black person. Both instances produce negative responses.

Many people respond extremely negatively to sexist language, language that is intrinsically offensive to one gender (usually the female) or another. Two areas seem to be of immediate concern: (1) using the masculine pronoun when referring to a noun that might apply to either sex, and (2) using *man* in occupational titles when the person holding the job might be either male or female. Many of us have been taught that when we use a noun of common gender, we should use a masculine pronoun when referring back to the noun. Thus, we may say, "A *doctor* should respect *his* patients' rights" and "A good *senator* communicates with *his* constituents. *He* lets them know what *he* is thinking." Many find such language objectionable, claiming its use as a fundamental cause of sex-role stereotyping. For the same reason, some individuals also find objectionable such words as chair*man,* sales*man,* line*man,* and so forth. As a public speaker, you must be sensitive to the potential associations that your language is likely to produce. You may mean no disrespect when you refer to a young *woman* in your audience as "the young *gal* in the back," but if that person takes offense, damage is done. Make an effort to avoid words your audience may find offensive.

Language Intensity

A public speaker can offer observations that reflect varying shades of negative or positive feeling—that is, the speaker can vary the degrees of departure from making a neutral comment.[12] Consider the following statements.

1. Acme Coal Company is *stripmining* in our county.
2. Acme Coal Company is *destroying* land in our county.

[10]Garfield, p. 3B.

[11]S. I. Hayakawa, *Language in Thought and Action,* 2nd ed. (New York: Harcourt Brace Jovanovich, 1964), pp. 44-46.

[12]John Waite Bowers, "Language Intensity, Social Introversion, and Attitude Change," *Speech Monographs, 30*: 345-352 (1963).

3. Acme Coal Company is *raping* land in our county.
4. Acme Coal Company is *infecting* the land of our county *with a cancer.*

Do you see a progression in intensity, with each successive statement more removed from the neutral position expressed in the first statement?

Research indicates that the intensity of a speaker's language may determine the speaker's level of persuasiveness, but the process may not occur in the manner suggested by common sense. We may suspect that the more intense a speaker's language is, the more persuasive the speaker will be. Studies have not, however, always found support for such a position. John Bowers, for example, discovered that speeches that use high-intensity language actually produced a *boomerang effect* in audiences: the audiences changed attitude but in the opposite direction to that which was advocated by the speaker.[13] Bowers speculates that when a speaker uses highly intense language, he or she may lose credibility with the audience. This loss of credibility leads to a change of attitude in a direction unintended by the speaker.

Along those same lines are some propositions pertaining to intensity of language put forth by Michael Burgoon, Stephen Jones, and Diane Stewart.[14] These researchers theorize that in the typical public-speaking situation, speakers who violate the expectations of their audience in a positive manner will achieve a change of attitude in the advocated direction, but when a speaker takes "an unexpectedly intense position," either no change or a boomerang effect will result. According to such a view, if an audience enters a public-speaking situation expecting the speaker to be intense or extreme in his or her presentation, the speaker will be most effective if he or she adopts a more moderate approach. Likewise, if the audience expects that the speaker will present a temperate or moderate presentation and instead presents an intemperate or intense speech, the boomerang effect or no change of attitude will result. Most of us would not expect a college president to deliver a speech that uses highly intense language. Accordingly, it may not be in the president's best interest as a persuader to use such phrases as "raping our educational system," "prostituting academic integrity," or "murdering traditional education"—all phrases high in language intensity.

What makes language intense? The answer is not altogether clear. Some have suggested that short, choppy words of Anglo-Saxon origin are more intense than longer words of Latin origin. Others have suggested that the familiar word is more intense than the word that is obscure. Little evidence exists to support such claims. We do know of at least two variables relating to the intensity of language: the presence of

[13]Bowers, pp. 351-352. See also Michael Burgoon and Lyle B. King, "The Mediation of Resistance to Persuasion Strategies by Language Variables and Active-Passive Participation," *Human Communication Research, 1*: 30-41 (1974).

[14]Michael Burgoon, Stephen B. Jones, and Diane Stewart, "Toward a Message-Centered Theory of Persuasion: Three Empirical Investigations of Language Intensity," *Human Communication Research, 1*: 240-256 (1975).

qualifiers and the metaphorical quality of the language.[15] Certain qualifying terminology seems to increase the audience's perception of the intensity of a speaker's language. Examine the following pairs of statements.

1. I ask for your *enthusiastic* assent.
2. I ask for your approval.

3. It was a *considerably less* arduous job than I anticipated.
4. It was easier than I thought it would be.

5. He is *totally* unworthy of praise.
6. He is undeserving of praise.

Research findings suggest that audiences perceive the first member of each pair as a more intense statement than the second statement. If you wish to make your language intensive, use qualifiers.

Metaphors, too, can make language intense. A metaphor is a figure of speech implying a comparison between two things that are not alike in most ways. Many of the phrases we use in everyday conversation are metaphorical. We speak of "burying the hatchet," being "up the creek without a paddle," and we say that someone is "hooked on drugs." We do not intend for such phrases to be interpreted literally, but expect a figurative interpretation. Some types of metaphors are perceived as high in language intensity; this is especially true of those referring to *sex* or *death*. "The coal company is *raping* the land," "He is nothing but a *pimp* for the establishment," or "We must not *prostitute* our values" are all sexual metaphors. Likewise, statements such as "Racism is the *cancer* of our land," "Liberalism is on its *deathbed* in our country," or "To adopt such a proposal is to *crucify* all who are poor" illustrate the death metaphor.

In summary, clarity is important, but it is not easily attained. As a public speaker, you must realize that your words will not always mean the same thing to all people. Occasionally, your audience, or at least some members of your audience, will assign a very different meaning to the words than you intended. Be aware, also, that words can produce strong positive or negative responses. The effective speaker is always sensitive to the potential ambiguity of language and its power to evoke emotional responses.

Economy

In Chapter 19, we observe that listening is hard work and that the process demands considerable expenditure of energy on the part of the listener. As a public speaker, you cannot force the members of your

[15]John Waite Bowers, "Some Correlates to Language Intensity," *Quarterly Journal of Speech, 50*: 415-420 (1964).

audience to listen to your speech, but you can make it easier—though not *easy*—for them to listen. Many public speakers unfortunately act instead as if they really do not care if the members of the audience listen to them; these speakers actually engage in behaviors that make listening and comprehending even more difficult. As John Wilson and Carroll Arnold observe, "A glaring fault in most speech making is the use of too many words. We spend words unwisely, using several where one would do. We clutter thoughts so that even when we do not obscure, we irritate with unnecessary circumlocution."[16] This statement leads us to suggest that economy is an attribute of effective style. Herbert Spencer, a theorist of the early part of the century, was well aware of the difficulties of commanding the attention of audiences. He wrote as follows:

> A reader or listener has at each moment but a limited amount of mental power available. To recognize and interpret the symbols presented to him, requires a part of this power; to arrange and combine the images suggested requires a further part; and only that part which remains can be used for realizing the thought conveyed. Hence, the more time and attention it takes to receive and understand each sentence, the less time and attention can be given to the combined idea; and the less vividly that idea can be conceived.[17]

We agree with Spencer that a speaker must make it as easy as possible for the listener to attend to the speech. Much of this book is devoted to suggesting behaviors that facilitate listeners' attention and comprehension. For example, in Chapter 8, we deal with the importance of presenting the speech in a well-organized and easily identified structure. If material is not organized in a form that is comprehensible to the listener, the listener must make a special effort to reorganize the information. Unless the listener considers the information to be vital, it is unlikely that he or she will expend the necessary energy to reorganize the speech. Instead, he or she is more likely to give up and attend to some stimulus that is more satisfying—daydreaming, perhaps. Language must not be difficult, redundant, nonrelevant, or excessive. How successful do you think Lincoln would have been at Gettysburg had he begun his now famous address as follows:

> Eighty-seven years ago, on July four, this government assumed jurisdiction pursuant to the Declaration of Independence as consummated by representatives duly authorized at the state level to sit as a policy making body at the very highest level. The discussions were oriented by the concept that all persons were in the same category as regards compliance with federal authority.[18]

---

[16]John F. Wilson and Carroll C. Arnold, *Public Speaking as a Liberal Art* (Boston: Allyn and Bacon, Inc., 1965), p. 269.

[17]Herbert Spencer, *The Philosophy of Style* (New York: Appleton, 1920), p. 22.

[18]William D. Grampp, "Words in Public," *Saturday Review,* September 20, 1952, p. 10.

Somehow, this tongue-in-cheek rewrite does not quite rival Lincoln's passionate prose. Lincoln expressed a similar thought, but he expressed it so much more eloquently and more economically, taking less than half as many words to make his point. Nevertheless, we caution that language is *effectively economical* only if it clearly and accurately expresses the speaker's thought. Being frugal with language pays dividends, but clarity should never be sacrificed in favor of brevity. We agree that economy in language is achieved through "the right choice of words, in right amount and best order for instantaneous intelligibility."[19]

Vividness

In his inaugural address, John Kennedy might have said, "Don't expect people to do things for you all the time. Do things for other people." Instead, he uttered a line that is now very much a part of our country's oral heritage: "Ask not what your country can do for you, ask what you can do for your country." In matters of foreign affairs, he argued, "Let us never negotiate out of fear. But let us never fear to negotiate." Consider the relative impact of some alternative phraseology: "We don't have to be afraid of anyone, but we should always be willing to negotiate with other countries." In comparison, this alternative is dull. It lacks the impressiveness, the liveliness, and the *vividness* of the original.

The language of the public speaker must be clear if communication is to occur, but if language is to have an impact, it also must be vivid. As Aristotle pointed out, "it is well to give the ordinary idiom an air of remoteness; the hearers are struck by what is out of the way, and like what strikes them."[20] When Franklin Roosevelt asked Congress to declare war on Japan, he did not say, "Last night Japan attacked Hong Kong, Guam, the Philippines, and Wake Island." Roosevelt communicated the same information, but with far greater vividness.

Last night Japanese forces attacked Hong Kong.
Last night Japanese forces attacked Guam.
Last night Japanese forces attacked the Philippine Islands.
Last night the Japanese attacked Wake Island.

Language takes on vividness when the speaker is creative, when the speaker takes the common and gives it a new twist, or when the speaker gives the ordinary idiom a sense of remoteness. The speaker should consider employing *figures of speech*: when artfully employed, these create vividness, primarily because of the images they produce in the minds of the listeners. One dictionary defines a figure of speech as "an

[19]Wilson and Arnold, *Public Speaking*, p. 269.
[20]*The Rhetoric of Aristotle*, 3.2.1404b, trans. Lane Cooper (New York: Appleton, 1960), p. 185.

expression in which words are used, not in their literal sense, but to create a more forceful or dramatic image."[21] Among the more common figures are the *metaphor, simile,* and *personification.*

The Metaphor

In this chapter, we have already described how certain types of metaphors contribute to the intensity of language. A good or fresh metaphor also increases vividness by painting a picture in the listener's mind. In fact, numerous metaphors have become very much a part of our ordinary speech. We frequently talk of "making a beeline," "going on the warpath," or "blazing a trail." When people change residences, they "pull up stakes." When a friend erroneously blames us for some action, we suggest that he or she is "barking up the wrong tree." When we resolve the conflict with our friend, we "bury the hatchet." These metaphors have been a part of our language for a very long time, but they are still useful. However, it is the new, the fresh, and the insightful metaphor that brings vividness to language. William Jennings Bryan knew the power of the metaphor. In 1896, he addressed the Democratic Convention and argued against the gold standard. So vivid was Bryan's concluding statement (a metaphor) that it will never be forgotten: "You shall not press down upon the brow of labor this crown of thorns, you shall not crucify mankind upon a cross of gold."[22]

The Simile

Similes express a comparison explicitly and use *like* or *as* to focus the comparison. The following are some very common similes:

solid as a rock	flat as a pancake
hard as a rock	teeth like pearls
sturdy as an oak	sweet as honey
easy as pie	cool as a cucumber
white as snow	soft as a feather
dead as a doornail	warm as toast
smooth as silk	high as a kite

As with the metaphor, the simile is most effective when it is novel. Those that we have cited are rather hackneyed. Frequently, the good simile expresses a relationship the listener experienced but never heard verbalized. For example, most of us have experienced insomnia on a hot summer night because of the heat. When a speaker observes that

[21]*The American Heritage Dictionary of the English Language,* ed. William Morris (Boston: Houghton Mifflin, 1976), p. 490.
[22]William Jennings Bryan, "The Cross of Gold Speech," in *William Jennings Bryan: Selections,* ed. Ray Ginger (Indianapolis: Bobbs-Merrill Company, Inc., 1967), pp. 37-46.

something is "as cool as the other side of the pillow," the imagery is immediately evoked and the meaning is clear.

The Personification

A third figure of speech is the *personification*—a figure in which inanimate objects or abstractions are given human qualities. Like metaphors and similes, the personification suggests a comparison. Note, in the following statements, that personifications give human form both to inanimate objects and abstract concepts:

1. Street lamps, dimly gleaming, trying to stay awake.
2. The admonishing finger of a church steeple.
3. Piers wading into the ocean on their centipede legs.
4. A lie can travel round the world and back again while the truth is lacing up its boots.[23]

There are yet other ways of producing images in the minds of your listener. Judicious language choices can stimulate the senses and cause the listener to generate images of sound, sight, touch, taste, and smell. Some of these features appear in General Douglas MacArthur's farewell address at West Point:

> I listen vainly but with thirsty ear, for the witching melody of faint bugles blowing reveille, of far drums beating the long roll.
> In my dreams I hear again the crash of guns, the rattle of musketry, the strange, mournful murmur of the battlefield. But in the evening of my memory always I come back to West Point. Always there echoes and reechoes: duty, honor, country.[24]

It has been our experience that most classroom speeches are just plain dull, primarily because of the lack of imagination with which student speakers employ our very rich English language. We have not attempted to be exhaustive with respect to the figures of speech at your disposal. We encourage you to build on our discussion, to be creative with language, to give novelty to the ordinary. Acquiring vividness is not an easy task for the public speaker. We recognize the difficulty involved, but as with so many things that are difficult to achieve, efforts you make in this area will be rewarded.

---

[23]Lew Sarett, William Trufant Foster, and Alma Johnson Sarett, *Basic Principles of Speech* (Boston: Houghton Mifflin, 1958), p. 351.

[24]Douglas MacArthur, "Farewell to the Cadets," in *Contemporary American Speeches*, 2nd ed., ed. Wil A. Linkugel, R. R. Allen, and Richard L. Johannesen (Belmont, Calif.: Wadsworth Publishing Company, Inc., 1969), pp. 284-290.

Propriety _____

Good style should be accurate, clear, economical, and vivid. It also must be appropriate. In fact, *propriety* may well be the most important characteristic of effective style. To say that good style has propriety is to imply that good speakers will have more than one possible style at their disposal and will be able to modify their language choices as a function of the (1) subject matter of the speech, (2) audience addressed, and (3) occasion of which the subject is a part.

Propriety and the Subject Matter

Aristotle reminds us that the style of a good speaker "should be neither mean nor above the dignity of the subject, but appropriate."[25] Imagine that you are giving a speech on tuning an automobile engine. Notice how absurd it would be to state the following:

> Open the bonnet of your modern miracle of transportation. Within you will find, standing there for all to see and perched majestically upon the top of your source of many horsepower, a circular object, an object whose mission it is to everfilter the engine's very breath of life.

Given the general purpose of such a speech, it would be more suitable to say, "Open the hood of the car. The large, round device sitting on the top of the engine is the air cleaner. It functions to filter the air that enters the carburetor." By contrast, should you be describing a battlefield scene with the purpose of producing within your audience a negative response to the scene you depict, it would be appropriate to use colorful and image-producing language.

Propriety and the Audience

Effective speakers also adjust their language choices to the audience they are addressing. Certainly, you would not want to use the same language when addressing a class of third graders as when speaking to an audience of college-educated individuals. Should you ever give the same speech to two such different audiences, you will find that the language of at least one of the two speeches will be *inappropriate*. To a group of behavioral scientists, it might be appropriate to say, "We undertook to assess the main and interactive effects of message structure, ability to organize, and gender within a $2 \times 2 \times 2$ completely crossed factorial design." To most other audiences, such a statement stands as undecipherable jargon and, hence, is inappropriate.

[25]*Rhetoric of Aristotle*, 3.3.2, p. 185.

Propriety and the Occasion

Language also must suit the occasion. Different occasions require various levels of language difficulty, sophistication, or familiarity. To exercise the same language options in a speech to the Democratic or Republican National Convention as you would exercise in a speech to a group of close friends probably would not lead to your acclaim as a speechmaker. Some occasions call for formal and highly vivid language. Other occasions suggest a straightforward, simple, and informal style. The effective speaker is able to adjust language to the situation.

Propriety and the Speaker

There is a definite range in which the speaker can adapt language to the demands of the subject, the audience, and the occasion. Specifically, the language you use as a speaker must always be appropriate for *you*. We are all aware of the politician who at election time attempts to sound like a factory worker when addressing a union meeting, a college student when addressing a campus group, or a business executive when speaking to a chamber of commerce. Such a ploy is not always very effective, and the speaker comes across not as one of the group, as he or she intended, but instead as an actor. Your audience will have certain expectations for you as a speaker, expectations formulated from prior knowledge they have of you. Should you violate their expectations in a negative manner, the result will not be favorable.

Propriety and Correctness

Earlier in this chapter, we indicated that speaking with grammatical correctness is an important component of accuracy. However, judging what is proper English is not always easy, and we frequently violate rules of strict grammatical usage with no ill effect. When we answer the telephone, we say, "This is him" or "Who would you like to speak to?" Although such language is not formally correct, most audiences would not be seriously disturbed by it. This suggests to us that some audiences will not be as sensitive to grammatical correctness as others might be. But we caution that a particular audience might tolerate grammatical incorrectness among themselves but have different expectations for a speaker. To adopt the language-usage level of the audience blindly is not always a good idea.

Enhancing Your Style as a Speaker

If you truly wish to become a more effective user of English, you must recognize that you have taken on a long-term task. Achieving good style is not something that happens overnight or within the term of your public-speaking or composition class. We now offer some suggestions for you to consider when striving for more effective style:

1. *Work for oral style.* We have made much of the differences between the written and oral style of a speaker. We know it may seem easier to you (at the moment) to write out your speeches and read them word for word, but because of these differences, we strongly advise you to practice extemporizing your speeches.

2. *Become a student of your own language.* Stop taking your style for granted. Begin thinking of it as a part of your speaking that can be improved if you are willing to expend the effort. Be alert for ambiguity in your language, for grammatical errors that you make consistently, for filler expressions ("ya know," "okay," "well," "and ah,"), and for words that you use incorrectly.

3. *Become a student of the language of others.* If you truly wish to improve your own style, you should find good role models to follow. Read widely and listen to live speeches. As you read and listen, you will learn to identify language choices that work, and you will be able to determine why such choices seem to be effective. Nevertheless, keep in mind that what worked for William Jennings Bryan, Everett Dirkson, or John Kennedy may not work for you. Your best approach may be to study good models not for the purpose of copying them but to identify their strengths and incorporate such strengths into a particular style suitable for you.

4. *Increase your word power.* How often in your reading have you come across an unfamiliar word that you simply passed over? If you do this very often, you are not taking advantage of an opportunity to increase your word power. Get yourself a good dictionary and use it. You may find a thesaurus helpful as well. When you are stuck for "just the right word" to express your thought, a thesaurus will be of invaluable assistance.

5. *Take advantage of your opportunities.* Throughout your college career, you will have many opportunities to take courses that will expose you to the works of great writers and speakers. We also advise you to write profusely and to speak often. You will never become a better user of language unless you experiment and practice with language. One can read and study the theory of golf all one wants, but improvement does not take place until one takes a club in hand and practices.

6. *Seek criticism.* Practice does not always make perfect. Practicing imperfections may only make these faults permanent. Therefore, as you experiment with language in both your writing and speaking, seek out good critics and ask them to appraise your work. Indicate that you are truly interested in improving your style and that you would appreciate honest criticism. Once you receive such commentary, consider it as carefully and as objectively as possible. Not all advice will be good, but keep an open mind to the suggestions of others.

Summary

1. Good style is *accurate, clear, economical, vivid,* and *appropriate.*
2. Accuracy has three components. Style is accurate if it best expresses the speaker's thought, if it is grammatically correct, and if it is precise.
3. Language can be accurate but still lack clarity. Meanings reside in message users, not in words. Sometimes words produce meanings in audiences that were not intended by the speaker. The good speaker is alert to potential misunderstanding and is very much aware that words evoke both denotative and connotative meanings.
4. A public speaker can offer observations with varying degrees of *intensity* and with varying degrees of departure from a neutral comment. Highly intense language can produce a *boomerang effect.*
5. At least two variables contribute to making language intense: the presence of qualifiers and the metaphorical quality of language. The most intense metaphors make reference to sex or death.
6. Using language that is difficult, redundant, nonrelevant, or excessive may cause your audience not to pay attention. Good language is *economical.*
7. The language of the public speaker must be clear if communication is to occur, but if language is to have an impact, it also must be *vivid.* Figures of speech give language vividness; they give a new twist to the ordinary.
8. Common figures of speech include the *metaphor, simile,* and *personification.*
9. Good style has *propriety.* That is, it is appropriate to the *subject,* the *audience,* the *occasion,* and to the *speaker.*
10. Enhancing one's style is a lifetime undertaking. Become a student of your own language and the language of others; increase your word power; take advantage of communicative opportunities; and seek and respond to constructive criticism.

Questions and Exercises

1. Your authors maintain that what we name things affects how we think about and respond to those things. How we respond to buying an executive-cut suit is certainly different than how we would respond to the offer to purchase a suit for fat men. Can you think of other names of objects or persons that produce favorable rather than negative responses?
2. Mentioned within this chapter are three components of language *accuracy.* List these three components and either find or construct an example of language that lacks one or more of the components.

3. How much importance do you place on grammatical correctness in effective speechmaking? Do you believe that "if it's understood, it's okay" or do you accept the position advanced by Kilpatrick, who considers it bad manners "to spit on the rules of grammar and usage"?

4. Put yourself in the role of an automaker introducing a new line of automobiles. Come up with names for an economy car, a sports car, a station wagon, a family car, and a top-of-the-line luxury machine. Compare your names with those of your classmates. Have the class arrange the names in rank order, and then discuss why the top names on the list were perceived as more favorable than those on the bottom.

5. Locate several examples of what you consider to be sexist and offensive language. Share your examples with your classmates. Do they share your perceptions? Why did you find the language to be offensive?

6. Suppose you wish to make the point that the administration of your college or university does not take the student viewpoint seriously enough. Write three sentences to express that thought, using increasing degrees of language intensity for each statement. Analyze your three sentences. What techniques did you use to increase intensity?

7. Choose any paragraph within the present chapter. See if you can rewrite the paragraph with greater economy of language than was exercised by your authors.

8. One way language achieves vividness is through the careful utilization of figures of speech. Examine several collections of short stories or other prose works and locate what you consider to be outstanding examples of metaphors, similes, and personifications.

9. Your authors maintain that of all the characteristics of good language, *propriety* may be the most important. What is meant by this term, and why is it viewed as such an important component of effective language?

Courtesy of the Lyndon Baines Johnson Library

Effective Delivery

OBJECTIVES

By the time you finish reading this chapter, you should be able to:

1. Enumerate, define, and list the advantages and disadvantages of four modes of delivery.

2. Explain how a speech might be presented to advantage by mixing the modes of delivery.

3. Define *paralinguistics* and list the components of the paralinguistic code.

4. Describe situations in which variation in volume would be appropriate or useful.

5. Define *pitch* and specify functions that are performed through variations in pitch.

6. Specify the normal rate of presentation and explain how variation in rate can convey differing messages.

7. Explain the roles of pauses and vocal quality in delivery.

8. Define *enunciation* and its components; articulation and pronunciation.

9. List the various nonverbal communication codes, defining each.

10. Explain the functions of the following five behavioral acts: emblems, illustrators, affect displays, regulators, and adaptors.

11. Provide descriptions of appropriate gestures, bodily movements, facial expressions, and eye contact.

12. Explain how the haptic, proxemic, physical appearance, chronemic, and environmental nonverbal communication codes apply to the public-speaking situation.

Imagine that you are in your public-speaking classroom and that it is the first day of a new round of speeches. Your instructor enters the room, makes some introductory comments, and calls upon Jack Williams to present the first speech. As Jack's name is announced, you direct your gaze to the corner of the room where Jack usually sits. There he is, slumped in his chair—unshaven, dressed in dirty jeans, a ripped T-shirt, and sneakers without socks. Jack rises and walks to the lectern, knocking the books off the arm of a classmate's chair in the process. Situated behind the lectern, Jack grips it with both hands and begins the speech. Immediately, you notice that he seems short of breath and that his voice is higher in pitch than you remember it to be. Jack proceeds and you listen, determined to pay attention to the content of the speech. Before long, however, your attention is diverted to Jack's right hand, which is in his pocket and engaged in the jiggling of what must be five dollars' worth of coins. You dismiss the behavior and resolve to refocus on what Jack is saying. In the process of redirecting your attention, however, you note that Jack's grip on the lectern has become rather intense. In fact, his knuckles now have become white, due to the pressure exerted by his grip. At this point, Jack announces, "There are three points I will focus on in this speech." Concurrently, he rips one hand loose from the lectern and holds up three fingers to reinforce his verbal statement. You cannot help thinking that the speech topic is potentially exciting, but that Jack is not very interested in it. In fact, he seems to be making it boring. You ask yourself why he is saying "okay" at the end of every other sentence and why he rarely looks up from his notes. Then you notice that he has just mispronounced two words and that he seems to be swallowing the ends of his thoughts—at any rate, you are having trouble hearing all that he says. Finally, Jack loosens his grip on the lectern and starts his trip back to his seat, announcing as he reaches the third row, "Well, I guess that's about it." Jack reaches his seat and tumbles into it, releasing a long sigh in the process.

Demosthenes, the foremost orator of the Golden Age of Greece, was not one to make Jack's mistake. Cicero tells us the following:

> The story goes that when Demosthenes was asked what is the first thing in speaking, he assigned the first role to delivery, and also the second, and also the third. . . .[1]

We, too, believe that delivery is of extreme importance. A speaker can have good ideas, clear organization, and dynamic language, but unless he or she delivers the speech effectively, the audience is likely to view the total effort as less than effective. In this chapter, we will focus on three principal topics: (1) modes or methods of delivering a speech, (2) vocal aspects of delivery, and (3) certain other nonvocal components associated with the presentation.

Options in Modes of Delivery

As the public speaker approaches the speaking situation, he or she must choose a mode or manner of delivery. Basically, the options available to the speaker involve (1) reading the prepared speech to the audience, (2) reciting the speech from memory, (3) extemporizing, (4) speaking impromptu, or (5) some combination of these methods.

Reading from Manuscript

On many occasions, speakers are justified in writing a speech out in its entirety and then reading it to the audience. In fact, when precision

---

[1]Cicero, *De Oratore,* III.56.213, trans. H. Rackham (Cambridge, Mass.: The Loeb Classical Library, 1942), p. 169.

in word choice or factual accuracy is of great concern, reading is in order.

You will undoubtedly find that there are times when it is of great importance for you to speak with accuracy and precision. As a member of your university's student senate, you may make proposals to your administration that are best presented verbatim and from a manuscript. Or, as chairperson of a committee, you may have to present reports requiring precision and accuracy.

Should you decide that your message is of such a nature that it is best read to your audience, keep in mind that most people do not read aloud very well. The majority of manuscript readers assume a position behind the lectern, place their speech on it, and commence reading—with little emotion, few or inappropriate pauses, limited vocal variety, minimal facial expressions, and brief and infrequent eye contact with the audience. In short, many manuscript readers give the impression that they are seeing the speech for the first time at the moment of delivery. In this day of ghostwritten speeches, such may often be the case.

Memorization

There is nothing wrong with a good memorized speech. But good ones are few and far between. It is our opinion that any gain resulting from memorizing a speech for presentation is outweighed by the extra energy expenditure required and the potential risks of forgetting. The advantage of a memorized speech is that it gives the speaker an opportunity to maintain constant eye contact with the audience. If you are good at memorizing, you might want to experiment with this mode of delivery, but it is our conclusion that the method has little to recommend it.

Extemporization

In earlier chapters, we recommended to you the extemporaneous mode of delivery. This type of speech is thoroughly researched, organized, and practiced in advance of presentation. The speaker electing the extemporaneous mode shares many preparation processes with the speakers who speak from manuscript or recite from memory. In fact, their preparation processes will be similar, if not identical, up through the stage in which a final, detailed outline is produced. Whereas the manuscript reader and the speaker choosing the memorized mode will use the outline to guide them in the writing of the complete speech, the extemporaneous speaker will adopt a different approach. Once the extemporaneous speaker has formulated the detailed outline, he or she will create an abbreviated form of the detailed outline to be used as speaking notes. With both outlines as a guide, the extemporaneous speaker will then rehearse the speech aloud, searching for appropriate word choices that relate the thought and detail of the complete outline but that are generated or cued by its abbreviated version. This will take considerable effort at first, but will become easier with practice and experience. You will discover that apt phrases and particularly vivid wording will stick in your memory and become a regular part of the speech; however—and to your advantage—you will not be saddled with a memorized speech from which you dare not deviate. Naturally, there may be a close resemblance between what you have decided on in rehearsal and what is actually presented, but there does not have to be. The extemporaneous speaker has flexibility to adapt the speech to the demands of the immediate circumstances. This feature is not available to the manuscript reader or the speaker who recites from memory.

There are many advantages to this mode of delivery. It is highly intelligible, and it allows a conversational quality to emerge in the speaker's presentation. It allows for adjustments dictated by the circumstances. The extemporaneous speaker can achieve a high degree of personal contact with the audience. He or she will most certainly become a skilled impromptu speaker.

Impromptu Speaking

As the name implies, impromptu speaking occurs spontaneously, giving the speaker little or no advance warning or opportunity for preparation. Each of us will have many opportunities to speak under such circumstances. Club meetings, church meetings, classroom discussions, political causes, and work groups all provide situations in which it will be necessary for speakers to address issues without the benefits of preparation time. Your ability to speak in this manner depends in large measure on how completely you have mastered the extemporaneous mode. We are convinced that becoming a good extemporaneous speaker will make you better at speaking impromptu.

Mixed Modes

You do not have to adopt a single mode of delivery to the exclusion of all others. Instead, you might decide that your primary mode of delivery will be extemporaneous but that certain quotations would best be read. Or a poem you intend to incorporate within the speech might have its greatest impact if it is recited from memory. As your speech develops, a certain audience response may suggest an idea that was not originally a part of your prepared speech but which could be beneficial; thus, you would speak impromptu on the topic. For most speaking situations, however, the extemporaneous mode will serve you best.

Vocal Aspects of Delivery: The Paralinguistic Code _____

"It isn't what he said but how he said it that bothered me." This type of statement suggests that messages are encoded *vocally* as well as verbally. Suppose you were to read the statement "I can't believe he hit her in the nose!'' The statement obviously expresses someone's surprise, but can you detect what has led to the surprise without actually hearing the words uttered? Was the speaker surprised that *he* hit her; that he *hit* her; that he hit her in the *nose;* that *he hit her* in the *nose;* or some other potential combination? Without actually hearing the speaker, it is difficult to tell exactly what has evoked surprise. Through vocal cues that accompany our words, we have the capacity to reveal our emotional state and to narrow the range of possible meanings that listeners might assign to verbal messages (our words). *Paralanguage* (paralinguistics) is the study of how vocal variables produce or temper the meaning of the words they accompany. The unusual and distinctive vocal accompaniments we can give to our words afford us genuine advantage in communicating delicate shades of meaning and mood. By employing variations in rate, volume, and pitch, and by judiciously using pauses, we can express concepts and feelings that go beyond the denotative definitions of the accompanying words. Certain aspects of voice collectively define the paralinguistic communication code. Taken as a group, these vocal aspects of delivery are termed the *vocal variables.* The manner and degree to which each is employed are options of the speaker. Let us examine these vocal aspects:

Volume

The volume (loudness) of sound is measured in decibels, with a quiet whisper registering 15 decibels, an average conversation at a distance of 3 feet 70 decibels, and the sound of a jet plane operating in a test chamber approximately 160 decibels. Sound approaches the threshold of feeling at approximately 120 decibels and becomes painful not far above this level.[2] Few beginning public speakers speak too loudly. In fact, most speak too softly. Many of our public-speaking behaviors are not as apparent as we perceive them to be.

As you undoubtedly know, vocal sound is made by forcing air through the trachea and across the vocal folds. The greater the force of this air, the greater the volume of the sound created. To increase force, it is necessary for a person to contract muscles of the stomach. In general, with higher degrees of contraction, greater force can be exerted and, hence, greater volume can be achieved. Most of us have the capability of speaking within a considerable range of volume and have no excuse for speaking so softly that we cannot be heard. Experiment with your voice. See what levels of volume you can achieve; see how variations in volume level can signify variations in mood; see how volume changes can add emphasis to the words, phrases, or sentences of your speech.

[2]Alexander Efron, *Sound* (New York: Rider, 1957), pp. 32-33.

Pitch

A second vocal variable is *pitch,* referring to the highness or lowness of the speaker's voice. More exactly, pitch refers to the location of a tone on a musical scale. Pitch is determined by the number of vibrations per second associated with a given sound. Slow vibrations produce low-pitched sounds; faster vibrations produce sounds of higher pitch. By increasing or decreasing the tension of the muscles that control the vocal folds, we are able to raise or lower the pitch of the human voice. Pitch is measured in cycles per second (cps) with human speech ranging between 125 and 8,000 cps.[3] The typical pitch of a male speaking voice is at about 250 cps (close to middle C), whereas the average female voice is about an octave higher.[4]

Pitch is an important aspect of the paralinguistic code. Through variation in pitch levels, a speaker can add liveliness, interest value, and color to a presentation. Through variation in pitch, a speaker can indicate surprise, disgust, or even satisfaction. In large part, the voice is like a musical instrument, but many fail to play it to its full potential. The best public speakers make full use of the range of pitch available to them. They recognize that appropriate variations in pitch clarify meanings, add interest, increase attention, and generally make listening a more pleasurable experience for the members of the audience.

Rate

Your rate is your speed of presentation. It is generally measured in words per minute (wpm). The average rate of a public speaker is approximately 150 wpm, but considerable variability exists among individuals. Seldom do speakers present their words so rapidly that the words are unintelligible. In fact, the listener has the capability of processing some types of information at speeds three or four times as fast as the information is typically presented. In some circumstances, particularly when ideas are complex, rate of presentation is an important concern. Often the *ideas*—not the *words*—are presented too rapidly. As a speaker, you should consider the complexity of your material, making allowances for the speed at which you present ideas, as well as considering the number of words per minute. See Chapter 19, pages 312-313, for a complete discussion of the effects of rate on comprehension.

It is also useful to consider what your rate is communicating to your audience. You certainly should wish to give the impression that you enjoy being there and that you appreciate the attention and interest. Some individuals speak so rapidly (and usually with little eye contact and expressiveness) that they give the impression that they would rather be elsewhere. Rapid rate can signify excitement, urgency, and enthusiasm, but it can also signify nervousness, lack of confidence, and a desire to be finished with the speech.

[3]William D. Brooks, *Speech Communication* (Dubuque, Iowa: W. C. Brown, 1978), p. 92.
[4]Brooks, p. 267.

Pauses

Pausing before or just after an idea can direct your audience's attention to the idea. Pauses are often associated with *rhetorical questions,* questions the speaker poses to elicit mental response in the audience members. For example, a speaker might begin a speech on fire safety by saying, "What would you do if a fire were to break out and block our usual exit from this room?" Consider how effective such a question becomes when it is followed by a pause instead of by the speaker rushing on ahead without allowing time for the audience to contemplate the potential answers to the question. Often, rhetorical questions are offered in a series: "Are you overweight? Do once comfortable clothes now feel tight? When is the last time you had any exercise? How many calories were in the food you ate yesterday—1000? 2500? 5000?" Such questions are of far greater value if the speaker pauses between them, allowing time for the mental response of the listeners.

Quality

Quality or *timbre* is the characteristic of a sound that distinguishes it from other sounds of the same pitch. It is this characteristic that allows us to distinguish between the sounds of a French horn and saxophone, each of which hits notes at the same level of volume. Through quality discriminations, we are able to determine if it is The Who singing our favorite song or another group attempting to imitate their sound. The quality of the human voice is determined to a large degree by physiological characteristics—length, thickness, resilience, and condition of the vocal cords; size and shape of the resonators; and general functioning of the entire respiratory and vocal production system. Nonetheless, you will want to take full advantage of whatever resources you do possess.

Enunciation

Enunciation is a term that includes both *articulation* and *pronunciation.* Good enunciation results from the proper production of sound and the combination of individual sounds to form words. Articulatory errors are usually characterized according to four types: substitutions, omissions, additions, and distortions. Elmer Fudd has a sound-substitution problem, evident when he suggests, "Look at that wascally wabbit wun!" Many speakers of a second language also make sound-substitution errors when speaking in the second language. Japanese people, for example, have the tendency to substitute *r* for *l* when speaking in English. Sound omissions are common in the speech of many people, particularly involving the *-ing* endings of words. Instead of saying talk*ing,* walk*ing,* and runn*ing,* many speakers shorten the words to talk*en,* walk*en,* and runn*en.* Others insert sounds that are not intended. *Film* becomes *filum* and *athlete* becomes *athelete.* Garbled sounds account for distortions, the final source of articulatory errors.

Whereas articulation is primarily associated with the distinctness of utterance, pronunciation involves the shaping of sound into recognizable symbols within the flow of oral discourse. Correct pronunciation involves proper uttering of vowel and consonant sounds and proper stress on the appropriate syllables of a given word. Articulating clearly and pronouncing correctly are important aspects of public speaking. Audiences *do* make judgments regarding a speaker's credibility based upon the speaker's enunciation. Do not take the chance of creating unintended and unwanted impressions within your audience due to sloppy articulation and unacceptable pronunciation.

Nonvocal Components of Delivery

Words serve as a primary tool of the public speaker. But the public speaker also communicates in codes that do not depend on words. As we have already observed, variations in volume, rate, pitch, emphasis, and periods of silence (paralinguistic variables) can add to or modify the meaning of verbal symbols (words). In this section, you will become familiar with additional nonverbal codes through which the public speaker intentionally or unintentionally communicates a message. Specifically, we will examine *kinesics, haptics, proxemics, physical appearance, chronemics,* and the *environment and its objects.*

Kinesics: Definition

Kinesics is the study of bodily movement, including gestures, movement of the body limbs and head, eye movement or behavior, posture, and facial expressions. Of the various nonverbal communication codes, it is one of fundamental import to you as a public speaker. To understand the kinesic code, it is useful to examine the functions of nonverbal behavioral acts. One classification system is suggested by nonverbal researchers Paul Ekman and Wallace Friesen.[5]

Emblems. Emblems are physical substitutes for words. They are usually produced by the hands and are frequently cultural-specific. The familiar "A-okay," the sign of the hitchhiker, the "thumbs-up" of early aviators, the forefinger drawn across the throat, the shrug of the shoulders, and the signals of an umpire or referee all have direct verbal equivalents. Emblems are frequently employed to substitute for words when circumstances require a substitution. Scuba divers, for example, employ emblems because vocalizing or writing could be accomplished only with considerable difficulty.

[5]Paul Ekman and Wallace V. Friesen, "The Repertoire of Nonverbal Communication," *Semiotica, 1*: 49-98 (1969).

Illustrators. Unlike emblems, illustrators do not have direct verbal equivalents. They are usually, but not always, intentional behaviors. In general, illustrators are used by a speaker to accentuate words; to indicate direction of thought; to draw pictures; to point to objects, events, or locations; to show spatial relationships; to indicate timing and rhythm; and to repeat or provide substitutes for words. Imagine one of your classmates standing at the podium, explaining how he scored the winning touchdown in last Saturday's game against Silo Tech. Notice how he acts out or draws the run both verbally and nonverbally, describing the positions of relevant players, indicating his path to the goal line, and repeating his actual physical movement during the play. Some individuals appear to be more adept at employing illustrators than others. The phrase "If you cut off his hands, he couldn't speak," suggests just such an individual. Illustrators, if properly employed by the public speaker, create color, excitement, and a sense of animation.

Affect Displays. Affect displays are those nonverbal behaviors that reveal our emotional response to some stimulus or set of stimuli. They are not intended to communicate, but others sometimes assign meaning to them. Affect displays frequently accompany a verbal message, but can occur independently or as a substitute for it. When we relate shocking news to others, seldom do they reply with, "I'm shocked." Instead, their facial expression and overall physical demeanor convey a nonverbal equivalent. When Ronald Reagan faced the press and answered questions regarding how his campaign staff secured secret papers from Jimmy Carter's White House, he tried very hard to control his affect displays, not wanting his emotional response to create a negative impression.

Regulators. Nonverbal communication is sometimes employed to regulate or control the flow of communication between individuals. This function is probably best observed in one-to-one communication situations. Regulators are nonverbal behaviors that interactants employ to change speakers, to encourage, and to signal a need for the speaker to slow down, speed up, repeat, elaborate, or even to stop. Most college professors can tell, without a timepiece, when their class period is drawing to a close, not because they have a built-in clock, but because they have learned to read the regulatory behaviors of their students. Notice how, when the end of a class period approaches, many of your classmates will begin to put books in backpacks, close notebooks, reach for coats and jackets, and so on. Some are so skillful at timing that they complete their regulatory behavior concurrently with the ringing of the bell that indicates the end of class. The good speaker must be sensitive to the regulatory behaviors of the audience and know when to speed up, repeat, supply additional amplification for a point, or even be aware of when it is time to draw the speech to a close.

Adaptors. Adaptors are physical behaviors employed to satisfy basic human needs. Scratching, rubbing, and adjusting clothing or hair are adaptive behaviors, as is smoking. Typically, adaptive behaviors are not intended to communicate a message, although others are likely to assign value to the behavior. Adaptive behaviors are usually practiced in private, and when they do occur in public, they take place most often in an abbreviated and unobtrusive manner. The nervous speaker frequently engages in a variety of adaptive nonverbal behaviors—pacing, shuffling the feet, tugging on an ear, rubbing the nose, wringing the hands, or constantly adjusting the hair. In most instances, speakers engaged in such behavior are not fully conscious of their behavior. All too frequently, others assign meanings to these actions: the listeners conclude that the speaker is nervous, inexperienced, lacking in poise, short on confidence, and so forth. At times, all of us will send unintended messages. Listen carefully to the feedback you receive from your instructor and classmates. Do you practice behaviors that detract from your message or that produce unintended meanings?

Kinesics: Application

It is possible to employ the kinesics code effectively within the public-speaking context. Naturally, the public speaker should be concerned with employing nonverbal behavior to clarify, amplify, and support the verbal message, not to detract from it or to create unintended meanings. Our discussion of applications of the kinesics code focuses on gestures, bodily movement and posture, facial expression, and eye contact.

Gestures. Gestures are movements of body parts, primarily the hands and arms, that are used to emphasize points, to substitute for words, to point to objects, to reenact previously performed actions, and to perform a host of additional functions. Many speakers are capable of making highly successful presentations without employing gestures, but for most speakers, the effective utilization of this aspect of the kinesics code adds to their presentation. The following suggestions will assist you in using gestures to best advantage:

1. *Gestures should spring from a strong inner desire to communicate.* Planned gestures are seldom effective. They do not appear spontaneous and usually are more of a distraction from the verbal message than a supplement to it. Good speakers are seldom consciously aware that they are gesturing. They are so concerned with communicating their message that they find words alone inadequate for expressing their thought. If you are able to acquire such an attitude, you too will find yourself gesturing naturally and expressively.
2. *Continuous gestures are seldom effective.* Some speakers appear to use gestures more to release tension than to communicate a message. These motions are known as adaptive nonverbal behavior. We have all observed the speaker who continuously waves one or both hands as he or she speaks. Here it is useful to keep in mind that *continuous emphasis is no emphasis at all.*

3. *Allow your gestures to mature and develop.* Perhaps you have observed speakers standing behind the podium, their arms flapping up and down as if they were shooing away a dog not visible to the audience. These speakers feel the necessity for enhancing their verbal message with gestures, but their nonverbal messages do not go quite far enough. Gestures should be strong and definite if they are to be useful. Should you find yourself a practitioner of such nonmature forms, do not dismay. With experience and some extra attention to the matter, mature and expressive gestures will develop.

4. *Avoid adaptive gestures.* Many of us, while delivering a public speech, will engage in the practice of one or more adaptive gestures. Perhaps you have had a teacher who continually juggled a piece of chalk as he or she lectured. Maybe you have observed a speaker who thrusts a hand in one pocket and proceeds to jiggle what sounds like five dollars' worth of quarters for the duration of the speech. As we indicated earlier, individuals are not usually aware that they are using adaptive gestures. Generally, these motions detract from the message and should be avoided. Should one of your classmates point out an adaptor you habitually employ, strive to eliminate it from your delivery.

Bodily Movement and Posture. Like gestures, the speaker's bodily movement should enhance the verbal message, not detract from it. Bodily movement should clarify, amplify, or support the verbal message. Keep in mind that you need not stand, rooted like a tree, behind the lectern for the duration of your speech. Feel free to move if it will accent an idea, indicate a change in direction of your thought, or help clarify a point. Again, we remind you that bodily movement, like gesturing, is sometimes used by speakers only to perform an adaptive function: to release nervous energy. The speaker who continuously shuffles the feet, rocks back and forth, shifts weight from one hip to the other, or paces back and forth across the speaking platform usually is calling attention away from his or her verbal message. Before long, an audience begins to focus attention on the behavior itself instead of on the total message. Earlier, we mentioned how the speaker can utilize physical movement to signify a change in thought. A good speech will have numerous *transitions*—words, phrases, and sentences designed to alert the listener to the fact that the speaker has concluded discussion of one thought and is ready to begin another. Thus a speaker might say, "Now that we have examined the financial impact of the proposal, let us next look at its social impact." Such a transition clearly indicates that the speaker is moving in thought. Physical movement during the vocalization of the transition stands as a highly satisfactory method of further symbolizing the movement of ideas.

We are not going to give you rigid rules about how to stand or position your feet during your speech. We will suggest, however, that your posture should not attract the adverse attention of the audience. Through your posture, you should communicate the message that you are alert, enthusiastic, poised, and respectful of your audience. Speakers who use the lectern to hold their body rather than their notes seldom create a desirable response in the audience. Keep in mind that through our legs and feet we may reveal emotional responses. The face and upper body may convey the message that we are in control of the situation, but the feet (crossed or in continuous shuffle) may be sending contradictory messages. Assume and maintain a relaxed posture—one that presents a pleasant picture to your audience.

Facial Expressions. The face has often and aptly been referred to as the "mirror of the soul." Through facial expressions, we are able to indicate feelings of joy, anger, sorrow, pity, surprise, and even love. Too few speakers, however, take full advantage of the communicative potential of facial expressions. Instead, they deliver their most exciting ideas from behind the most deadpan of expressions. If videorecording facilities are available to you, we encourage you to take advantage of them. Most people are surprised to see how they appear to others. Most of us discover that our face is not nearly as expressive as we would like it to be, or that our face seems to be sending unintended messages. Here again, we observe that speakers who are excited about their topic, who believe in their message, and who have the strong desire to communicate, are the speakers who are the most effective.

Eye Contact. One of your authors recalls taking a college class from an instructor who rarely, if at all, maintained eye contact with his students. Alternately, the instructor would focus his gaze on the ceiling, to his right, and out a window. Needless to say, his lectures were not interesting. Research evidence suggests that audiences expect the speaker to maintain eye contact with them and that the degree of eye contact maintained by the speaker is related to audience perceptions of the speaker's credibility.[6] Some speakers, perhaps the instructor just mentioned, avoid eye contact with the audience because of feelings of fear. Somehow, they withdraw themselves from the situation by avoiding the communicative exchange accompanying eye contact. Other speakers may ignore their audience—not out of fear, but because they have no genuine respect for the listeners and are indifferent to their response. Most speakers recognize the need to maintain eye contact, but many fall short simply because they have not practiced their speech well enough to leave the printed page for any extended period of time. Through eye contact, the speaker reveals a desire to be communicative, and through the maintenance of eye contact, the speaker is able to follow the

[6]See Martin Cobin, "Response to Eye-Contact," *Quarterly Journal of Speech, 48*: 415-418 (1962), and Steven A. Beebe, "Eye Contact: A Nonverbal Determinant of Speaker Credibility," *Speech Teacher, 23*: 21-25 (1974).

responses of the audience. Do not be inhibited by your notes. Let them assist, not dominate, your presentation.

Haptics: Definition

We all make decisions to touch another person or to avoid touching. To what extent do we comunicate through this behavior or its absence? To what extent is *touch* a communication code? These questions are the subject matter of *haptics*—the study of touching behavior.

The public speaker usually employs this nonverbal code to only a very limited degree. The realities of the public-speaking situation are such that it is neither possible nor desirable for the speaker to wander among the audience. Some speakers, however, are able to incorporate within their total presentation elements of the haptic code. The speaker who hugs the person who introduces him or her, who during the introduction walks out into the audience to shake hands with friends and acquaintances, who warmly shakes hands with the people seated on the platform, who leaves the podium at the conclusion of the address to talk with members of the audience, shake their hands, pat them on the back, or to be a target of touching, is engaged in behaviors that have potential communicative value. We are not always sure how the audience interprets such nonverbal activity, but many speakers seem to believe that the act of touching shows their general affability and their concern and respect for the audience.

Proxemics

Anyone who has lived in a college dormitory understands that each of us has an inherent need for space to call our own, a place to escape from contact with the outside world. *Proxemics* is the name given to the study of the use and perception of both social and personal space. The use of social space has long been a subject of interest to psychologists, architects, anthropologists, and more recently, city planners. Much research has focused on how different seating positions of small groups affect the nature of communication networks that are established, the leadership style employed, the ability of the group to accomplish tasks, and a great variety of additional variables. More generally, however, the study of proxemics focuses on needs for territory and personal space.

Many public speakers seem to regard the area behind the lectern or speaker's stand as a kind of personal space. Student speakers often become anxious when the lectern has disappeared on a day that they are scheduled to speak. The lectern, even when it is very small, seems to act as a barrier that separates the speaker from the audience. Positioned behind the lectern, numerous speakers feel more secure. They have created, perhaps, a kind of aesthetic distance between themselves and their audience. We offer this observation nonjudgmentally and certainly do not recommend that you seek refuge behind a speaker's stand.

Physical Appearance

In Chapter 7, we cited scientific evidence to support the assertion that in particular circumstances physically attractive individuals may be more effective sources of influence than individuals lacking in attractiveness. But we need not look only to research studies for support for this view. The life experience of each of us is rich with anecdotal evidence suggesting that physical appearance (body type, hair, odor, skin, and so on) is a dimension of nonverbal communicative behavior—that others do assign meanings to various aspects of physical appearance. Good grooming, cleanliness, and a well-dressed look are probably insufficient in themselves to produce influence—at least on matters of considerable import to an audience—but slovenliness certainly has the potential for producing influence not intended by the speaker.

We are not going to suggest how to dress for success, nor will we argue that all *endomorphs* (short and basically pear-shaped individuals) should make every effort to become *mesomorphic* (athletic and well proportioned). But we will remind you that your physical appearance does have message value.

Chronemics

Have you ever considered how time is employed to communicate messages to other people? This is the subject matter of *chronemics*. How do you feel about a public speaker who speaks longer or shorter than appropriate for the occasion, a teacher who lectures so long that you are late for your next class, dinner guests who arrive 45 minutes late or early, or a doctor who keeps you waiting until four o'clock for a one o'clock appointment? We send messages—not always intentionally—by how fast we walk, speak, eat, or pause between utterances; through our punctuality or lack thereof; through the time we allow for given appointments; and through additional behaviors that relate to the utilization of time.

The public speaker must develop an awareness of the potentialities of time as a communication code. Here are some suggestions concerning the utilization of time:

1. *Arrive for your scheduled speech on time.* To be late for a public speech is insulting to your audience.
2. *Determine how long an appropriate speech should last.* This involves knowing your place on the program.
3. *Keep your promises to the audience.* Perhaps you have heard a speaker say, "Today I'm going to speak for about 20 minutes." Thirty-five minutes later, the speaker is still going strong and the audience is uneasy, if not infuriated. Likewise, the speaker who promises the audience time for questions and then does not follow through may not evoke a desirable response from the audience.

4. *Use time to indicate your favorable attitude toward the speaking event.* Arriving only seconds before you are scheduled to speak, and running for the exit as you deliver the last words, may send unintended negative messages.

The Environment and Its Objects

Many who study nonverbal communication concern themselves with the extent to which the *environment* and *objects* within it influence the amount, flow, and nature of communicative activity. Good teachers are aware of the effects of environment on learning, and they make every effort to select and structure classrooms in such a way that the learning environment facilitates the accomplishment of course goals and objectives.

In your role as a public speaker, you frequently will have only limited, if any, control over the environment in which you speak. The location of your address typically will be predetermined. You will be fortunate if those who arrange for you to speak will give careful thought to the nature of your speech, your manner of presentation, the size of the expected audience, and so on. Naturally, you will want to suggest modifications in the physical environment that can make your presentation as effective as possible. You may wish to make requests about temperature, ventilation, or seating arrangement; location of the speaker's lectern or audiovisual materials; and elimination of noise sources that might detract from your presentation.

A Concluding Note _____

Within this chapter, we have addressed a large number of vocal and nonvocal considerations that relate to the delivery of your speech. We have divided our discussion into neat, seemingly discrete categories, addressing standards of good practice within each category. But these categories must be *integrated* if the speaker is to display an effective delivery. A beginning golfer is frequently so involved in remembering how to stand, grip the club, swing, and follow through that the result is less than satisfactory. A beginning speaker is likely to find himself or herself in similar circumstances if he or she tries to think of each delivery variable as unique and independent. It is our experience that the speakers who are truly involved in their speech, who have a strong and sincere desire to communicate their message, and who have genuine respect for their audience have few delivery problems. We believe that if you can acquire or maintain such an attitude, your delivery will contribute to the success of your speech.

Summary

1. There are four primary modes of delivering a speech: reading from manuscript, memorizing, extemporizing, and speaking impromptu.
2. Paralinguistics is the study of how vocal variables produce or temper the meaning of the words they accompany. Elements of the paralinguistic code include volume or loudness, pitch, rate, pauses, quality, and enunciation (articulation and pronunciation). Each element of the paralinguistic code is a vocal aspect of delivery.
3. Verbal and nonverbal communicative behaviors are inextricably related to each other within the total communication system. Authorities have identified at least six ways in which verbal and nonverbal communication codes are related: repetition/redundancy, substitution, contradiction, complementation, regulation, and accentuation/emphasis.
4. Kinesics is the study of bodily movement, including gestures, movement of the body limbs and head, eye movement, posture, and facial expression.
5. Nonverbal behavioral acts serve as emblems, illustrators, affect displays, regulators, and adaptors.
6. Gestures should spring from a desire to communicate, be definite, mature and develop, and enhance the verbal message.
7. Haptics is the study of touching behavior and how it creates or modifies meaning.
8. Proxemics is the name given to the study of our use and perception of both social and personal space.
9. The physical attractiveness of a speaker may influence the response of the audience.
10. Chronemics investigates how messages are communicated through time-related variables.
11. The environment and its objects compose a nonverbal communication code that can influence the amount, flow, and nature of communicative activity.

Questions and Exercises

1. Your text lists five possible modes of delivery. List and define them, and explain why your authors generally prefer one mode over the others.
2. What advantages and disadvantages are associated with presenting a speech from memory?
3. Under what circumstances might it be appropriate to read a speech rather than present it extemporaneously?
4. Observe several public figures delivering a speech. What modes of delivery do they employ? To what degree would you judge their effectiveness to be related to their skill at delivery?

5. Think back to Chapter 7. To what degree would you associate skill in delivery with high speaker credibility? Are certain dimensions of credibility more strongly affected by the speaker's delivery skills than are other dimensions? If so, which ones and why?

6. Identify the vocal aspects of delivery that collectively define the paralinguistic communication code.

7. With respect to their functioning as nonverbal communication codes, define *kinesics, haptics, proxemics, physical appearance, chronemics,* and the *environment.*

8. Formulate a set of rules that should govern the nonverbal behaviors of a speaker. Be prepared to defend your rules before your classmates.

9. At one point in this chapter, your authors refer to the possibility of revealing emotional responses through unintended nonverbal behaviors. Explain how this might occur, and identify particular nonverbal behaviors that might be associated with such emotional leaks.

Principles to Practice

Victor Alleman, UFW

14

The Nature of Informative Speaking

OBJECTIVES

By the time you finish reading this chapter, you should be able to:

1. Explain what is meant by cognitive and affective instructional goals or learning outcomes.

2. List four cognitive and three affective goals or outcomes.

3. Describe how the following serve as sources of attention: humor; action, variety, and change; the old and the new; proximity; concreteness; the vital; and suspense.

4. Recall two requisites of understanding and provide a definition of each.

5. Explain what it means to translate, interpret, and extrapolate.

6. Differentiate between long- and short-term memory, describing how information is transferred from one memory system to another.

7. Provide a definition of *interest* and explain its relationship to nonvoluntary attention.

8. Define *attitude* and *intervening variable.* Explain the relationship between attitudes and learning.

9. Explain how developing appreciation can be considered a purpose of informative speaking.

Ours is an age of information, a time when vast amounts of factual data abound. Television, radio, news and specialty magazines, newspapers, and books constantly bombard us with information about everything from matters of personal hygiene to issues of national and international policy. We seem to have an almost insatiable appetite for information, evidenced by the growth and development of such new sources as cable television and computerized data bases. Technological innovations constantly increase either the amount of information available to us or our ease of obtaining access to the information. Nevertheless, a need will continuously exist for human beings to interpret, integrate, and explain information to others.

Whenever we communicate, we affect others in some way. Whether we intend it or not, communicating changes the other person—and ourselves. Sometimes communication results in changes in the behavior of others and is a direct result of our persuasive efforts, but other less observable changes also occur. When we share our knowledge, attitudes, beliefs, and values with another person, we add to the other person's information base. We provide the person with new data to add to his or her existing storehouse of knowledge. The data will very likely change how the receiver of the message views, interprets, and responds to future events. In this chapter, we focus on the types of speaking that will enable listeners to gain understanding. The goals of the speaker are either to add to an information base already existing within an audience or to create an information base where none yet exists.

When you speak to gain understanding, your general purpose is obviously to *inform*. But additional, and perhaps more specific, purposes might be involved. Suppose you are interested in the welfare of animals. Assume that it has been exceptionally hot in your area for an extended period of time, and you have observed numerous instances of animals suffering as a result of the heat. You have been assigned to give an informative speech to your classmates, and you decide that speaking on "Caring for Pets in Hot Weather" is both a timely and a relevant topic. Your general purpose is obvious—you are going to inform. But what exactly do you hope to achieve through your message to fellow class-mates? Obviously, you hope they *attend* to and *comprehend* your message—that is, that they focus on and interpret it as you intend. Do you also hope they *retain* the information for future reference? Do you hope your classmates will at some future time *apply* the information? Do you aim for them to develop *interest* and positive *attitudes* about pet care? All of these goals are reasonable and plausible. When we speak to inform, a variety of subpurposes or goals also is likely to be operative. We have grouped these aims into two categories: *cognitive* and *affective*.

Cognitive Goals or Outcomes _____

In your role as an informative speaker, you are like a teacher, charged with the responsibility of increasing the knowledge base of a set of learners (your audience). Cognitive instructional goals are those that emphasize the acquisition and utilization of knowledge.[1] Here we focus on four primary cognitive goals: *perception, understanding, retention,* and *application*. You will notice that these goals are ordered on a dimension of complexity. By this, we mean that it will be relatively easy to gain the audience's perception of your message, but more difficult to gain their understanding. It will be even harder to present your message in a manner that encourages its retention. But your greatest challenge will be to increase the knowledge level of your audience in such a fashion that they can actually apply their new information to some future task. You also will note that the specified cognitive goals (learning outcomes)

[1]Our discussion here is based on principles contained in Benjamin S. Bloom, *Taxonomy of Educational Objectives: The Classification of Educational Goals. Handbook I: Cognitive Domain* (New York: David McKay, 1956).

are hierarchical. That is, as we move up the dimension of complexity, the new goal subsumes those below it. To express this in another way, we might say that before an audience member can understand, he or she must perceive; before an audience member can retain, he or she must understand; before an audience member can apply knowledge, it must be retained. Cast in the light of our example regarding pet care, we would suggest that one's ultimate goal within such a speech would be to have members of the audience actually treat their pets in the ways you specify. In order for that to occur, your audience will have to recall and understand the information. This is not possible unless they have initially perceived or attended to it. Now let us look more closely at each of these instructional goals or learning outcomes.

Attention and Perception

One necessary goal of any speaker is to gain and sustain the attention of the audience. Unless the audience first attends to the message, there is no possibility that they will be influenced by it. James Winans, borrowing on the theories of William James and Edward Titchener, made *attention* the basis of his comprehensive theory of public address. According to Winans's view, persuasion is achieved only if the speaker can gain fair, favorable, and undivided attention.[2] We would go a step further, to suggest that influence in general, not just persuasion, is dependent upon achieving the attention of the audience. An individual cannot be affected by what he or she does not perceive or attend to. As a speaker, you will have the attention of your audience until you do something to lose it. As you rise to speak, you change the perceptual field of your audience, because you are a moving and attention-getting stimulus. When you begin to speak, most audiences will accord you attention out of courtesy and convention. They will subsequently attend to you and your message until other, more attractive stimuli present themselves. It will be wise to remember that the attention of the audience is fleeting. The speaker must constantly capture, and then recapture, their attention. Yet, what you hope to capture is not just attention, but *favorable* attention. Should a speaker decide to disrobe during the course of a speech, the striptease would evoke attention, but it would not be the kind that would contribute to a favorable audience perception of either the speaker or the message. With these thoughts in mind, we are ready to examine some *sources of attention*.

Humor. Humor can provide the salt and pepper for any kind of speech, if applied judiciously. We all like a good joke, but the astute speaker must keep in mind that humor, if inappropriately employed, can have highly negative, if not disastrous, results. Telling a supposedly funny story that fails to amuse can have devastating effects on a speaker's self-confidence. Having one's punchline greeted with silence

[2]See James A. Winans, *Public Speaking* (New York: Appleton, 1915).

or a few nervous chuckles can be most unnerving for even the most experienced orators among us. In Chapter 20, we discuss humor in greater detail and provide some guidelines for its use.

Action, Variety, and Change. Changing the perceptual field of your audience will command their attention. There are many ways in which public speakers can alter the listening environment of their audience. Physical activity brings about one such environmental change. Animated and energetic speakers draw more attention than do their static and lifeless counterparts who stand rooted behind the lectern throughout an entire speech. Bodily movement, facial expressions, and gestures reinforce and call attention to the speaker's verbal message. So does the effective employment of paralinguistic cues (see Chapter 13). Through vocal variety—variation in rate, pitch, volume, pauses, and so forth—the speaker signals changes in mood, emphasis, and direction of the speech. The less static, and the more enthusiastic, vibrant, and varied your total presentation is, the more likely it is that you will be able to command the attention of your audience. Consistency brings monotony, which brings a straying of audience attention. Naturally, whatever action, variety, or change you bring should be consistent with the emotional level and the thought content of your speech.

The Old and the New. Old wine, friends, songs, and automobiles have great appeal to many of us. The familiar has an unmistakable fascination, but it can also be boring. There are times when a friend approaches you, eager to relate a joke he or she has just heard. You sense your friend's enthusiasm and anticipate your own pleasurable response to an uproariously funny story. Before the friend gets far, however, you discover that you heard the story days, or even years, before. What happens to the attention you are according your friend? Chances are it dissipates, and your mind wanders while your face continues to display a polite grin. You do monitor the story, but only to the degree necessary for you to laugh at the expected point.

Like the very familiar, the completely new can produce this effect. When we are presented with a totally new idea, we have to be convinced to sustain our attention on it. It is interesting, we say, but what is it and how does it relate to those things I already know? This is our point: both the old and the new have great attention-getting value—if they are carefully intertwined. We are comfortable with the familiar, but fascinated by the new. Speakers who can extend the knowledge of their audience by relating new information to information already a part of the audience's knowledge base will be attended to. Speakers who only rehash the old, or who concentrate on the unfamiliar, will find the level of attention accorded to them by the audience is less than they have desired.

Proximity. Closely related to the familiar as a source of attention is what we label *proximity*—the use of nearness in time and space or the close association of your subject with the immediate audience. When you make direct reference to the person who introduces you, when you single out and recognize friends who are in the audience, when you make reference to the occasion, or when you acknowledge those seated on the speaker's platform, you are utilizing proximity as a source of attention. Many of the best speakers are careful observers of the events preceding their time to speak. They seem to make mental note of all happenings that interest the audience, and then, when it is their turn to speak, they relate their topic and approach to those events, including references to the presentations of previous speakers. Experienced speakers are aware of the potential benefits of arriving for a speech well in advance of the designated time. Their early arrival allows them to interact with members of their future audience, to learn some of their listeners' recent history, to discover old acquaintances, to share an experience with an audience member—and then to incorporate these factors of proximity within their scheduled speech. Few techniques are more effective in securing audience attention.

Concreteness. Have you ever attended a lecture and left, thinking, "I understood every word the speaker said, but not a single idea"? Frequently, it is the abstract, vague, and ambiguous speaker who receives such a response. James McBurney and Ernest Wrage discovered a rather curious speech excerpt that will help to illustrate this point:

> Political reactionaries today may advertise haughtily their venal verdure, personally and through equal venal media, spread themselves like the Biblical green bay tree—Laurus Nobilis—and claim that the power of gold is supreme, but what doth it avail them; it, too, shall pass away like a drunkard's disturbing dream and be lost forever in fathomless nothingness long before their life's bad book shall have found its last resting place in oblivion's uncatalogued library.[3]

The meaning of this passage is obscure to everybody. A speech with many such passages would not maintain audience attention for any extended period of time. Although we understand the words, the search for ideas is difficult and perhaps not worth the effort. Abstract language all too frequently encourages lack of audience attention. By contrast, concrete and specific language seems to demand listeners' attention. In Chapter 12, we discussed the values associated with specificity of language. When you read the word *car,* what image does it evoke in your mind? You probably create a picture of your own or family vehicle. By making the term *car* specific—through mentioning model names such as Corvette, Porsche, 280ZX, Rabbit, Edsel, Model T—a speaker or writer can evoke images of power, speed, contour, economy, or even rattle. The specific word seems to have greater appeal than the abstract. Concrete illustrations also have greater attention-getting value than vague generalizations do. A speaker can go on at great lengths discussing, in the abstract, the dangers associated with drinking and driving, but

[3]*Congressional Record,* February 14, 1950, Appendix, p. A1122, cited in James H. McBurney and Ernest J. Wrage, *The Art of Good Speech* (Englewood Cliffs, N.J.: Prentice-Hall, 1953), p. 356.

watch ears perk up when the speaker begins to relate an anecdote regarding a particular instance in which drinking and driving resulted in unhappy consequences.

The Vital. Audiences will attend to those ideas and language which promise either to threaten or to improve their personal lives. Several years ago, one of your authors was negotiating to buy a parcel of land on which he planned to build a new home. The land was outside the city limits, and it appeared to be secluded and seemingly ideal. Shortly before the negotiations were completed, your author picked up the daily newspaper and immediately focused on a headline announcing that stripmining was about to be initiated in the immediate vicinity of his planned home. It was with more than casual attention that he read the accompanying article. Although it is not always prudent to threaten your audience with disaster or to promise them eternal bliss, you should recognize that those parts of your speech that touch on the fulfillment of your listeners' basic human needs will attract their attention. Your role, whether you are speaking to inform, to effect change, or to reinforce, is always to relate your positions to the needs of your listeners—to provide them with a reason for attending to what you have to say.

Suspense. On a Monday morning not long ago, a friend related what for him was a most unhappy experience. The friend, an avid fan of our university football team, was unable to attend Saturday's game. His disappointment at missing it was somewhat mitigated, however, when he learned that the game would be videotaped and broadcast late Saturday night. All Saturday afternoon and evening, he avoided any information source that might reveal the outcome of the game. He looked forward to sitting before the television and responding as if the game were live. It was 11:30 P.M., and as the kickoff was about to take place, his wife appeared and stated, "Why don't you go to bed? There's no use staying up late to watch a game we lost." Our friend continued to watch the game, but not with the same enthusiasm or interest. The suspense was gone; the outcome was known. Suspense builds audience interest and secures attention.

Securing favorable audience attention, then, is a primary goal of the informative speaker. Audiences cannot understand, recall, or apply information if they have not been attentive. The sources of attention—humor; action, variety, and change; proximity; concreteness; the vital; and suspense—if artfully employed, can assist the speaker in the continual quest first to capture and then to recapture the favorable attention of an audience.

Understanding

A second potential cognitive instructional goal of the speaker is to promote understanding within the audience. A recent cartoon depicted Dagwood Bumstead visiting his optometrist. In one frame, the doctor instructs Dagwood to cover his right eye and read the eye chart, a task that Bumstead easily accomplishes. In the next frame, the optometrist indicates that Dagwood should cover his other eye and read. This time, the result is less satisfactory, with Dagwood reporting that he can see nothing at all. Within the last frame of the cartoon, we learn why. Our hero has covered his other (the left) eye, but continues to cover the right, following the first instruction. This cartoon shows that the possibility always exists that your message will not be interpreted as you intend. Now we examine two requisites of understanding: *knowledge* and *comprehension.*[4]

Knowledge. Consider the following passage. Read it carefully, for once you have done so, we will ask questions about what you read.

> Aristotle was a Greek philosopher who lived from 384 to 322 B.C. He is famous for his *Rhetoric,* a book on the theory of speechmaking. His work is organized in three books: the book of the speaker, the book of the audience, and the book of the speech. It was Aristotle who first classified artistic proofs (those created by the speaker) into three catgories. *Ethos*, or ethical proof, was created by the character of the speaker. *Pathos,* or emotional proof, was brought about by arousing the emotions of the audience. *Logos,* or logical proof, involved the employment of evidence and reasoning to bring about belief. Aristotle was the first of the "big three" classical rhetorical theorists, the others being Cicero of the first century B.C. and Quintilian of the first century A.D.

Now, without rereading the passage on Aristotle, see if you can answer the following questions:

1. In what year was Aristotle born?
2. In what country did Aristotle live?
3. What was Aristotle's profession?
4. How is Aristotle's *Rhetoric* organized?
5. What is *ethos*?
6. Did Aristotle do his writing before or after Cicero?
7. Did Cicero live before or after Quintilian?
8. What did Aristotle classify as forms of artistic proof?

Chances are that you could answer these questions. Your training and past experience as a student have undoubtedly made you a good learner of specific, factual information. To the extent that you successfully recalled the answers to our questions, you have acquired *knowledge*— that is, you have been able to recall specifics included in the message. Our questions have asked you to recall a date (Question 1), a place (Question 2), a profession (Question 3), a method of organizing (Question 4), the meaning of a term (Question 5), a sequence or movement in time (Questions 6 and 7), and a specific classification scheme (Question 8)— all specific facts included within our written message. Sometimes it is

---

[4]Here again our discussion is based on Bloom, *Educational Objectives.*

important for the informative speaker to impart knowledge to the listener, particularly because knowledge is a prerequisite for performing higher-level cognitive tasks. For example, before a learner (listener) could be expected to construct a logical argument based on the Aristotelian concept of *logos,* he or she would have to know what the concept meant and what operations Aristotle associated with the construction of such an argument. Knowledge, defined here as *specific, factual data,* has little value in its own right but is necessary as a prerequisite for *comprehension.*

Comprehension. Adding to the knowledge base of the listener is not always an easy task. Effecting comprehension in your listener is even more difficult to achieve. Comprehension requires knowledge of specifics but goes beyond to impose more complex demands on the listener. To illustrate what we mean by comprehension, let us again use the technique of presenting you with information and then asking questions about what you read. Read the following passage carefully:

A distribution or set of test scores can be symbolized as the X_i distribution. Σ is a Greek letter used to stand for "the sum of." The number of scores in a distribution of scores is symbolized by N. Not infrequently, distributions of scores are "summarized" by finding one value to represent the distribution's central tendency and another value to represent the degree of variability present within the distribution. The mean, symbolized as $\overline{X}$, is one possible measure of central tendency. Algebraically, we can define the mean as

$$\overline{X} = \frac{\Sigma X_i}{N}$$

The variance (S_2) is one potential measure of variability. It is defined as the average squared deviation of raw scores from a distributions mean.

Consider the following items, all requiring *only* the recall of information actually presented in the passage.

1. What does X_i symbolize?
2. What letter is used to stand for the number of scores in a distribution?
3. What is the meaning of Σ?
4. List one measure of central tendency.
5. List one measure of variability.
6. Write the formula for the mean.

How did you do? The tasks' demands were relatively easy. To perform successfully, all you had to do was recall information presented in the passage. In no way did you have to go beyond the presented information to accomplish any of the posed tasks (the questions). Did you comprehend what you read? Can you *translate, interpret,* and *extrapolate* from what you read? Here again is a set of tasks based on the passage. Try your hand at accomplishing them.

1. Write an algebraic formula for calculating the variance of a distribution of scores.
2. Explain in your own words how a mean of a distribution of scores is calculated.
3. Why is the variance defined as "the average *squared* deviation . . . from the mean" and not just "the average deviation from the mean"?

You probably notice that the tasks have become a bit more difficult. Each task requires that you go beyond the information presented in the passage if you are to accomplish it successfully. In the first instance, you were required to *translate* from prose to algebraic notation. The second question asked you to *interpret* or explain in different language symbols a portion of the passage. The final task required you to *extrapolate* and discover a new principle—the sum of deviations from a mean is always equal to zero.

In short, a second potential cognitive instructional purpose requires the speaker to promote or facilitate *understanding*. The goals might consist of speaking to increase the knowledge level of an audience or speaking to effect comprehension.

Retention

Do you still remember the date of Aristotle's birth? If you do, we would be surprised. You probably forgot the date seconds after responding "384 B.C." to Question One. As an informative speaker, you obviously hope that your audience will not only perceive and understand your message, but also that they will *retain* it for further use. Why did you forget, assuming you did, the date of Aristotle's birth? Probably you forgot because you knew of no good reason to remember it. Psychologists would explain that the date was never transferred from your short-term to your long-term memory system. Have you ever had the experience of looking up a telephone number and dialing it, only to hear a busy signal? Seconds later you decide to try again but discover you have already forgotten the number. Once we dial the number, not anticipating that we might get a busy signal, our need to remember the information no longer exists and we forget.

It was the great psychologist William James who first distinguished between a short- and long-term memory store. He described these as *primary* and *secondary* memory systems.[5] According to James's view,

[5]William James, *Principles of Psychology* (New York: H. Holt, 1890), vol. 1, pp. 643-689.

information in primary memory never leaves consciousness, whereas information in secondary memory has been absent from consciousness for some time. In addition, James maintained that the retrieval of information from primary memory was essentially easy and effortless, while retrieval from secondary memory was far more difficult and complex, requiring active search processes and considerable energy expenditure.

Exactly how and why information is moved from short- to long-term storage is not known, but presumably the movement is a function of whether specific nerve cells are subjected to either brief or repeated excitation. Return to the case of the telephone number. Suppose we call this number regularly and have become frustrated by continually thumbing through the telephone book in search of it. We have "decided" it would be desirable to locate the number in our long-term memory system so that we might retrieve it as necessary. Once again, we look up the number, this time for the purpose of moving it from short-term to long-term storage. How do we accomplish such a task? Probably through *rehearsal* or by *coding* the number in a fashion designed to facilitate recall. Rehearsal would simply involve repeating the number, silently or aloud, until such time that it could be retrieved after an intervening elapse time. Coding is more complex. Telephone numbers, of course, are seven digits long, requiring the retention of seven discrete pieces of information to store the number successfully. But what if the number of discrete units could be reduced (chunked) to one? Suppose our friend's number were 569-2589. A little creativity results in the discovery that 569-2589 spells out LOY-ALTY. Now we have one piece of information (descriptive of our relationship with our friend) to recall rather than seven. Obviously, other coding strategies are possible—rhymes that include key dates, names, and so forth.

Application

Application centers on the degree to which your listeners are able to *apply* the information you present to a specific and concrete situation. When your speech instructor lectures on methods of organizing a speech, for example, he or she does so with the goal in mind that you will actually utilize the organizational methods in your own speeches—that you will actually apply the knowledge that you *comprehended* and *retained*. As a learner, it is relatively easy to comprehend what is meant by a concept such as *chronological order* and even to retain the definition for a test. But it is more difficult to produce a speech with the main points arranged as a chronology. Likewise, your geometry instructor might consider it useful for you to remember that the area of a circle is πr^2, but he or she would be more pleased if you could then actually calculate areas.

Affective Goals or Outcomes

Informative speakers obviously hope that their message will be perceived, understood, and possibly put into practice. There are, in addition, other purposes sometimes associated with informative speaking. The informative speaker frequently hopes also to achieve goals that are *affective* in nature—that pertain to the emotions or feelings of the audience. Specifically, some potential affective goals of informative speaking are to develop *interests, attitudes,* and *appreciations.*[6]

Developing Interest

Most of us seem to know what it means to be *interested* in something. We often observe that a feature was "really interesting," or, conversely, "very boring." Although the term *interest* is used with great frequency, psychologists have had considerable difficulty settling on a definition of the term. Some have defined it as an emotional involvement of like-dislike associated with attention to an object.[7] In Chapter 19, we discuss the nature of attention and identify three types or phases: involuntary, voluntary, and nonvoluntary. Involuntary attention is the type we accord to sudden and abrupt changes in the environment (lights going out, doors slamming, books falling, and so forth). Voluntary attention requires conscious effort, whereas nonvoluntary attention seems effortless and is the type we accord when some stimulus or set of stimuli promises or proves to bring us satisfaction. When a speaker creates nonvoluntary attention within the audience, he or she has awakened high interest in the message. Thus, from our point of view, nonvoluntary attention and high interest are basically equivalent concepts.

Obviously, you will want to create a high level of interest in the content of your informative speeches. But how is this accomplished? One way is by demonstrating that the information you present will be of either present or future value to your audience. Show your listeners how the information you present will improve their lives in important ways. Can you show how learning the information contained in your speech will lead to the greater physical well-being of your listeners? Can you show how a mastery of the content will make your listeners' futures more secure? Can you demonstrate to your listeners that by mastering the content of your speech they can gain the friendship and respect of those whom they most admire? Can you link the listeners' comprehension of your message with needs that they may have to self-actualize—to be all that they can be? If you can address these questions positively through your treatment of a topic, you are on your way to creating high interest in your subject.

[6]Our discussion here is based on David R. Krathwohl, Benjamin S. Bloom, and Bertram B. Masia, *Taxonomy of Educational Objectives, Handbook II: Affective Domain* (New York: David McKay, 1964).

[7]W. D. Commins and Barry Fogin, *Principles of Educational Psychology,* 2nd ed. (New York: Ronald Press, 1954).

Developing (Shaping) Attitudes

We ask the students in our public-speaking classes to present a speech, the general purpose of which is to be informative. In the class discussions that follow each speech, it has often become apparent that members of the audience disagree about the purpose of a given speech. Some class members maintain that the speech was, in fact, *informative,* but others insist that the thrust of the speech was clearly to *persuade.* Who is right? It is difficult to tell, but let us consider a case in point. Mae Tong presents a speech, the thesis of which is "The whale is fast becoming an endangered species." In her speech, she presents carefully documented evidence that shows a rapid decline in the whale population. Mae also maintains that the decline has been caused by the indiscriminate taking of these sea-going mammals by Russian whalers, who operate in violation of international agreements. From our brief description, how would you classify Mae's speech? Is she speaking to *inform* or to *persuade?*

The way we answer this question is probably not all that important. Most likely, Mae's speech accomplishes a purpose in between informing and persuading. Prior to her speech, many of the members of the audience had never really thought much, if at all, about Russian whalers. But following Mae's speech, a number of these same individuals felt highly negatively about the illegal taking of whales and the people who did so. Although Mae thought she was fulfilling the assignment—informing—by providing information on the declining whale population, she was also forming (shaping) attitudes where they did not previously exist.

We are not born with attitudes. None of us enters the world with either positive or negative feelings regarding race, religion, abortion, capital punishment, drugs, or education. Attitudes are learned predispositions that teach us to act in one way as opposed to another. Social scientists consider attitudes to be *intervening variables*—that is, they act as internal mediators of behavior and intrude between the presentation of some stimulus and an overt response. Many of our attitudes are information-based. In Chapter 6, we presented such a theory of attitude, observing that attitudes are the product of the beliefs we hold about some object, event, person, and so forth, and our evaluation of those beliefs. The informative speaker should be aware, then, that one effect of expanding the information base of the audience may be to create attitudes that did not exist previously.

Developing Appreciation

A final affective instructional goal or learning outcome of informative speaking relates to *appreciation.* Like interest and even attitude, appreciation is a somewhat slippery concept—it is difficult to define. Perhaps you are currently enrolled in a course, the goal of which is to enhance your *appreciation* of art or music. How do you know when your appreciation has been enhanced? What does it mean to *appreciate* something? In the *Dictionary of Education,* Carter Good defines *appreciation* as "an emotionally fringed awareness of the worth, value, or significance of anything."[8] Your authors attend many professional conferences where researchers report the results of various studies they have conducted. The style of such reports is straightforward and factual. The researcher usually presents a review of literature, hypotheses that were tested, procedures, results, and conclusions. More than occasionally, audiences leave those reporting sessions by asking, "Why would anyone want to research that topic?" or "How does that research advance our understanding of communication?" Clearly, such responses reveal a lack of appreciation on the part of the listeners. It is wise to keep in mind that your informative speech will evoke some degree of appreciative response in the audience. Audience members will be making judgments regarding the worth, value, and significance of your topic and treatment of it.

By way of summarizing our discussion of the purposes of informative speaking, we reiterate that the purposes are many and varied. Typically, when people think of informative speaking, they consider it to be a situation in which one individual provides information to a group of receivers. We have attempted to illustrate that the outcomes of informative speaking can be both cognitive and affective. Some outcomes are intended and others are unintended. We also want to make it clear that the purposes we specify are only potentially operative. A particular speech may have any or all of the specified instructional goals and produce any or all of the specified learning outcomes.

Summary

1. When you speak for understanding, your general purpose is to inform, but additional and more specific purposes—cognitive and affective—also are involved.
2. Cognitive instructional goals or learning outcomes are those emphasizing the acquisition and utilization of knowledge. There are four primary cognitive goals: perception, understanding, retention, and application. These goals arrange themselves on a hierarchically ordered dimension of complexity.
3. Attention-perception is necessary before any learning can occur. Individuals cannot be affected by what they do not perceive or attend to. The sources of attention—humor; action, variety, change; proximity; concreteness; the vital; and suspense—if artfully employed, can assist the speaker in the continual quest to capture and then recapture the favorable attention of an audience.

[8]Carter V. Good, *Dictionary of Education* (New York: McGraw-Hill, 1959), p. 34. Reprinted by permission.

4. The two requisites of understanding are knowledge and comprehension. Knowledge involves the recall of specific factual data, and it results from a relatively simple form of learning. Comprehension requires knowledge but also involves translation, interpretation, and extrapolation.

5. As an informative speaker, you will want your audience to perceive, understand, and retain your message. Human memory is theorized to be of two types: short- and long-term. Before information is retained, it must be moved from short-term to long-term storage. How this process is accomplished is not totally clear, although rehearsal and coding appear to be involved.

6. The highest (most complex) cognitive instructional goal or learning outcome is application, which requires the perception, understanding, and retention of message information.

7. Affective instructional goals include developing interests, creating attitudes, and promoting appreciation.

8. Interest and nonvoluntary attention are similar concepts.

9. Attitudes are learned predispositions to act in one way as opposed to another. Attitudes are termed intervening variables: they act as internal mediators of behavior and intrude between the presentation of some stimulus and an overt response.

10. Appreciation is an affective instructional goal or learning outcome. It is defined as an emotionally fringed awareness of the worth, value, or significance of anything.

Questions and Exercises _____

1. This chapter presents four cognitive goals or outcomes of informative speaking: perception, understanding, retention, and application. Briefly describe what is involved within each goal or outcome.

2. The cognitive goals of instructional speechmaking are argued to be hierarchically ordered. Explain this position.

3. James Winans maintains that persuasion is achieved only by gaining fair, favorable, and undivided attention. Your authors extend this notion to informative speaking as well. Explain the role played by attention in informative speech.

4. Enumerate the sources of attention, providing an illustration of each "source" in operation.

5. Your authors maintain that knowledge—meaning factual data—has little value in its own right but is necessary as a prerequisite for comprehension. List and define three categories of comprehension, explaining why factual data are a prerequisite for each.

6. Memory is frequently subclassified as either *primary* or *secondary*. How do these differ from each other? What techniques seem to facilitate the movement of data from short-term to long-term storage?

7. How would you differentiate between a cognitive and an affective instructional goal? List and define three potential affective goals of instructional speech.
8. With which of the three forms of attention (involuntary, voluntary, and nonvoluntary) would you most closely associate the affective goal of developing *interest*?
9. Define an *attitude* and explain how behaviors are mediated by attitudes. Here it would be useful to clarify what is meant by an intervening variable. Why may an attitude be so classified?
10. Specify a circumstance in which a speaker might have developing appreciation as the primary goal of an informative speech.

15

Informative Speaking: Principles to Practice

By the time you finish reading this chapter, you should be able to:

1. Identify the types of informative speeches and provide an example of each.
2. Identify a number of learning principles of special interest to the informative speaker.
3. Explain the relationship between the retention of a message and the degree of structure contained in the message.
4. Explain what is meant by a structured cue and list three such cueing techniques.
5. Describe the subsumption theory of learning and explain how it relates to informative speaking.
6. Define such terms as *presummary, transition,* and *summary,* providing an example of each.
7. Identify the various types of visual aids and provide some rules for their use.
8. Explain the relationship between language choices and comprehension.
9. Describe proactive emphasis and its relationship to learning.
10. Differentiate between repetition and restatement and explain their relationship to learning.

Those who engage in informative speaking do so with a number of purposes or goals. As we saw in Chapter 14, the many potential purposes or goals of informative speaking can be placed into two categories—cognitive and affective purposes. Cognitive goals emphasize the acquisition and utilization of knowledge. Affective goals strive for the development of interest, the creation of attitudes, and the promotion of appreciation for a topic or cause. Not only does informative speaking have multiple potential purposes, but it also occurs in a variety of settings. Within this chapter, we will first present the three most common settings in which informative speaking occurs. Second, we will focus on some principles of learning that will be of special interest to the informative speaker. In our final section of the chapter, we will provide practical advice to the informative speaker. This advice delineates ways in which the speaker can put fundamental principles of learning into practice.

Settings for Informative Speaking

As a public speaker, you will have many opportunities to present informative speeches. Your hobbies, professional training, travels, and organizational affiliations will equip you with special knowledge and competencies worth sharing with other people—and you will be asked to share them. Sometimes, you will be asked to explain how things work or how some task might be accomplished. At other times, people will want to know about your trip to Japan, England, or Switzerland. They will be interested in your answer to such questions as "What is pornographic literature?" or "What is academic freedom?" Although no standard system exists for classifying informative speeches, we think it is convenient to consider them according to the following three types: speeches of process, speeches that report, and speeches that provide exposition.

Process Speeches

Very frequently, we are exposed to explanations of processes. Your calculus teacher tells you how to solve quadratic equations; your English teacher describes how you should write a term paper; your psychology professor explains how the brain processes stimuli; your computer science instructor explains how the computer translates inputs into binary code. Daily, you are exposed to dozens of messages—in the form of speeches—that concern processes.

There are basically three kinds of process speeches: (1) speeches that explain how things work, (2) speeches that provide instructions on how some task might be accomplished, and (3) speeches that inform the listener about criteria to employ in completing a given task. When you describe how plants add oxygen to the environment or how television converts electronic signals to the pictures that we see, you are explaining *how a process operates*. Speeches that detail how to make candles, how to care for a pet in hot weather, or how to treat a snakebite focus on providing a set of instructions relating to *the accomplishment of a given task*. Finally, when you inform your audience about how to select good firewood or what to look for when buying a used car, you will be *detailing criteria* to be employed by the audience when they accomplish a given task.

Our classification system does not mean to produce mutually exclusive categories. Sometimes the speaker will find it necessary to incorporate aspects of each type within a single speech. A speaker telling us how to buy a used car might give a set of ordered instructions; might provide us with criteria to be employed when checking brakes, compression, ignition, exhaust, and so forth; and yet might also find it necessary to explain how an internal combustion engine operates.

Oral Reports

Someone once defined a camel as "a horse that was put together by a committee." Although we do not subscribe to such a pejorative view of committee work, we do recognize that some organizations have as many or more committees as they have individuals on their membership rolls. Someone has to report committee findings to the larger group. Fact finding is a task more efficiently performed by a subdivision of an organization, not by the total membership. Thus, a church considering the purchase of a computer will appoint a committee to survey its clerical workload; a city considering the awarding of a cable television franchise appoints a committee of citizens to gather the facts; and a university appoints a committee to ascertain the benefits and liabilities of changing from the quarter system to the semester system. A committee report is one form of informative speaking.

It is not only committees, or their spokespersons, who make reports. Sales managers report the latest sales figures to their supervisors, researchers report the results of their efforts to the scholarly community, teachers report on new instructional techniques that are being employed in the school systems. Representatives of organizations attend conventions and training sessions and then report their individual experiences and observations to the larger group. Professors returning from sabbatical leaves are frequently asked to report on their activities to colleagues and supervisors. A student returning from a tour of duty with the Peace Corps and a local resident who returns from travels to Poland and Russia will find themselves much in demand as public speakers, with many audiences interested in reports of their experiences. The mayor of a city reports to a meeting of the Chamber of Commerce, informing them about what the administration is doing to attract new industry to the city.

Speeches of Exposition

In a general sense, expository speaking is that speaking which explicates or elucidates; thus, all informative speaking might be classified as exposition. Here, however, we are utilizing the term in a more specialized sense. We consider expository speaking to be interpretive, involving situations in which the speaker provides his or her own definitions of concepts or understandings of events or series of events. When you explain "What Democracy Means to Me," you are engaged in expository speaking. When you offer your definition of freedom, pornographic literature, love, phenomenology, rhetoric, conservatism, or any other concept, you are presenting an expository speech. Likewise, the speaker who lectures on "Light and Dark Images in the Poetry of John Milton," or "Symbolism in *The Old Man and the Sea*," is engaged in expository speaking.

People have an almost insatiable appetite for information and a desire to have others organize, translate, and interpret that information.

Informative speaking serves a highly important function in society. Through it, we learn how tasks are accomplished and how processes are performed. We discover information that guides our future decisions and determines our policies. We learn of the experiences of others and how different people interpret the world around us.

Principles of Learning

How do individuals "learn" the information contained within informative speeches? Many theories explain how people learn—these explanations range from Sigmund Freud's system of psychoanalysis to B. F. Skinner's theory of operant conditioning. Rather than recount numerous learning theories, we will focus on some characteristics of listeners (learners). The learning principles we present are of particular relevance to the informative speaker and are derived from a list of learning principles enumerated by learning theorist C. M. Charles.[1]

1. *Individuals learn best when they are instructed at their level of competence.* If your speech consistently rehashes material already known by the audience, little learning will occur. Likewise, should you speak too abstractly, or include highly complex explanations, or use terms not understood by your audience, you will inhibit learning. It is important to anticipate the competence level of your intended audience and plan the speech accordingly. You want to challenge your audience with the content of your speech, but you also want them to understand you.
2. *Fatigue, boredom, and frustration inhibit learning.* It is a wise speaker who recognizes when the audience has heard enough. People who are tired are not going to be good listeners. People who discover nothing new, exciting, or useful in what you say, are going to be bored. People who do not understand what you say will become frustrated.
3. *Motivation facilitates learning.* Instilling within your listener a desire to acquire the information contained in your speech will be worth the effort. It is always good practice, during the preparation of your speech, to ask, "Why do my listeners need to know this information?" If you cannot come up with a good answer to this question, you may encounter problems. You may be the foremost authority on the Brown Recluse spider, but the garden club might not be interested in learning about the insect's courtship practices. Listeners will be motivated to learn those things that promise to fulfill their needs, that promise to make their lives more enjoyable and productive.

[1]Adapted from C. M. Charles, *Educational Psychology: The Instructional Endeavor* (St. Louis: C. V. Mosby, 1972), pp. 354-361.

4. *Attention is a learned response.* Audiences do make an effort to attend to what you have to say. As we indicated earlier in this chapter and elsewhere (see Chapter 19), one form of attention is *voluntary,* a form that requires a conscious effort by the listener. The audience member who thinks to himself or herself, "Well, I'm here. I might as well listen to what the speaker has to say" is about to exercise voluntary attention. Do not disappoint the listener. However, remember that no speaker, no matter how polished, can expect to maintain the constant and undivided attention of the audience. Audience members will attend to you and your speech for a time, but will tune you out and then back in numerous times during a speech. If you consistently disappoint your listeners, you are likely to extinguish their attending behavior.

5. *Emotional involvement increases retention.* People remember those things that are associated with the comic, tragic, sorrowful, hateful, spiteful, lovable, and so forth. If you want an idea to be remembered, anchor it to an emotional response within your audience.

6. *Reinforcement speeds learning.* A rat can be conditioned quickly to press a lever if its press is followed by an immediate reward (a pellet of food). A pigeon can be taught to avoid going to a certain area of its cage if it receives an electric shock each time it wanders there. We do not mean to suggest that humans behave in exactly the same way as lower life forms, but we do have at least one thing in common with the rats and the pigeons: reinforcement (positive and negative) affects our learning. Even though the speaker cannot provide immediate reinforcement for learning, he or she can make use of principles of reinforcement. Your audience will learn if you can demonstrate that the material of your speech will result in either a positive consequence or in the avoidance of an unpleasant circumstance.

7. *The organization of a message can promote learning.* Have you ever assembled toys for children? Toys such as doll houses, baby carriages, bicycles, and wagons come with the understated instruction "Some Assembly Required" printed inconspicuously on their box. If you have tried to put the toys together, you know that the clarity and order of instructions have a great deal to do with whether or not a task can be successfully completed.

8. *Sensing relationships enhances learning.* We have commented that listeners attend best when the speaker intertwines the old with the new, the familiar with the unfamiliar. You will promote the learning of your message if you show your audience how new information within your speech is related to what they already know.

9. *Overlearning improves retention.* Many of us have been in a play and have been required to memorize a number of lines. In attempts to remember those lines, we read through the script numerous times and then tried to recite the lines from memory, using the script to prompt us until we could successfully recall each line without the

script. But our efforts did not stop with one successful trial. We recited the lines over and over again, until we felt we could repeat them in our sleep. Here again, the public-speaking situation and the conventions operative within it typically preclude the audience reciting the idea until it is retained. But the speaker can provide a kind of vicarious rehearsal for the audience. By repeating or restating key ideas, by including transitions that conclude one thought and show movement to the next idea, and by summarizing important sections of a speech, the speaker provides the listeners with multiple exposure to the same idea. This increases the probability that the repeated idea will be retained.

10. *Individuals remember best those materials they consciously intend to remember.* When you undertake the task of informing your audience, part of your responsibility as a speaker will be to provide cues about the relative importance of the ideas contained in your speech. If an idea is important, tell your audience. Think of the times an instructor has said, "This is important to know for the test." Did you remember the item in question? If an idea is important, cue your audience. Naturally, however, you would not want to overuse such a technique.

Instructional Strategies: Principles to Practice _____

Now that we have provided a set of principles that govern either how or what individuals understand and retain, let us turn to some specific techniques that a speaker might employ to put learning principles into practice. We organize our discussion around *organizing for clarity, providing structural cues, employing visual aids, making effective language choices,* and *providing emphasis.* Note the sample outline and speech at the end of the chapter. In the text of the speech on word processing are bracketed items that employ the specific principles discussed here.

Organizing for Clarity

Individuals retain more information from highly structured speeches than they do from speeches of lesser structure.[2] In Chapter 8, we

[2] Ernest Thompson, "An Experimental Investigation of the Relative Effectiveness of Organizational Structure in Oral Communication," *Southern Speech Journal, 25*: 59-69 (1960); Ernest Thompson, "Some Effects of Message Structure on Listeners' Comprehension," *Speech Monographs, 34*: 51-57 (1967); Arlie A. Johnson, "A Preliminary Investigation of the Relationship Between Message Organization and Listener Comprehension," *Central States Speech Journal, 21*: 104-107 (1970); Richard F. Whitman and John H. Timmis, "The Influence of Verbal Organizational Structure and Verbal Organizing Skills on Select Measures of Learning," *Human Communication Research, 1*: 293-301 (1975); and Tom D. Daniels and Richard F. Whitman, "The Effects of Message Introduction, Message Structure, and Verbal Organizing Ability Upon Learning of Message Information," *Human Communication Research, 7*: 147-160 (1981).

discussed clarity and patterns of organization in greater detail. Here, we stress again that clarity of organization is present when your audience can identify your thesis, main points, and supporting ideas. It is present when listeners can see the relationships you intend for them to perceive between and among the various levels of subordination into which your speech is divided. In a typical experiment to test the effects of organization on learning, a researcher would ask experts to outline the speech and assess their agreement with respect to the thesis, main points, subpoints, and appropriate subordinations. Should the outlines produced by these experts show high agreement, the researcher would consider the message to be organized. Next, the researcher would create a low-structure version of the information contained in the original message, possibly by randomly ordering the sentences, paragraphs, or thought units of the original message. After producing the high- and low-structure messages (original and random), the speaker would expose the two different but equivalent audiences to one or the other messages and would administer some measure of their learning (usually a multiple-choice test) following exposure to their respective messages. Such experimentation typically reveals that organization does affect learning. Listeners recall more from organized than from disorganized messages.

Examine the outline of our sample speech (see pp. 244-246). Notice how the thesis emerges as the last main point in the introduction. Also observe how the main points are phrased in structures that are parallel both gramatically and in thought. Look closely at subpoints. They, too, maintain the concept of parallelism.

Providing Structural Cues

Although high structure produces learning, it is effective only if it is detectable by the listener. Richard Whitman and John Timmis administered the Goyer Organization of Ideas Test to a group of college students and subsequently classified the group members as possessing either high or low verbal organizing ability. They then exposed the individuals to either a highly structured message or a randomly ordered version of the same information. Although the researchers found that the highly structured version produced more learning than the message of lesser structure, they also discovered that those who profited most from organization possessed high verbal organizing ability. In explaining their findings, the researchers argued, "The low ability organizers were not able to 'capitalize' on the high structure sequence to the same extent as the high ability organizers. . . . It may also be that low ability organizers are not particularly astute with regard to recognizing structure when it does, in fact, exist; consequently, the low ability organizer is not penalized by the absence of a structure that he would not perceive if it were present."[3]

[3]Whitman and Timmis, "Influence of Organizational Structure," p. 300.

What can you do to facilitate the audience's perception of your organizational structure? Fortunately, there are many effective structural cueing techniques.

The Presummary. Psychologist David Ausubel proposed what is termed *subsumption theory.*[4] He argued that if a message is first previewed at a high level of generality and inclusiveness, it will be better retained. According to this view, the general preview provides the learner with conceptual anchors for the information contained in the message. The preview provides learners with conceptual categories into which they can organize information. Orientation material performs such a function and is frequently included in a speech's introduction. This type of material includes whatever information your audience needs in order to understand your speech or your approach to the topic. Whenever you devote a portion of your introduction to explaining how the material of your speech is related to or is different from what the audience already knows, you are employing what is known as *subsumption theory.*

In addition, informative speakers frequently find it useful to include within their introduction a *presummary* or statement of the main points that will be contained in the speech. The following is an example of such a statement:

> Yes, Japan is a country with many faces [speaker's thesis]. But to illustrate that further I will first of all describe its varied topography; next, its mixture of the traditional and the modern; and finally, the various religious and cultural differences found in Japan [preview of the main points]. Now let us take a look at the country's varied topography [transition to the first main point of the speech].

Through this preview of key ideas, the audience is alerted to at least the major points that will be developed in the speech. The presummary of our sample speech (see pp. 247-251) occurs within the third main point of the introduction. The main point is actually a statement of the thesis of the speech. The subordinate points forecast the content that is to come in the speech's body.

Transitions. With presummaries we cue the audience, alerting them to our organizational structure. The *transition* is another cueing device at our disposal. Transitions are words, phrases, clauses, and sentences that show either the relationship between ideas or movement from one idea to the next. Words and phrases such as *next, in addition to, another reason why. . . , also,* and so forth alert the listener to our movement in thought or to a relationship we perceive between two ideas. A complete transition is one that concludes a previous thought and shows movement to the next. Note the following statement: "Now that we have identified the causes of anorexia nervosa, let us next look at its treatment." Such a

[4]David P. Ausubel, *Educational Psychology: A Cognitive View* (New York: Holt, Rinehart & Winston, 1968).

phrase leaves little doubt that the speaker is finishing one idea and is about to introduce a new one. Transitions are like road signs—they alert the audience to your flow of ideas, just as the road sign indicates the way traffic is expected to flow. In our sample speech, the major transitions are in parentheses, but other transitional words also appear in the actual text of the speech.

Summaries. Usually people associate summaries with the conclusion of a speech. Certainly, the conclusion should usually include a summary of the major ideas, but summaries can occur at other points in a speech as well (theoretically after each main point). Do not, however, overuse the device. If you get into the pattern of summarizing each idea, the audience will come to expect your summary and will either ignore your initial presentation of an idea or will lose interest altogether. Notice main point 3 of our sample speech outline (see p. 244). Within this point, the speaker not only restates the thesis of the speech, but also briefly summarizes the three main topics around which the speech is developed.

Employing Visual Aids

Can you imagine Julia Child explaining how to make some exotic dish without also showing us the ingredients, telling us how they are mixed, and providing examples of how the dish looks at various stages of completion? Consider how difficult it would be to put together an automotive engine or even a model airplane without diagrams to supplement verbal instructions. Imagine the plight of a building contractor who lacks blueprints or an electrician who does not have a schematic diagram. In many circumstances, you will find it necessary to supplement words with visual aids.

Types of Visual Aids. Technically speaking, visual aids are divided into two groups: those that amplify the effectiveness of transmitting or receiving sensation, and those that contribute directly to the process of teaching and learning.[5] In the first group are movie projectors, screens, chalkboards, television sets, videorecorders, opaque and overhead projectors, and so forth. In the second group are objects, models, photographs, diagrams, maps, charts and graphs, and movies.

1. *Objects.* Sometimes there is no substitute for the real thing. If you are explaining the characteristics a dog must have to win confirmation trials, there is no better visual aid than an actual champion canine. If you are teaching your audience to identify trees from their leaves, will not the display of actual leaves prove useful?
2. *Models.* Sometimes the complex nature of an object makes it more feasible to display a model rather than the object itself. To explain how the knee joint operates, a speaker could best employ a model of the knee. In fact, physicians use such a model when explaining

[5]Len S. Powell, *Communication and Learning* (New York: American Elsevier, 1969), p. 96.

injuries to patients and in the training of future doctors. Models serve a useful simplifying purpose, particularly when the object they represent is complex. The model can be made to include only those details that are relevant to a particular speech.

3. *Photographs.* Using photographs to illustrate or amplify a point can be highly effective. Certain speech topics seem to require pictures or slides to amplify the verbal message. Imagine how dull and unsatisfying it would be to hear a speech on techniques that guarantee good picture taking if the speaker did not present photographs to illustrate the results of both proper and improper techniques.

FIGURE 15-1 Histogram (bar chart) furnished courtesy of George Hinkle, Ohio University Computing and Learning Services.

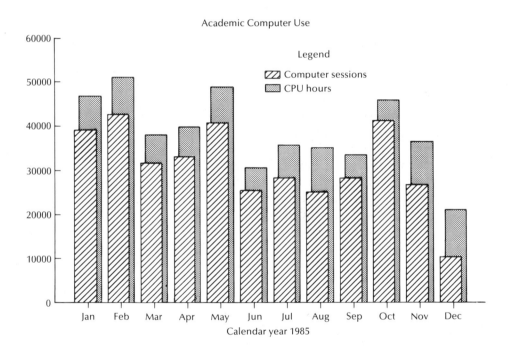

4. *Diagrams.* Without presenting a diagram of the playing field, could you explain how soccer, hockey, football, or rugby is played? Does the diagram of a sentence help display the relationships between its words, phrases, and clauses? A frustrated student of grammar might answer "no" to our last question, but most of us would agree that diagrams add clarity to verbal messages. Like the model, the diagram can be a simplified version of what it is intended to represent, displaying only those features of immediate interest.

5. *Maps.* Certain spatial relationships can best be communicated when the words used to describe them are supplemented with a map of the relevant territory. Without maps of the areas, it would be hard to explain to an audience the present controversies in the Middle East or Central America. Similarly, if a speaker wished to point out how transportation costs contribute to the price of imported oil, he or she could display a map that locates oil-exporting countries.

FIGURE 15-2 Frequency Polygon furnished courtesy of George Hinkle, Ohio University Computing and Learning Services.

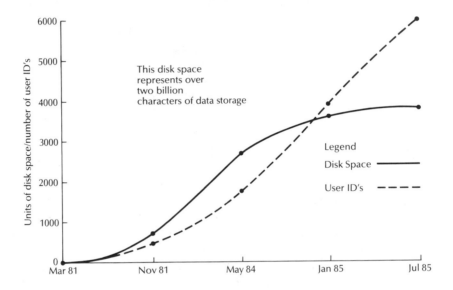

6. *Charts and graphs.* These visual aids are useful whenever you find it desirable to summarize or condense large amounts of information or to display trends. A sales manager reporting the latest sales figures might find it useful to prepare a chart that displays products as column headings and sales areas as row headings. Each entry at a particular row and column might list units sold within a specified time period. Graphs, as well, display trends easily and quickly.

7. *Movies.* Occasionally, the public speaker will find it desirable to include a movie as a part of the total presentation. Speakers sometimes use movies to provide their audience with orientation material, material the audience must grasp if they are to understand the content of the speech that follows. For example, an audience might have a better understanding of a speech on the effects of nuclear bombs if they were first to see a film of a nuclear explosion and its aftermath.

FIGURE 15-3   **Pie Chart furnished courtesy of George Hinkle, Ohio University Computing and Learning Services.**

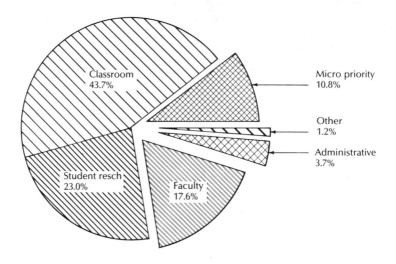

Total shared resource accounts...12,189

Speakers have a wide array of visual aids available to clarify, amplify, or support their message. They frequently also have choices regarding the mode through which those visual aids are displayed. Photographs, for example, can be shown in black and white or color. They can be made into slides and may be projected onto a screen in an enlarged version of the original. Diagrams, maps, charts, and graphs also can be displayed in a variety of ways—on the chalkboard, through photocopies, on an overhead transparency, and so forth. Movies, too, might be presented via a projector and screen or possibly via videorecorder and television. When deciding on the appropriate mode for displaying a visual aid, you will want to consider the costs and benefits of each possible mode. Keep in mind, however, the fact that a visual aid has no positive effect if the audience cannot see it.

Using Visual Aids Effectively.   Used effectively, a visual aid can attract favorable attention, supplement a verbal message, hold attention, illustrate relationships, simplify the complex, or even summarize large bodies of data. Here are some suggestions for using visual aids:

1. *They must be relevant.* Visual aids should provide support for your ideas, rather than support for you. Do not allow the visual aids to be the dominant part of your presentation. Their role is to clarify, amplify, or support your ideas, and they should never become a distracting factor.

2. *They must be seen easily.* The audience must be able to see your visual aids. All too often, we have heard a student speaker say something like, "I know this is too small to see, but if you could see it, you would notice. . . ." If you should choose to display a chart, diagram, or graph on an easel or some other support, be sure that your body does not obstruct the view as you make reference to the visual. A pointer might prove desirable. If you display an object or model, be sure that your hands do not obstruct the view of your audience.

3. *The speaker must maintain audience contact.* Many people have the tendency to talk *to the visual aid* and not to their audience. Make specific references to your visual aid, pointing to or otherwise indicating the exact feature you want your audience to see. Maintain a high degree of eye contact in the process.

4. *Visual aids should be covered.* Keep visual aids covered or otherwise out of the view of your audience until you are ready to use them. When you are finished with them, again remove them from view. If a visual aid is effective, it will have attention-getting value. You do not want the audience to attend to your visual aid before or after you have displayed it—that would detract from your message.

5. *Visual aids should be kept simple and clear.* Include only essential details in visual aids. It is usually better to use several simple charts or diagrams to make a point than to display one that is complicated. Accuracy, of course, must not be sacrificed to achieve simplicity.

Language Choices

Your language choices will have much to do with whether or not the audience comprehends and retains your message. Written and oral styles are quite different from one another. Oral style has more personal references, more first-person pronouns, shorter thought units, more repetition of vocabulary, more monosyllabic and familiar words, and more self-references, qualifiers, and "allness" terms such as *everyone, always,* and *never.*

Various measures have been devised to quantify the degree of reading-difficulty present in a given passage.[6] By assessing such variables as sentence length, number of syllables per hundred words, and number of familiar words, these measures are able to predict the educational level that a reader would need in order to understand the passage. Usually, when oral and written styles are compared through these readability formulas, written style emerges as more difficult to comprehend. Without belaboring the point, we urge you to cultivate an oral style. Do not read your speeches. By extemporizing (see Chapter 13), you will naturally

[6]See, for example, Rudolph Flesh, "A New Readability Yardstick," *Journal of Applied Psychology, 32*: 221-233 (1948) and Edgar Dale and J. S. Chall, "A Formula for Predicting Readability," *Educational Research Bulletin, 27*: 11-20 (1948).

include elements of the oral style and encourage the audience's retention of your message.[7]

Providing Emphasis

We have detailed a variety of techniques that, if artfully employed, promote the receiver's learning of information. We have suggested that an organized structure, if recognized by the listener, enhances learning. We also have observed that visual aids and oral style favorably affect learning. Now we provide a series of miscellaneous techniques that the speaker can use to emphasize ideas and encourage in listeners the retention of those ideas.

Proactive Emphasis. When speakers employ words and phrases that direct the listener to retain an immediately following idea, they are employing *proactive emphasis*. "Remember this," "now get this," and "this is important" are all examples of proactive emphasis. Under certain experimental conditions, proactive emphasis has had positive effects on enhancing learning.[8] We suspect this technique has its greatest impact when the speaker uses it sparingly and only in conjunction with truly important ideas. To preface every or even a majority of ideas with proactive emphasis would put the speaker in the same state as the little boy who cried "wolf" too often.

Repetition or Restatement. Restate your ideas. If you have ever heard a formal collegiate debate, you may have noticed that the speakers repeat their major ideas throughout their speeches, primarily so that the judge of the debate is sure to note these points. Restatement also invites stating an idea more than once, but with new and different language symbols. (Repetition, too, promotes retention, but audiences regard this method as overused.)[9] Restatement appears to accomplish the same goal and offers the audience greater variety. Interspersing repetition and restatement of important ideas seems to be a desirable course of action.

Voice and Body. In Chapter 13, we described how vocal variables and physical activity can shape the meaning an audience assigns to a verbal message. Here we mention that certain elements of a speaker's delivery also can emphasize an idea and encourage the audience's retention of the idea. In one study, A. T. Jersild discovered that pausing before an idea, raising the voice to introduce it, and gesturing and banging on the table in conjunction with an idea all serve as successful means for emphasizing the important points of a speech.[10]

[7]Gordon L. Thomas, "Effect of Oral Style on Intelligibility of Speech," *Speech Monographs, 23*: 46-54 (1956).

[8]Charles R. Petrie, Jr., "Informative Speaking: A Summary and Bibliography of Related Research," *Speech Monographs, 30*: 79-91 (1963).

[9]Petrie, pp. 79-91.

[10]A. T. Jersild, "Modes of Emphasis in Public Speaking," *Journal of Applied Psychology, 12*: 611-620 (1928).

These, then, are a number of techniques available to the speaker to maximize the retention of information. The recall of information can be affected by choices made by the public speaker. It is not a given. Experiment with these techniques and see if you can make your audience members more effective listeners.

Summary

1. Informative speeches can be classified according to three types: speeches of process, speeches that report, and speeches that provide exposition.
2. Individuals learn best when they are taught at their level of competence. Fatigue, boredom, and frustration inhibit learning; motivation facilitates it. Attention is a learned response. Emotional involvement increases retention; overlearning improves it. Reinforcement speeds learning; organization promotes it; sensing relationships enhances it. Individuals remember best those materials they consciously intend to remember.
3. Numerous techniques help the speaker put learning principles into practice. Clear organizational structure affects learning. Providing structural cues promotes learning, as do visual aids, oral style, and variables relating to voice and bodily movement.
4. Among those structural cueing techniques that affect learning are presummaries, transitions, and summaries (final and internal).
5. Visual aids (objects, models, photographs, diagrams, maps, charts and graphs, and movies) can amplify, clarify, and support the speaker's message. Visual aids should be relevant, easily seen, definite, simple, and clear.
6. Oral style improves the intelligibility of a speaker's message.
7. A variety of techniques gives emphasis to an idea. The techniques include proactive emphasis, repetition and restatement, pausing before an idea, raising the voice to introduce an idea, gesturing, and banging on a table.

Questions and Exercises

1. Provide three thesis statements appropriate to each of the types of informative speeches: process, report, and expositive.
2. This chapter enumerates ten learning principles (see pp. 230-232). Choose three that you believe have had the most impact on your own learning and explain why these three have been so effective.
3. What characteristics does a well-organized speech possess?
4. Researchers have discovered that people who are skillful organizers might profit more from well-organized messages than people who

are lacking in the ability to organize. What justification can you offer to support this finding?

5. Explain the subsumption theory of learning and enumerate some techniques that are at the disposal of the public speaker for capitalizing on subsumption principles.

6. What functions are served by transitional phrases and how do they facilitate learning?

7. Make a list of informative speech topics. Suggest two visual aids that would be appropriate for each.

8. What characteristics constitute a good visual aid? Can you provide examples of unsuccessful visual aids that you have observed speakers using? Why did you find them less than effective?

9. Define *proactive emphasis* and explain the role it can play in promoting learning.

Sample Speech Outline
Word Processing: A Key to Scholarship

Introduction

I. In recent years, the availability of microcomputers and related software packages has increased dramatically.
   - A. The number of home computers has increased.
   - B. The number of microcomputers in business has increased sharply.
   - C. The number of microcomputers on the college campus has increased greatly.

II. Word-processing programs are a vital tool of the microcomputer user.
   - A. A word-processing program is a canned set of instructions that allows even a naïve computer user to accomplish sophisticated text manipulations.
   - B. Many good programs are available.
      1. WordStar has been the industry standard for a number of years.
      2. WordPerfect is rapidly becoming a dominant package.
      3. Other programs of some significance include PeachText, Volkswriter, PerfectWriter, DisplayWrite, and AppleWriter.
      4. The cost of a good word-processing program varies from $75 to over $500.

III. The ability to command a word-processing package can enhance your scholarship.
   - A. Word processing can increase your productivity.
   - B. Word processing can compensate for the lack of skills that the poor typist has.
   - C. Word processing can improve your writing skills.

(Transition: Now let us go on to consider each of these three claimed benefits in greater detail.)

Body

I. Word processing can increase your productivity.
   - A. A word processor minimizes the agonies of writing.
      1. Sophisticated on-screen editing is possible.
      2. More than one document can be edited at a time.
      3. Footnotes are easily incorporated.
      4. Documents are easily combined.
   - B. Document management can be very efficient.
      1. Documents (files) can be renamed, reordered, and erased with little difficulty.

    2. Massive amounts of data can be stored in a very small space.

  C. Many word-processing programs have a mail-merge capability.

    1. The same letter or other information can with great ease be sent to different individuals.

    2. The documents resulting from mail merging can be highly personalized.

(Transition: Not only do word-processing programs make you more productive, but they can also polish your final product.)

II. Word processing can compensate for the lack of skills that the poor typist has.

  A. Erasures and white-outs do not appear on the final product.

  B. Page formatting can be changed easily.

    1. Margins are set and changed easily.

    2. Pages can be automatically numbered.

    4. Justification is possible.

    4. Hyphenation can be eliminated.

  C. Different fonts and pitches are frequently addressable.

    1. Twelve-, fifteen-, and seventeen-pitch are frequently available.

    2. Many printers allow a choice of different fonts or type-faces.

  D. Word processors take the guesswork out of footnote location.

    1. Footnotes can be at the bottom of the page or at the end of the text.

    2. Space requirements for footnotes are automatically calculated.

(Transition: Yes, word-processing programs can make you more productive and help you to produce better-looking papers. But there is an even more important benefit that might be realized.)

III. Word processing can improve your writing skills.

  A. Research studies indicate that students using word-processing programs develop improved attitudes toward writing.

    1. Improved attitudes lead to more actual writing.

    2. Improved attitudes lead to collaborative writing with other students and the teacher.

  B. Word-processing programs produce files that can be analyzed by other writing-assistance programs.

    1. Spelling checkers can be utilized.

    2. Thesauruses can be employed.

    3. Grammatical and syntactical programs can be used.

Conclusion

I. Microcomputers and word processors are fast becoming a part of our world.

II. They can be an important tool for today's college student.
    A. I encourage you to learn more about them.
    B. Once you have tried a word processor, you will not want to go back to your typewriter.

III. Word processing can make you a better student.
    A. You can be more productive.
    B. You can produce professional-quality final copy.
    C. You might even become a better writer.

Sample Speech

Word Processing: A Key to Scholarship

I'm sure that I don't have to point out to any of you that the availability of microcomputers and related software packages has increased dramatically in the last few years. A number of you may already have microcomputers, or your families may have them. As we look over the past five years, we can see the dramatic increase in the number of home computers that have been put into operation. We also look in the business community and we can see that a business nowadays that does not have microcomputing facilities is no longer on the cutting edge. Finally, we can look to college campuses and we see, once again, a very, very dramatic increase in the availability of microcomputers. In fact, in the September 4, 1985, issue of *The Chronicle of Higher Education,* it was observed that 1985-86 might well be called the "year of the microcomputer" on the college campus. Many institutions have already been heavily involved in microcomputing. Among them are such schools as Brown University, Carnegie-Mellon University, and Dartmouth College. This year is going to see a new wave of involvement that will sweep across the country. Lehigh University, for instance, is scheduled to expend $20 million this year on a computer network, and it will encourage all of its entering students to purchase a Zenith microcomputer. Other institutions, like Franklin and Marshall College, will also be urging this fall's freshmen to purchase microcomputers. Part of this emphasis comes from observing what has happened in other colleges that have required microcomputing of their students. Drew University in 1984 required all of its freshmen to own and use a microcomputer, and it saw a 49 percent increase in enrollments.

The microcomputers alone don't do much good unless they have the software to drive them. A very important part of any software is what is called a word-processing program. A word-processing program, basically, is a set of instructions that allows even a very naive computer user to accomplish the most sophisticated text manipulations. Many good word-processing programs are available. Perhaps you have heard of some of them. For many years WordStar has been the industry standard. WordPerfect is rapidly becoming a dominant package in the word-processing area. Other programs of some significance include PeachText, Volkswriter, PerfectWriter, DisplayWrite, and AppleWriter. The cost of a good word-processing program varies; generally they are quite inexpensive, ranging in price from $75 to $500.

Today I am going to be talking in a general sense about word processing. I am not going to advocate one word-processing program, but instead I want to speak about word processing as a generic term, and I want to observe for you that [THESIS FOLLOWS] the command of a good word-processing program can enhance your scholarship.

[PRESUMMARY FOLLOWS] I'm going to talk about this in three areas today. I'm going, first of all, to show you that word processing can increase your productivity as a student. I'm going to show you that word processing can compensate for your lack of skills if you are a poor typist. And I'm going to observe that word processing might well improve your writing skills.

[TRANSITION FOLLOWS] Now let us go on to consider each of these three claimed benefits in greater detail. First of all, I would observe that [MAIN POINT I FOLLOWS] word processing can increase your productivity as a student. All of us have experienced certain agonies whenever we have been engaged in writing. [SUBPOINT IA FOLLOWS] Well, a word processor can minimize these agonies. Word processing provides very sophisticated on-screen editing techniques for you. You are able to erase words, whole lines, whole paragraphs, a complete document; you are able to move words, phrases, sentences, and paragraphs from one position in a document to another position. You are able to work on more than one document or file at a time. You can also easily insert superscript numbers for the purposes of footnoting. And speaking of footnoting, do you have the same problem that I have—judging the amount of space that should be left at the bottom of the page in order to incorporate a footnote and leave the appropriate margin? Well, a word-processing program can take care of this for you automatically. Footnotes are easily incorporated, either to appear at the bottom of pages or at the end of a document that you are preparing. A good word-processing program also allows you to combine two separate documents without retyping one document and appending it to another. Another advantage that can make you more productive is that a word-processing program provides for easy and effective document management. Documents, or files, as they are typically called in computer jargon, can easily be renamed, reordered, and erased.

[SUBPOINT IB FOLLOWS] And speaking about document management, massive amounts of data can be stored in a very small space. Many of you probably have problems in your dorm room, finding room for all of the materials that are required of you in a given quarter. Microcomputers store information on what are called floppy disks. As you can see, they look very much like a 45 rpm phonograph record. This particular disk, which I am displaying, has a capacity of 360,000 bytes. Now, a byte is generally equivalent to a character. If your term paper runs 35 to 40 pages, including your footnotes, there would be as many as 40,000 bytes of information. So you see one of these small floppy disks could contain up to nine term papers. And as you see, the space required to store those nine term papers is considerably different than if you had to store a hard copy of each of those particular papers.

[SUBPOINT IC FOLLOWS] In addition, many of the good word-processing programs have what are called mail-merge programs. These allow you, with great ease, to send the same letter or other information to different individuals. A set of names and addresses is prepared and stored in one file, and a second file contains the letter that you would like to send to each of the persons on your address list. At the time of printing, then, the letter or document that you have prepared is merged with the set of names and addresses you have prepared, to produce an individualized letter to each of the persons on your list.

[TRANSITION FOLLOWS] Not only do word-processing programs make you more productive as a student, but they can also polish your final product. I'm not a very good typist, but [MAIN POINT II FOLLOWS] I can produce professional-quality documents through the use of my word-processing program. When I'm sitting at my typewriter, I probably use more white-out than any three persons at this university. I also frequently make erasures. When I'm finished with my typewriter-produced document, it typically doesn't look very nice. I'm dissatisfied with the product that results. With my word-processing program, I can make all my changes right on the screen. It doesn't matter how many times I change a word, how many times I make a correction. [SUBPOINT IIA] These will not be reflected in the final product that is produced.

Many times I have sat down to type my term paper in final form and have discovered that once I got into the typing I didn't like the margins that I had set, or I didn't like the indentation that I had used for paragraphs. My only choice had been to retype it, providing, of course, that I was sufficiently dissatisfied to go through that ordeal once again. But with the word-processing program, that is no longer a hassle. I can set my margins and my indentations and print the copy. I can examine the copy, and if it proves dissatisfactory, all I have to do is go back into my word-processing program, change my margins, change the indentations, change the locations of page numbers—whatever I wish—and reprint the document. This can be done in a matter of minutes, and it certainly takes the agony out of the typewriting process.

[SUBPOINT IIB FOLLOWS] Page formatting is easily changed. Margins can be set and changed easily; pages can be automatically numbered. Do you like to have your text right-justified? That is, do you like to have the letters in the right margin all line up with one another? Are you plagued with hyphenation problems—that is, you get to the end of a line of a text and you don't know exactly where to place a hyphen in a word? Well, in word-processing programs many times you can demand "hyphenation off" and the program will format your text in such a fashion that hyphenations do not appear. Your text is spaced across a given line to the point where hyphens are not required.

[SUBPOINT IIC FOLLOWS] Another way in which a word-processing program can make your product appear more professional is by making available to you many different fonts and pitches. A good dot matrix printer will allow the user to select from among 10 characters per inch, 12 characters per inch, or even 17 characters per inch in the output that is produced. Now to explain what that means, most of you probably have a typewriter that is either pica or elite. Pica type has 10 characters per inch; elite type has 12 characters per inch; and most typewriters don't have the capacity of producing 17 characters per inch as a dot matric printer might have. Also, few of you have choices in your typewriter with respect to the kind of font that you use or the kind of type that you use. Those of you with IBM Selectrics, for instance, might have a typing element or ball that you can replace to produce typefaces like Prestige Elite, Bookface Elite, or a variety of others. Many dot matrix printers have this same capability of allowing the user to select from a variety of type styles or fonts in the production of the final product.

As I mentioned earlier, word processing can make you a better typist by taking some of the guesswork out of locating footnotes. [SUBPOINT IID FOLLOWS] In a good word-processing program, footnotes are easily prepared. You can choose between placing them either at the bottom of the page, as some professors require, or at the end of the text, where it is generally easier to display them. The space requirements for footnotes are automatically calculated.

[SUMMARY AS TRANSITION FOLLOWS] Yes, word-processing programs *can* make you more productive and help you to produce better-looking papers. But there is an even more important benefit that might be realized from the use of word-processing packages. [MAIN POINT III FOLLOWS] It is conceivable that consistent use of a word processor may make you a better writer. Here the final verdict is not yet in. The area of study is relatively new. But a handful of research studies done in this particular area do provide promising evidence that using word processors might well improve the writing abilities of the students who use them in a consistent fashion. [SUBPOINT IIIA FOLLOWS] One thing that has been noted is that students using word-processing programs have developed improved attitudes toward the actual writing process. [SUBPOINT IIIB FOLLOWS] These improved attitudes have led to collaborative writing between students and even collaborative writing with the teacher. [SUBPOINT IIIC FOLLOWS] In addition, word-processing programs produce files that can be analyzed by other writing-assistance programs.

A good word-processing program comes with a spelling checker. Here a student can compare word for word his or her document against the dictionary of the spelling checker and detect any errors that might occur. A good word processor might also have a thesaurus. Here the student can select a word that he or she would like to have an alternative for and find a variety of suggestions from which to choose. Some writing-assistance programs will also do an analysis of your grammar. They will point out when you have incorrect usages, when you have subject-verb disagreement, and when you have unusual syntax.

[CONCLUSION BEGINS] Yes, microcomputers and word processors are fast becoming a part of our world. They can be a very important tool for today's college students. I encourage you to learn much more about them. Once you have tried a word processor, I'm sure you'll be much like me—you won't want to go back to your typewriter. [RESTATEMENT OF THESIS AND BRIEF SUMMARY FOLLOW] Yes, word-processing programs can make you a better student; you can be more productive than you are now; you can produce professional-quality final copy; and finally, you might even become a better writer if you are willing to spend a little time up front to learn the skills associated with microcomputing and word processing.

Courtesy of Bill Fitzpatrick, The White House

16

The Nature of Persuasive Speaking

By the time you finish reading this chapter, you should be able to:

1. Explain what it means to change people's minds and behavior.
2. Relate the explanation of change to establishing a precise goal for your persuasive message.
3. Explain the general strategy for constructing persuasive messages.
4. Explain the needs for arousal of motives in persuasive speeches.
5. Explain how to adapt ten basic motivational appeals to a variety of message situations.

Speeches that modify thoughts or behavior are persuasive. Persuasion involves providing receivers with information that leads them to make decisions to alter their thoughts and behaviors. The key terms in this definition are *information, decisions, thoughts,* and *behaviors.*

The word *information* is used in a broad sense to include not only facts, figures, authoritative reports, and opinions, but also information about feelings. A typical persuasive speech presents sound evidence and reasoning and adds information about how receivers should feel toward that evidence and reasoning. For example, a persuasive speech that presents facts about pesticides may also add motivational information about why the audience should fear the effects of pesticides. It may go on to specify what people should do to prevent those effects from occurring.

The term *decisions* emphasizes the point that receivers are in charge in persuasive speeches. It is receivers who *decide* whether they will go to the trouble of changing their minds or modifying their behavior. No matter how important your subject may appear to you, unless receivers agree that your topic is important, you will have little chance of altering thoughts and behaviors.

The term *thoughts* refers to beliefs, attitudes, values, stereotypes, and other concepts that you might use to refer to what takes place inside the human head. Simply and generally stated, when your speech convinces receivers to think differently, the receivers decide to change their minds or their behaviors.

The term *behaviors* means those things that you can see others do. Sometimes you can see the look of sudden insight on the faces of your receivers, but most of the time changes of mind are not visible. Receivers may, however, demonstrate their changes of mind by signing a petition in support of the position you advocate in your message. After a successful speech on the importance of renewing tetanus shots, you may see receivers lining up at the campus health service. Or if your receivers decide that one presidential candidate is better than another, then that belief should lead them to vote for the better candidate.

When you prepare a speech to modify thoughts or behavior, you usually prepare one that provides evidence and reasoning and adds motivational information in order to get receivers to reach a decision to think or behave differently. In this chapter, we will emphasize methods of persuading receivers to alter their thoughts and behaviors. We will discuss establishing a goal for your persuasive message, general planning for persuasion, and specific planning for persuasion.

Selecting a Goal for Your Message

In persuasion, the setting of a clear goal is essential to success. Failure to establish one is the most common reason persuaders do not succeed.[1] If you do not know the kinds of thoughts you wish your classmates to have as a result of your speech, there is little reason to expect your listeners to accept your views. If you do not know the modifications in behavior you wish to achieve, it is improbable that your audience will decide to behave as you wish. The more specific you can make your goal, the better. General acceptance of your thesis may be appropriate in some situations, but greater specificity usually makes for more effective persuasion. To set specific goals, ask yourself questions like these: What arguments and evidence do you want your audience to remember? Do you want them to be able to repeat your points to others? Do you want them to sign a petition you will circulate at the end of your speech? Do you want them to write to their Congresspersons? Do you want them to purchase a product? To the extent that you can identify exactly the kinds of thoughts or behaviors you wish audiences to have, you are more likely to achieve the results you wish.

[1]Kenneth E. Andersen, *Persuasion: Theory and Practice,* 2nd ed. (Boston: Allyn and Bacon, Inc., 1978), p. 124.

General Planning for Persuasion ——————————————————————

Persuasion involves three interrelated steps:

1. Identification of some need of your receivers.
2. Selection of information that helps your receivers decide that the need is important or pressing.
3. Selection of additional information that helps your receivers decide to follow your recommendations to fulfill that need.

These steps follow a model, based on learning theory, proposed by Carl I. Hovland.[2] Though other theoretical explanations have advantages in some situations, this approach seems to fit most of the situations you are likely to encounter in the classroom or elsewhere. Stated simply, it says that once you have selected a need held by receivers, you provide content cues that arouse motivation. Having aroused that motivation, you supply recommendations about how the receivers may fulfill the need that has been aroused. Those recommendations involve the receivers' decisions to alter thoughts or behaviors. In many, if not in a majority of cases, the most reliable desire of your receivers is the desire for sound information to help them to make rational decisions. Even where strong emotions are involved, the speaker who appeals to reason will be most likely to get receivers to make decisions corresponding to his or her intentions.

How Do These Steps Work?

First, as you identify your receivers' needs as a basis for your persuasion, you must decide how to direct your arousal cues. You must choose whether to direct these cues at (1) the individual receivers themselves, (2) their loved ones, (3) their possessions, or (4) humankind in general.[3] If, for example, you were to speak against nuclear weapons to an audience of young parents, it might be more persuasive to focus on the effects of nuclear war on their children than on themselves, their possessions, or humankind in general. If you were trying to convince your classmates to become more security-conscious in their dormitories, then it might be more effective to focus on the loss of prized possessions than on personal dangers.

[2]Carl I. Hovland, Irving L. Janis, and Harold H. Kelley, *Communication and Persuasion* (New Haven: Yale University Press, 1953), pp. 64-65.

[3]Gerald R. Miller and Murray A. Hewgill, "Some Recent Research on Fear-Arousing Message Appeals," *Speech Monographs, 33*: 377-391 (1966).

Second, you must determine the extent to which you want your receivers to feel the need as important and compelling. The stronger the need or want aroused, the more likely people are to respond to it. It may seem, on the surface, that vivid descriptions of disasters will prove to be most effective. If you are urging a ban on nuclear weapons, slides of Hiroshima and of the terrible burns and disfigurements the survivors received might seem likely to get people to sign a nuclear-ban petition. Although this thinking is generally correct, exceptions to this rule abound. When people find information too emotionally arousing, they may not respond as you wish. Instead, they may do one of three things: (1) They may decide that the situation is so bad that they will not think about it and will consequently cease listening to the speech; (2) they may decide that the situation is so bad that there is nothing that can be done; or (3) they may engage in the age-old human practice of attacking the bearer of bad news—that is, they may become angry with you.[4] It is important that you exercise care in selecting arousal cues. You do want to convince your receivers that the matter is pressing and important enough to produce a decision. At the same time, though, you should not overstate your case.

The most neglected step in the persuasive process is the third step: recommendations—that is, selecting materials that help receivers reach decisions to fulfill the need aroused. In the case of a nuclear ban, you must find information that will convince the audience that signing the petition will enable them to reduce the anxiety you have created.[5] If you cannot provide such information, it is unlikely that your audience will decide to think or behave as you intend. Frequently, convincing the audience that a subject is important is easier than providing them with adequate mechanisms for meeting the need you have aroused.

There is a myth about persuasion that leads speakers to neglect the recommendation. The myth is that it is not the speaker's responsibility to offer a way of meeting the needs that the speaker arouses. Students often point to problems like overcrowded classes, high tuition, and unresponsive officials in colleges or in government. However, students seldom accept the responsibility for recommending measures for correction. The myth is often expressed by sentences such as "They can figure out what to do for themselves." In the abstract, this statement is true, for reasonably intelligent people can usually determine how to change a situation. However, studies have shown that in the concrete, particularly in persuasive speaking, people do not figure out solutions for themselves.[6] An instructor may inspire a student to try for the grade

---

[4]Irving L. Janis and Seymour Feshback, "Effects of Fear-Arousing Communications," *Journal of Abnormal and Social Psychology, 48*(1): 78-92 (1953).

[5]Howard Leventhal, "Fear Communications in the Acceptance of Preventive Health Practices," *Bulletin of the New York Academy of Medicine, 41* (ser. 2, no. 11), pp. 1158-1160 (1965).

[6]Carl I. Hovland and W. Mandell, "An Experimental Comparison of Conclusion Drawing by the Communicator and by the Audience," *Journal of Abnormal and Social Psychology, 47*: 581-588 (1952).

of A on an assigned term paper. But unless the student knows how to write an A paper, the student is not likely to receive this grade. In persuasion, the more specific and precise the speaker can make the recommendation, the greater is the likelihood that the speaker will get the response he or she intends.

In summary, general planning for persuasion involves selecting receiver needs, providing information that leads receivers to decide that the need is pressing or important, and providing additional information to help receivers decide on the changes in thought and behavior that will fulfill the need. The ways of selecting the need, making it pressing or important, and developing effective recommendations are discussed extensively in the following section.

Planning for Motivation _____

What motivational appeals can you use to facilitate your persuasive attempts? What needs can you use? How can you make them important? How can you develop effective recommendations that enable your receivers to meet those needs? The answers to these questions depend on understanding motivational appeals. Motivation has been described as the "processes or conditions which. . . describe how . . . behavior is initiated, maintained, guided, selected, or terminated."[7]

Beliefs, attitudes, and values are one set of concepts that you may evoke to produce energy and direction (these choices are discussed extensively in Chapter 2). When you provide information that leads to evocation of a belief, attitude, or value, the receiver will respond with thoughts or behaviors consistent with that attitude. Those who study human motivation in psychology and physiology refer to two additional, relatively powerful sources of motivation, called *drives* and *motives*. Drives refer to those predominantly physiological motivators that we share with other animals—hunger and thirst are examples. Motives refer to learned motivational patterns that humans employ to fulfill their physiological and psychological needs. The achievement motive or the need for self-esteem are examples. In some cases, the drive state operating as the basis for a motive is obvious, but in most cases, the learning component is more important.

Motives and Motivational Appeals. The list of appeals that motivate humans is probably endless. One of the most widely used textbooks in the area of persuasion draws on H. A. Murray's classic work for a list of twenty-eight such appeals.[8] These diverse appeals

[7]Richard A. Littman, "Motives, History and Causes," in *Nebraska Symposium on Motivation,* ed. Marshall R. Jones (Lincoln: University of Nebraska Press, 1958), p. 136.

[8]Winston L. Brembeck and William S. Howell, *Persuasion: A Means of Social Influence,* 2nd ed. (Englewood Cliffs, N.J.: Prentice-Hall, Inc., 1976), pp. 93-95.

range from orderliness (the need to organize and put things away), to autonomy (the need to be independent), to rejection (the need to be separate from others), to exposition (the need to teach and explain things to others).[9] If you are like students in one of the authors' persuasion classes and you leaf through the advertisements in a magazine aimed at people your age, you can usually identify ten to twenty different motivational appeals that appear in the front of the magazine. Near the back of the magazine, you will find still other appeals, many of which are not aimed at the higher human motives. The diversity in the appeals that motivate humans is so great that trying to discuss them all would require several chapters and perhaps a whole book. We have selected ten appeals that are commonly used by persuaders. We think that our discussion will aid you in most of the persuasive speeches you prepare. Nevertheless, we hope you will also be sure to analyze any situation and audience you face with the thought in mind that the most effective appeal is the one that fits the specific situation and its audience.

Persuasive speakers appeal frequently to the following ten human qualities or needs:

1. The desire to make rational choices based on sound information.
2. Fear and anxiety.
3. Anger or frustration of goals or desires.
4. Success and achievement.
5. Pity.
6. Humor.
7. Affection.
8. Self-esteem and pride.
9. Power or the ability to influence or control others.
10. Contemporaneity.

The Desire to Make Rational Choices Based on Sound Information. Sound evidence and reasoning can convince many receivers to support an idea. The persuader must exhibit clear and cogent reasoning in these cases. For many topics, the potential for changing ideas or behaviors rests on a thesis that is supported by reasons for something to be changed, some workable method of making the change, and an explanation of how the receivers will benefit from the change. Should the United States adopt a system of health-care payment similar to Medicare for all citizens? Should our country cease to develop nuclear weapons? Should capital punishment be eliminated? Should tuition be increased? Should dormitory restrictions be relaxed or increased? An appeal to listeners' desires to make rational choices is potentially an effective way to change minds or to get signatures on petitions. The

[9]Henry A. Murray, _Explorations in Personality: A Clinical and Experimental Study of Fifty Men of College Age_ (New York: Oxford University Press, 1938), pp. 142-143.

ways to appeal effectively to this desire are discussed more extensively in Chapter 11. Keep in mind that such appeals need not be coldly logical in the sense that mathematical demonstration is logical. Cogent arguments are the things humans rely upon to enable them to predict and control the future; in the long run, these arguments are the most effective of all persuasive appeals.

Fear and Anxiety. Appeals directed at human fears constitute a widely studied subject in the literature of persuasion. The chief reason for the extensive study is that humans, like most animals, have a great deal to fear. Unlike most animals, however, humans have the ability to think and imagine the many terrible things that may occur. Making a receiver fearful requires the speaker to bring up content cues that describe the threatening agent. The speaker must also explain how the threat applies to the receiver and must provide recommendations about how the receiver can cope with the threat. Examples of general classes of threatening agents are such things as diseases, injuries, possibilities of failures, loss of things the individual values, the possibility of becoming like someone loathed, and so on. In short, people fear harm to themselves and to the other people, things, and ideas they hold dear. The greater the fear, the greater an individual's motivation to deal with it. This generalization probably applies to many other kinds of appeals, provided that the recommendations for dealing with the appeals are adequate. The exception noted earlier in this chapter (p. 256) applies. The greater the anger, the more likely the receiver is to act against the source of his or her frustrations; the greater the pity, the more likely the receiver is to offer the recommended aid and succor; the greater the affection, the more likely it is that the receiver will act protectively; the greater the appeal to rationality, the more likely the receiver is to act logically. Most experiments support these findings on fear,[10] and the viewpoint that "stronger is better" appeals to common sense.

Anger or Frustration of Goals and Desires. On the surface, appealing to the angry feelings of your listeners should seem to be an almost ideal technique of persuasion. You can offer cues that arouse anger in your receivers and offer those receivers some way of alleviating the anger that corresponds with your purpose. The urgency associated with being angry should yield a high probability of receiver compliance. Unfortunately, arousing anger also has risks for the persuader.

The technique of arousing anger requires the speaker to identify the receivers' expectations toward an individual, organization, or object.

---

[10]Graduate students in persuasion seminars regularly report that at least forty-five studies generally support the idea that higher levels of fear persuade better than lower levels. These studies deal with such topics as dental hygiene, smoking, tetanus, driving practices, fallout shelters, alcohol abuse, surgery, tuberculosis, roundworms, eye damage due to a solar eclipse, stair hand rails, pain killers, health maintenance organizations, sunlamp exposure, population control, the energy crisis, sunburn, and cheating.

The speaker must then note failures to meet those expectations. When a speaker tries to get people to vote against an incumbent political candidate, a frequent technique is to arouse anger toward that candidate by noting past promises that raised voter expectations and that have not been met. "Henry Smith promised more jobs, but there are fewer jobs available in his district than when he was first elected" and "Smith promised lower taxes, but most of us are paying 50 percent more in taxes" are typical cues that can be offered when anger is to be directed at an individual. "The university pledged to each of you the opportunity to study what you wished to study; instead it requires you to take courses that represent departmental interests rather than your own needs and interests," is a typical cue designed to arouse anger toward an institution. "Machines make errors. All of us have spent hours trying to straighten out problems created by computers" is a typical cue that is used to arouse anger toward an object.

As we have noted, however, appeals to anger involve risks to the speaker. First, anger tends to be a relatively urgent feeling. It is an unpleasant emotion for most people, and unless there is an opportunity to block it quickly and effectively, people may rid themselves of anger in ways that may run contrary to the speaker's persuasive purpose. The most obvious target for unrelieved anger is the persuader himself or herself. Second, even when quick and effective action is possible, anger is difficult to control, and it may spread to other matters. Though the speaker's attempt at arousal and his or her recommendations may appear perfectly in balance, the odds are good that for many receivers, the resulting degree of arousal will be much greater than the speaker anticipated.

Success and Achievement. Success and achievement are strong motivators in modern America. The idea of a beautiful house or apartment in the "right" neighborhood, a trendy, expensive automobile or two, regular vacation trips to the Bahamas, Aruba, or Hawaii, eating out frequently, and having the income to support all these activities are goals for many Americans. Even Americans who are less materialistic are inclined to set personal goals and to work hard to achieve them. Most of us want to be perceived as successful, and we are constantly motivated to do a good job. Shelves in bookstores often contain 30-50 self-improvement titles; these illustrate as clearly as anything the desire of Americans to be even better than they are in interpersonal relationships, in losing weight, in building their bodies, or in making successful complaints.

The desire of students to improve themselves is usually strong (or else they would not be students). Your classmates are thus particularly likely to respond to a speech that demonstrates how they can enhance their probability of success or personal achievement.

Pity. If you can demonstrate to your audience that there are others who are less fortunate than they are and proceed to show the audience how a change in their thinking or behavior will benefit those less fortunate persons, you have a good chance of producing the change you seek. Individual Americans donate millions annually to various charities. Most of that money is donated to aid people who are, in some way, less fortunate than the donors. Few people, when confronted with a verbal picture or photograph of a starving child or someone with a severe handicap, can resist an appeal for a few dollars of aid. Such appeals are made so frequently, however, that people learn to avoid hearing them. Nevertheless, resisting is difficult, and as a persuader, you should recognize that this kind of appeal can be particularly strong. In fact, most Americans believe that making contributions is a duty, even when the degree of misfortune is minimal. Many buy bonds, for example, to aid a government whose debts are sizable, even though these same people may be opposed to deficit spending.

Although appeals in this area have a great chance of success in the short run, the long-run consequences of such persuasion may not be positive. Content cues are designed to make the receiver feel sorry for someone or some group. Your appeal should offer a recommendation that says that people can exchange their sorrow for positive feelings by giving up some of their money or other resources. But the content cues you present usually amount to a demonstration that the person or group has a defect and that they should be pitied. In short, you demonstrate that the person or group is less capable than the receiver. Such messages have a dual effect. The receiver may come to perceive the handicapped as the persuader has portrayed them—as less capable and consequently as stigmatized. Worse still, the descriptions may influence the persons who have the handicap to begin to think of themselves as less capable.

Humor. Experimental studies of the effects of humor on persuasion raise questions about its efficacy in persuasion. Despite these studies, experience indicates that humor, in some instances, facilitates acceptance of a persuasive thesis. President Reagan uses humor to blunt criticism of his policies and himself. He is not alone. Effective speeches given by officials who are attacked in the press begin frequently with good-natured, sometimes pointed humor. Humor works to blunt negative attitudes and to pave the way for answers designed to change those attitudes.

In addition, humor may give the speaker a chance to make related appeals and to urge corrective action. Famous comedians seem to have considerable success in arousing audiences to laughter and then making appeals for funds to aid the unfortunate or to support the government's policies. Cartoons, satire, and other methods of poking fun at stereotypical behaviors seem to be socially acceptable and are somewhat effective means of getting people to consider changing their thinking and behavior. On the whole, providing cues that first arouse the audience to smiles or laughter works well enough to be used extensively.

The most common error of speakers who employ humor is that they concentrate on producing laughter and then misinterpret the laughter as a sign of effectiveness. Instead, speakers should concentrate upon exactly what they are trying to achieve by the use of humor. Always remember that when humor is to be used for persuasive purposes, it should be used as a means to an end.

In Chapter 20, we explain the use of humor in more detail.

Affection. Affection operates to produce protective thoughts and actions. At least three kinds of cues seem to arouse it, and, in most cases, the recommendations that follow arousal are designed to reinstate it or to intensify it. Your receivers tend to feel affection for the attractive or beautiful, for the young and helpless, and for pleasant recollections of shared experiences. Thus, you may arouse protective feelings toward the environment by describing or otherwise picturing its beauty, just as you can inspire feelings for an individual by cues designed to show his or her attractive qualities. Descriptions of kindness, the use of whimsical humor, and concern build feelings of affection. Politicians everywhere like to be seen kissing or holding babies, comforting the sick in hospitals, or joking with friends or constituents. It is hard to disagree with someone for whom you feel affection. The only caution to follow in arousing affection is to avoid becoming sickeningly sweet (cloying) or maudlin and overly sentimental. Recommendations that follow affection should provide the receiver with advice about how to think or behave protectively toward the object of the affection. If you were organizing a campaign for political office, you might help your audience remember some of the obstacles overcome in past campaigns. Following the arousal of affection through these shared memories, you might specify the difficulties likely to be encountered in the coming campaign, urging your audience to avoid becoming discouraged. If you were trying to persuade your classmates to join a group of which you are a member, you might focus on the kinds of activities the group enjoyed in the past. You would then recommend joining the group to enable your listeners to enjoy such activities in the future.

Self-esteem and Pride. An appeal to self-esteem and pride is one of the easiest for the persuader to use. And so is its opposite—lowering self-esteem or shame. Most humans are so far from perfect, and so want to achieve perfection, that anything you say or do that indicates some step toward or away from a more perfect state has significant effects upon them. Suppose you spend considerable time preparing your speech, paying particular attention to your dress and grooming before class. You meet a friend on the way to class who says, "Say, you'd really look great today if it weren't for that outfit." Your positive feelings are likely to change. Studies have shown that a speaker can produce positive feelings in an audience by expressing sincere liking for its members.[11] You can produce strong negative feelings by telling the audience you dislike them.

In using self-esteem as the predominant appeal, you may describe beliefs, attitudes, values, or behaviors of the audience of which they should be proud or ashamed. Such an approach might work if you wished to persuade a group to donate funds for a civic project. If you are in a position from which you can sincerely compliment the audience on their leadership in the community, their past concern and generosity, and their hard work on the behalf of projects, then your appeal for support may be successful. In some situations, however, it may be more effective to point to their failure to exercise leadership, their failure to work on behalf of worthwhile projects, their past indifference to the needs of the community, and their habitual penny pinching. This method might shame them into making the desired commitments.

Generally, your authors have observed that building pride and self-esteem is a most effective way to persuade. Although there are occasions in which the opposite approach is both appropriate and effective, these are comparatively rare and have to be handled with caution. The general consequences of listeners' low self-confidence are reduced performance, depression, and unwillingness to try something new and different. We recommend, therefore, that before you use lowering of self-esteem as a primary appeal, you should make sure that the situation you confront is one of the comparatively rare ones in which the lowering technique will be effective, such as when you need to eliminate over-confidence to ensure high levels of performance.

Power or the Ability to Influence or Control Others. To suggest that a persuader motivate receivers by appealing to the human desire for power may appear paradoxical in a book devoted to communication. Persuasion ends and coercion begins when the receivers' acceptance of the message becomes contingent upon the ability and willingness of the source to use rewards and punishments. Power and coercion have evil reputations. Yet the human desire to have and hold resources that other humans want or need is neither rare nor necessarily evil. In our society, the desire for what some classify as economic, political, spiritual, and technological powers is considered a legitimate and socially useful motivators.[12] Even more subtle forms of power, with names such as expert power, referent power, and legitimate power, are considered as positive, rather than negative forces if properly used.[13] Power, and the

[11]J. Mills, "Opinion Change as a Function of the Communicator's Desire to Influence and Liking for the Audience," *Journal of Experimental Social Psychology, 2*: 152-159 (1966).

[12]Carl G. Gustavson, *A Preface to History* (New York: McGraw-Hill Book Co., 1955), pp. 180-183.

[13]John R. P. French, Jr. and Bertram Raven, *Studies in Social Power,* ed. Dorwin Cartwright (Ann Arbor, Mich.: Institute for Social Research, 1959), pp. 150-167.

coercion that implements it, gained a negative reputation largely because of abuses (and its abuses are extensive and widely publicized). As Aristotle noted, "The wrongs, if any, that are done by men in power are not petty misdemeanors, but crimes on a large scale."[14] As a result of the reputation and abuses of power, appeals to gain enough of it to escape the control of others are as effective as appeals based on ways to acquire it. Power's negative reputation means that most appeals to power are called by other names. But, whenever a message motivates by providing cues about how receivers can acquire the wherewithal to control things or people, the appeal is to power—even if it is termed "financial security," "self-confidence," or "independence."

The persuader invokes the power appeal by cues that indicate that the receiver is being threatened, bribed, or otherwise manipulated by someone or some organization that controls resources the receiver wants or needs. Recommendations follow that specify the method by which the receiver can become the controller rather than the controlled. More often than not, the cues establishing the control focus upon abuses associated with the control. Typical of this appeal are messages designed to get us to vote for a candidate who promises to free us from red tape and bureaucracy, or the presentations that promise us greater control over our own lives. A strong American tradition is based on the idea that we should be free of debt and be beholden to no person. If you can demonstrate to your classmates how rules or other restrictions imposed by the institution restrain or coerce them, and how a change in rules will free them, then you can probably get most of them to vote for the change or sign the petition urging it. If you can show your classmates how taking certain classes or acquiring certain skills will enable them to exercise greater control over others (perhaps by leading to higher-level positions in their chosen occupations), then it is likely that they may decide to take those classes or acquire those skills. Finally, we note that it is probably unfortunate that power has acquired an evil reputation. That reputation leads us to look for ways of discussing use of power and coercion in pleasant-sounding, disguised terminology. As a result, though we often threaten and promise to gain compliance from others, we pretend that we are doing something else and thus fail to see clearly the implications of what we are doing.

Contemporaneity. Most of us set for ourselves several long-term goals, such as marriage and raising a family, achieving certain levels of income or prestige in our work, obtaining the means to engage in our favorite kinds of recreation, and so on. Despite these long-term goals, we also value involvement in today's world. Even though giving up a weekly movie for a year would enable us to save a sum that could be

[14]Aristotle, *The Rhetoric of Aristotle,* trans. Lane Cooper (New York: Appleton-Century-Crofts, 1932), p. 140.

considerable (after it had earned interest for the next fifteen years), we prefer to keep up with the movies rather than save the money. We want to be knowledgeable about contemporary trends in fashion, politics, or social problems. Consequently, one basis for changing ideas or behavior is to link the change to the appeal to be contemporary. If you wish to persuade a friend to update his or her wardrobe, you may point to advertisements and articles in magazines to demonstrate how far out-of-date the friend has become. This appeal is frequently used by our national leaders to get us to support development of what are currently called "new weapons systems." The technical and military reasons for weapons improvements are seldom clearly presented to the public. Instead, modernness or the importance of currency are emphasized, and we generally yield to such appeals without being aware of why the weapons system is an improvement over previous systems. Advertisers frequently use similar tactics, calling their products "new" or "improved." Great drama still surrounds the introduction of new automobile models each year. There is a large variety of topics for which you can present cues showing that thinking or behavior is out-of-date and that a change is necessary. With many people, such appeals are highly effective. However, there is one caution to keep in mind when using an appeal to contemporaneity: it is not enough to show that something is simply new. The basis of the appeal should be that there is a better way of thinking or behaving, not just a new way.

Summary

1. Changing thoughts and behaviors involves getting a *receiver* to reach a *decision* to make the change.
2. Adjusting to receivers is the job of the persuader.
3. Express the effect you desire as precisely as possible to achieve the greatest persuasive effect.
4. Motivation is defined as arousing and directing behavior.
5. Effective persuasion is achieved by arousing motivation through content cues that specify feelings and that advise ways of dealing with those feelings.
6. Persuasion is most likely to occur when there is a balance between motivational arousal and the recommendations for how the receiver is to deal with that arousal.
7. When imbalance between arousal and recommendation occurs, receivers may become angry with the speaker. They may fail to pay attention to the remainder of the message or may decide that the message does not apply to them.

8. In most persuasive situations, the speaker should appeal to the following: (1) the desire to make rational choices based on sound information, (2) fear and anxiety, (3) anger or frustration of goals or desires, (4) success and achievement, (5) pity, (6) humor, (7) affection, (8) self-esteem and pride, (9) power or the ability to influence or control others, and (10) contemporaneity.

Questions and Exercises

1. Interview a few friends about the significant changes in their thinking or behavior that resulted from persuasion. What led them to reach a decision to change their minds or behavior? Be prepared to describe briefly to the class how each of these examples of persuasion worked.
2. With a small group of classmates, discuss the advertisements that you think are most effective in the magazines you read, the newspapers you read, and on television. Are there noticeable differences in the nature of the advertisements that appeal to you in each of those cases? Why do you think these differences exist?
3. Watch television for a limited period of time, such as 30 minutes or one hour. How many attempts at persuasion take place during the commercials? Describe a person who was persuaded by appeals presented during the time you watched. Do the appeals cause you to become interested in products that you might actually purchase? Are college students and their needs largely ignored in television advertising? If this is so, why do you think it is so?
4. Consider the list of appeals given in this chapter while you look through a copy of your favorite magazine. Try to identify the appeals used in each of the major advertisements in the front of the magazine. Do the same thing with those that appear in the back of the magazine. Are there differences in the appeals used in the front and toward the end? If there are, why do you suppose these differences exist?
5. Review the advertisements that you took note of for Question 4. Do any of them use appeals that are not among the ten listed in this text? Which are they?
6. Find a brief, persuasive speech and write a criticism of it, paying attention to the way in which it arouses informational or other needs and the way in which it provides recommendations that enable the individual to deal successfully with the needs aroused.
7. With friends or classmates, compile a list of the issues in which humor has been influential in helping you to accept some idea or try some behavior. On the basis of the list you generate, be prepared either to defend or to reject the thesis that "humor is ineffective in persuasion."

8. Repeat the procedures of Question 7, applying them to each of the other appeals mentioned in this chapter. The appeals can be divided up among your classmates. The people in the class assigned to each appeal should be prepared to report on what they have found. In the end, you may wish to decide which kinds of appeals are most effective, least effective, most frequently used, and least frequently used.

John Duricka, Associated Press

17

The Forms of Persuasive Speaking

OBJECTIVES

By the time you finish reading this chapter, you should be able to:

1. Identify three kinds of persuasive speeches.
2. Recognize controversial topics and know how to express them as convincing, stimulating, and actuating theses.
3. Analyze the topic you have selected in terms of identifying audience needs, making those needs pressing and important to your listeners, and producing recommendations for audiences consistent with convincing or stimulating or actuating.
4. Name the specific requirements you will need to fulfill in order to give successful persuasive speeches.

This chapter deals with the preparation of the three basic kinds of persuasive speeches: the speech to convince, the speech to stimulate or inspire, and the speech to actuate. Persuasive speeches modify thoughts and behaviors; therefore, these speeches must commence with a topic that is, in some respect, controversial. The controversy may be immediate (as in the speech to convince and the speech to actuate), or it may be anticipated (as in the case of the speech to stimulate). The nature of the controversy in speeches to convince and actuate must be such as can lead to changes in receivers' current thinking. This chapter begins with a discussion of how to discover controversial topics suitable for the various forms of persuasive speeches; this is followed by a description of the general nature of each form. The chapter concludes with specific advice about preparing and presenting each type of speech.

Selecting a Controversial Topic

When selecting a topic for a speech, you will want to begin with an inductive review of your own experience. For speeches that convince and speeches that actuate, your review would focus on a list of the topics you argue about, or would potentially argue about, with your friends, family, or classmates. For the speeches that stimulate and reinforce, your review would focus on a list of topics you would like to use to produce more intense feelings among these same people. These are topics about which you and your audience agree, but about which you think they should be more concerned.

Public-speaking students report that they spend more time searching for topics than on any other speech-preparation activity. Help is available if your inductive search of possible topics fails to produce a suitably controversial theme. Records are kept on controversial matters, and catalogs exist that list the principal pro and con arguments surrounding these matters. You may be able to find a number of such books, both old and new, in your library. If you make a comparison, you will notice striking similarities between the controversial issues in the old and new books. Table 17-1 presents a list of controversial subjects based on an examination made by your authors of just such sources.[1] It suggests at least forty-two controversial topics. To see how controversial topics might begin to be translated into persuasive speeches, study Table 17-2. Five topics have been broken down into representative pro and con theses for possible speeches to convince, stimulate, and actuate. Not all topics, of course, lend themselves readily to all three kinds of persuasive speeches.

TABLE 17-1   Controversial Topic Areas

1. Advertising	22. Examinations
2. Alcohol Use	23. Farm Subsidies
3. Animal Rights	24. Federal Grants
4. Armaments	25. Foreign Languages
5. Athletics	26. Gambling
6. Automobiles	27. Government
7. Birth Control	28. Gun Control
8. Broadcasting	29. Homosexuality
9. Capital Punishment	30. Inheritance Taxes
10. Censorship	31. Intelligence Tests
11. Churches	32. Judges and Juries
12. Civil Disobedience	33. Medical Costs
13. Congress	34. Minimum Wage
14. Criminal Sentencing	35. Minority Rights
15. Cults	36. Newspaper and Magazine Reporters
16. Divorce	37. Nuclear Weapons
17. Education	38. Private vs. Public Schools
18. Emigration	39. Public Lands
19. Employee Rights	40. Social Programs
20. ERA	41. Sterilization
21. Euthanasia	42. Tax Laws

[1]A useful source of such information is Anne Robinson, *Pros and Cons: A Newspaper-Reader's and Debater's Guide to the Leading Controversies of the Day* (London: Routledge & Kegan Paul Ltd., 1977).

TABLE 17-2   Topics and Possible Thesis Sentences

Armaments

Pro Theses:

Convincing: America should produce and deploy the M-X missile.

Stimulation: Burial in Arlington cemetery is the highest honor for the American soldier.

Actuation: Students who oppose cuts in military spending must write their Congressperson today.

Con Theses:

Convincing: Americans should refuse to produce further offensive weapons systems.

Stimulation: The Vietnam Memorial symbolizes a mistake America must avoid repeating.

Actuation: Students who oppose the use of space for military weapons deployment (Star Wars) should call the White House Comments Office.

Censorship

Pro Theses:

Convincing: Federal legislation should prohibit violence in programming directed at children under 12 years of age.

Stimulation: True romance blossomed in the strictly censored early movies.

Actuation: Sign my letter protesting R- and X-rated movies that exploit women.

Con Theses:

Convincing: Laws that interfere with freedom of expression should be repealed.

Stimulation: The cuts in movies made by TV network censors are ludicrous.

Actuation: Sign my letter to the Chief of Police protesting his or her policy of confiscating X-rated movies.

Education

Pro Theses:

Convincing: The Federal Government should set and enforce funding standards for public schools in the United States.

Stimulation: School days are happy days.

Actuation: Write the Superintendent of Public Instruction protesting corporal punishment in the schools.

Con Theses:

Convincing: No college should admit students who were in the bottom half of their high school class.

Stimulation: Poor teachers are the best preparation for the "real world."

Actuation: Sign this petition urging the faculty to impose mandatory and uniform student evaluation of our instructors.

Gambling

Pro Theses:

Convincing: This state should legalize gambling.

Stimulation: Las Vegas is the fun capital of the world.

Actuation: Write your state representative, urging him or her to support legalization of gambling in private social organizations.

Con Theses:

Convincing: The Federal Government should prohibit state-sponsored lotteries.

Stimulation: Gambling is our society's chief moral problem.

Actuation: Sign this pledge refusing to participate in or support gambling.

Table 17-2 *(continued)*

Tax Laws

Pro Theses:	Con Theses:
Convincing: Federal taxes should be set at levels sufficiently high to prevent federal deficits.	*Convincing:* The United States should Constitutionally prohibit taxes that, in aggregate, lead to a tax rate above 25 percent of an individual's earned income.
Stimulation: Taxes are the price we pay for America.	*Stimulation:* Americans should be angry about taxes.
Actuation: Give your parents this brochure explaining why they should support the upcoming tax bill for funding higher education in this state.	*Actuation:* Join me in petitioning our Congressperson to abolish taxes on student wages.

The Speech to Convince

The speech to convince begins with a thesis that contradicts the viewpoint likely to be held by many or most of the members of the audience. It argues that evidence and reasoning support the opposing thesis and urges the audience to change their thinking or behavior because of the strength of that evidence and reasoning. If most of your classmates felt that an all-volunteer army provided effectively for national defense, a speech to convince might support the contrary thesis, that the volunteer defense force should be replaced by a force composed of 50 percent draftees. You might argue that the intellectual and moral quality of the volunteers is low; that efforts to adapt modern technology to the abilities of the volunteers is costly; and that the level of readiness to fight of such a force is hard to maintain. You could also argue that the intellectual and moral qualities of draftees would be higher than that of the volunteers and that the draft would consequently reduce costs and enhance the force's readiness to fight. If your arguments were supported by appropriate facts, opinions, and statistics, and if your evidence were tied together by cogent reasoning, then your receivers might decide that reinstituting the draft to staff our military forces is a wise idea.

The Speech to Stimulate or Inspire

The nature of the speech to inspire or stimulate is clearly expressed by Sarett, Foster, and Sarett in their classic text. They point out that such speeches are given when "the need is for inspiration, for intuitive insight, for strengthened loyalties, heightened devotion to ideals, pleasure and the relaxation of tensions, or strengthened bonds of human fellowship."[2] The thesis of a speech to stimulate or inspire calls for the audience to intensify their existing feelings about some matter. Two kinds of topics are commonly chosen. First, an individual whom the audience accepts as hero or villain may be selected as the subject. The speech might praise a national leader or Olympic athlete, or it might attack a historical figure such as Adolph Hitler or Joseph Stalin. Second, the speech to stimulate or inspire may attempt to intensify feelings about some attitude or value. Frequently, people who give sermons choose these kinds of topics. The people attending the service already accept the basic values of their church, and the sermon attempts to motivate the audience toward more enthusiastic acceptance of those values.

Supporting materials selected for the speech to inspire or stimulate should be chosen for their value in helping the audience envision your ideas. If you can select illustrations, examples, or even statistics that contain elements to lead your receivers to repeat those supporting materials to one another and to others, you will have achieved your goal of stimulating. The process underlying the selection of such materials has been studied systematically by scholars such as Ernest G. Bormann and his associates.[3] The essential features of this process center around receiver thinking called *fantasy themes* and *rhetorical visions*. When you were younger, you may have attended a movie or watched a regular television program, and as a result you might have assumed the role of your favorite character. You may have put on a cape made of a bath or dish towel (if the hero or heroine wore a cape) and may have tried to act like that character. These acts constituted your fantasy theme. And if you and your friends organized a play or little drama that continued for several days, in which each of you portrayed roles from the movie or program, you were involved in a rhetorical vision. Adults sometimes become involved in a message in a similar way. They see or imagine themselves involved in new and different ways that nevertheless are consistent with their personality. As people discuss a speech or event, they interpret what has occurred in a manner that redefines roles in the group. In recent times, the most notable example of such an event occurred in the months after John F. Kennedy's inaugural address. People quoted that address and began to play roles consistent with their own fantasies and their friends' visions about the somehow "changed" nature of the world. Those who are interested in exploring the matter further will discover a thorough analysis of it in José Ortega y Gasset's (1833-1955) *Revolt of the Masses*.[4]

[2]Lew Sarett, William T. Foster, and Alma Johnson Sarett, *Basic Principles of Speech,* 3rd ed. (Boston: Houghton Mifflin Company, 1958), p. 482.

[3]Ernest G. Bormann, "Fantasy and Rhetorical Vision: The Rhetorical Criticism of Social Reality," *Quarterly Journal of Speech, 58*(4): 396-407 (1972).

[4]José Ortega y Gasset, *The Revolt of the Masses* (New York: W. W. Norton and Co., 1932), p. 204.

The Speech to Actuate

The speech to convince aims at gaining intellectual acceptance of the thesis. The speech to inspire aims at heightening existing feelings. But a speech designed to produce action goes beyond intellectual acceptance and heightened feeling; it aims at an overt response. There are three basic requirements for a speech that aims to activate. First, the thesis must be controversial, but controversial in a different way than in the speech to convince. The thesis that calls for action opposes the audience's tendency to do nothing about the matter at hand. If the audience favors the intellectual position that supports the action, the task of the speaker is comparatively easy. However, if the audience opposes the intellectual position that supports the action, the task of the speaker is difficult. The key element remains, however—the thesis requires the audience to act.

Second, moving people to act usually requires that the speech be demonstrably more compelling than in the case of the speech to convince. To move people to act, the speaker often must select the appeal that has the strongest motivational properties available consistent with the thesis. For example, you may wish to emphasize pity if you aim to get the audience to pledge money to relieve hunger in a developing nation facing famine. You may wish to describe the ravages of disease due to lapsed immunizations if your object is to get the audience to sign up for injections at the campus health service.

Third, you want to select an action that the audience can perform with comparatively little effort. Generally, in both the classroom and the outside world, these types of speeches lead to such actions as signing petitions, making pledges, signing up for appointments, trying a sample of a product or a food, signing up for a demonstration of the product, signing up to receive more information about an issue, or such specifics as filling out a voter registration form, purchasing a ticket for a play or athletic contest, or wearing a campaign button.

On occasion in the classroom, and frequently in the outside world, the clearest example of the speech to move to action is the sales pitch. When sales pitches are given by one or a few individuals to many, it is almost always the case that they are given in controlled situations. It is possible to provide a generic description of such a speech. Some of the elements can be adapted to the classroom situation. In the generic situation, the audience is gathered together by means that ensure that a large number of people attend. For revival meetings, for example, great efforts are made through personal contact to assure the appearance of a crowd. Real estate developers offer free trips to development sites, and department stores may send invitations to certain customers for fashion shows. By one means or another, a crowd is gathered. The persuasive event usually takes place in surroundings that flatter the individuals who are invited. The well-known auditorium or stadium is featured in revival meetings, the most prestigious motel (or one that sounds as if it is prestigious) is used for the development presentation, a carefully appointed ballroom is made available for the fashion show. Even humbler gathering places such as tents are usually well decorated. The sizable audience is then packed into the available space. Closeness to others causes people to do what others in the group are doing. This tendency to follow the crowd is increased when the size and closeness of the group are increased. Many times, shills will be planted to get a desired response started. They may applaud on cue, or rise at appropriate times, or sing loudly and clearly. They may ask leading questions, and they certainly will be the first to sign up for the property or to make the purchase of the new gown. Finally, the event will almost always involve having the group do something together, whether it be singing, turning to the people nearby to make introductions, or drinking and eating together. The persuasive presentation often involves a variety of activities other than speaking. If the persuaders can afford it, a movie or tape that supports the endeavor will be presented, often featuring a prestigious source. Testimonials by "folks just like yourselves" will also be featured. The formal sales pitch itself comes only after the listeners have been stimulated by the group and the entertaining activities. At that point, the audience may be tired by the length of the event. It is common for the pitch to take place in the late afternoon of a long day or in mid-evening of a tiring day.

Preparing and Giving the Persuasive Speech _____

The model of persuasion explained in Chapter 16 serves as the guide for the practical matters of preparing and giving the speech to convince, the speech to stimulate or inspire, and the speech to actuate. The discussion of preparation in our current chapter is divided into (1) identifying the needs of the receiver as the basis for appeal, (2) making the information presented pressing and important for receivers, and (3) making appropriate recommendations for action. These sections are followed by a checklist that identifies the information and thinking that the persuader should complete in order to ensure a successful presentation. An example of a speech or description of speeches concludes each section.

Preparing the Speech to Convince

The aim of the speech to convince is to get the audience to accept the thesis and supporting arguments as their own. The specific goal will depend upon the topic. Keep in mind that you are trying to get receivers to decide to give up their current way of thinking about your topic and to accept the position that you advocate. You may wish for the audience to master your thesis and its major supporting arguments. You may even want them to repeat certain evidence you cite when they discuss the topic with friends at some later time.

Identifying Receiver Needs. The major need of the receivers in the speech to convince is the desire to make rational choices based on sound information. It is in the speech to convince that the advice given in Chapters 10 and 11 should be followed most carefully. Not only should you use evidence and reasoning as the primary reasons for accepting your thesis, but as the chapter titles indicate, you also want effective use of that evidence and reasoning. This means that you will take care to make your use of evidence and reasoning explicit for the audience. If your speech is based on causal reasoning and factual evidence, then you will highlight demonstrations that your reasoning meets the appropriate tests of causal reasoning and the appropriate tests of factual evidence.

While your appeal will be based on the needs to make rational choices, you may make use of additional motivational appeals as well. Most worthwhile topics for convincing speeches offer the opportunity for such appeals. A young man in a public-speaking class presented an excellent convincing speech designed to get the audience to set aside stereotypes they held of student athletes. The speech used humor, affection, and a small amount of pity to supplement the major appeal based upon facts about athletes' grade points, selection of major areas of study, career success not directly related to athletic achievement, and how these things were accomplished in spite of compressed study time due to practice schedules.

Incorporating Pressing and Important Information. An effective speech to convince leaves little doubt in the mind of the audience as to why they need to change their thinking about the matter at hand. It focuses upon reasons why the change requested is pressing. Convincing people that mandatory seatbelt laws should be enacted might be done by citing gross annual traffic death and injury statistics for the nation as a whole. It will be more convincing, however, if you are able to break the statistics down and identify the number of students in your institution or your class who are likely to be injured in the next months. So it is with the best speeches to convince. The speaker selects materials that indicate to receivers why the problem bears directly on them, their loved ones, their positions, or the institutions and ideas they hold dear.

Making Recommendations. Throughout this book, we have stressed the importance of being as specific as possible in almost all public speeches. The recommendations for the speech to convince suggest the alterations in thought that are necessary for achieving a rational approach to a problem. In the speech to convince, this means that the audience must know basic facts and must be able to repeat basic arguments. In short, a set of recommendations in a speech to convince gives the audience the wherewithal to defend the position you would have them adopt. A recommendation like "There are three key facts to remember," followed by a reiteration of the facts, is the kind of recommendation you should make. So is "There are three steps that led to this conclusion that I hope you will remember," followed by a restatement of those steps. Finally, in many speeches to convince, the recommendations will include information about how to answer or refute those who advocate other positions. For example, you might say, "The chief arguments from the other side on this issue are. . . ." You would then arm your audience with ways to counter these alternate views.

Giving the Speech to Convince. This checklist should enable you to review the major qualities of an effective speech to convince:

1. Is your topic controversial? Will your presentation convince the members of the audience to alter their ways of thinking?
2. Have you found more evidence than you will be able to use? If not, get more. If you do, then select the evidence that will be most convincing to the audience.
3. Are you able to construct a Toulmin diagram of your overall reasoning? (See p. 160.) Are you able to tell whether you employ cause, sign, analogy, or example reasoning? Are you able to show that your argument meets the tests of that form of reasoning?
4. Do you have materials that take advantage of other motivational appeals besides the desire to make rational decisions? Will those materials make the audience want to accept your evidence and reasoning?
5. Do you have materials to show the audience why it is important or pressing that they change their thinking *now*, instead of weeks or months from now?
6. Have you paid particular attention to transitions and summaries, so that your reasoning will be abundantly clear and easy for the audience to follow?
7. Have you thought of possible rebuttals the audience might raise while you are speaking? Do you have answers?
8. Do you have clear recommendations for the audience to follow?

An Example Speech to Convince. This speech is a slightly edited version of an effective speech to convince given by a college student. Most of the speaker's materials come from two scholarly sources and her analysis of one novel. The sources are the following: (1) Erich Segal, *Love Story* (New York: Harper and Row, 1970); (2) Frank D. Cox, *American Mariage: A Changing Scene* (Dubuque, Iowa: Wm. C. Brown Company, 1976); and (3) Paul C. Glick, *American Families* (New York: John Wiley and Sons, 1957).

Postpone Marriage

Two adolescents fall hopelessly in love. They battle their parents' disapproval and marry anyway. Romeo and Juliet, we know, have a love that will last forever. In the book *Love Story,* Jenny and Oliver marry while they're still in school and they remain in love throughout their marriage. Youthful marriages may work in movies, but they rarely have a happy ending in real life. How many of you have boy friends and girl friends? I bet you fantasize about what marrying that person would be like. Not to say you're going out to buy the ring tomorrow, but I bet you've thought about it.

Today, I'm going to give you some good reasons why you should wait until later to get married. I'll show you some ominous statistics of divorce rates among young couples. I'll show you the pressures that cause the frequent splits, the burdens that are involved, and then I'll wrap it up with some reasons why kids get married early.

Here's a graph taken from a book on the breakdown of marriages. [Refers to a graph drawn on a large sheet of paper that gives age brackets of first marriage on the horizontal axis and percentages of remarriage on the vertical axis.] It reports the results of a study done on marriages during the 1940s and 1950s. You may say this isn't an illustration of our time and that it isn't appropriate and doesn't apply to you. But if you'll remember how rare and socially unacceptable divorce was back then, and compare it to these statistics, then you'll realize it's pretty startling and it's a forewarning of what our statistics will be like. Down at the bottom it shows the age of the bride when she first married. [Points to the horizontal axis on the graph.] The brackets are 14-17, 18-19, 20-21, 22-24, 25-29, 30 and above. Over on the left, you have the percentage that were remarried by 1954. [Points to the vertical axis on the graph.] The line representing women who were married in 1945 shows a consistently low divorce rate until you come to the brackets representing women who married before 20; then it rises from 20 percent to well above 20 percent. The line for those married in 1949 looks the same. It is slightly elevated, though it rises abruptly to above 30 percent when the 20-21 age bracket is reached. In the 1951 marriages, the rate was 40 percent overall, with a tremendous rate for those under 20.

In this second chart, the bride's age is plotted against the number of couples parted after five years. Of 50 couples married before 19, 26 percent were divorced, while of 89 couples in the 20-24 year age bracket, only 6.8 percent were divorced.

The book *American Marriage: A Changing Scene* says that every study and statistic of the past 30 years shows that age is definitely associated with the success or failure of a marriage, with the critical cutoff point being about 19.

Youthful marriages usually fail because there are so many pressures put on the kids. If the couple isn't mature because of age or lack of development, they're going to have an even tougher time facing problems. Maturity includes the physical, social, emotional, and spiritual aspects of human growth. One authority says that early marriages involve people who have met the requirements for sex and reproduction. However, these requirements are not enough to sustain the marriage through the early trials. The wider significance of marriage needs emotional maturity to develop.

Also, those who marry early miss out on a lot of experience dealing with other people. They don't have the chance to make mistakes with previous boy friends or girl friends, because they are automatically thrown into the big leagues. Few couples escape the feeling that they're missing out. They sometimes feel a bitter resentment and eventually blame their spouse for trapping them. These pressures are increased tenfold when the couple starts out with a child. If the kids are married while still in college, they face a lot of financial burdens. The parents cut off all the money, which includes the tuition. The fund cutoff means that they have to go out and get a job, study, go to classes, and give attention to their spouse. Even if they marry right out of college, they still have to look for a job and pay rent and other expenses. The book *American Families* says that the inexperience and emotional instability that characterize these situations are often made worse by housing and economic difficulties. And this is a time when earnings are small and initial expenses are heavy. And the combination of emotional immaturity and financial and housing difficulties often proves to be overwhelming for young couples.

Why do people marry young? A lot of times, it's to escape an unhappy situation and to find a substitute security, or the union could be visualized as deliverance from a personal problem that seemed insurmountable. The people need closeness, companionship, security, or support, or they need to escape from an intolerable home situation. But these things are exactly what makes the couple unprepared to deal with the pressures of marriage.

Now that you've seen the odds young couples are up against, I hope you'll remember a few things. When couples are dating, similarities are usually stressed and their differences are pushed into the background. But after a few months, the differences surface and have to be faced. And also everyone is more patient and loving and caring when they are secure with themselves and with their environment. I hope from my speech you realize the odds that you're up against and weigh the pros and cons. One study indicates that the portion of remarried women among those who were married before 20 is three times as high as those between 22 and 24.

The things I've mentioned in my speech—statistics, immaturity, emotional and financial burdens—should give you reason enough to wait until you're older to get married. Don't become just another divorce statistic.

Preparing and Giving the Speech to Stimulate or Inspire _____

Preparing the Speech to Stimulate or Inspire

The general goal of the speech to stimulate or inspire is to get the audience to increase the intensity of their thinking or behavior. Keep in mind that in this type of speech the audience already agrees with your thesis in the abstract. Your job is to convert that abstract agreement into an agreement that is more intense and concrete.

Identifying Receiver Needs. As you analyze your audience to discover areas in which you may inspire them, you will want to learn exactly what need their current beliefs fulfill. Do they think that a former President you are about to praise was great? What does that belief accomplish for them? Do they hold a particular opinion about this President because it enhances their self-esteem? Do they believe it because the President was an underdog and because they pity underdogs? Is discovering that this President was really a good one a contemporary or fashionable thing to do? If you want to inspire your classmates to have a greater degree of school spirit, how can you determine the meaning of school spirit for them? Does it help to enhance their pride in their institution and consequently in their own accomplishments? Does it lead them to fulfill their desires for success and achievement? If you are to succeed in stimulating or inspiring, you must discover why members of your audience hold that current position. Only then can you develop your speech around the need or needs that led to that belief.

Incorporating Pressing and Important Information. The chief means of making the needs pressing and important in the speech to stimulate is through the use of vivid language. Each of us varies in our ability to use language that is vivid and poetic, but each of us has the ability to move toward vividness and the poetic. Fortunately, in most situations a move in that direction is all that is necessary. If our language and delivery are more intense than normal, then those familiar with our habitual language and delivery will recognize that our subject is more pressing and important than usual. Assuming that what we say makes sense, the audience will respond appropriately.

Making Recommendations. As with the speech to convince, the recommendations to the audience in the speech to inspire or stimulate dwell on what you wish the audience to do. The listeners should, however, focus on the thoughts and information that will reproduce the strengthened feelings aroused by your speech. After you have inspired the audience with stories of the courage and decisiveness of a great president or athlete, your recommendations should suggest to the audience situations they might face themselves in which the stories would be relevant and should be recalled. You would go on to explain how their recollection would help them imitate the president or an athlete so that they would have the courage or decisiveness to deal effectively with their own problems.

Giving the Speech to Stimulate or Inspire

This checklist should enable you to review the major qualities of an effective speech to stimulate or inspire.

1. Have you selected a topic and a viewpoint with which your audience agrees but for which the agreement is weak or unenthusiastic?
2. Have you analyzed your receivers to determine how their current opinions meet their personal needs?
3. Have you discovered the important evidence and reasoning that will serve as a sound basis for increased strength in the receivers' commitment to their position?
4. Have you taken pains to work on the phrasing of your main points and other ideas that you want the audience to think about and remember? Are the phrasing and language you have selected more vivid and elevated than the language you usually use in your speeches?
5. Have you taken pains to demonstrate to the audience how they will benefit from the increased enthusiasm you have helped them experience about this topic?
6. Have you made your overall organization climactic? Does the speech build to a big finish?
7. Have you rehearsed enough to ensure a smoother-than-usual presentation?

An Example Speech to Stimulate. Recently a young woman gave a speech to her public-speaking class on the topic of increasing positive thinking in order to increase personal happiness. For most of her classmates, the speech asked for only an intensification of their existing beliefs and attitudes. For this group of classmates, the speech was certainly stimulating or inspirational. The speech that follows has been edited, but for the most part it reflects a good student speech.

Positive Thinking

This is the kind of day it would be easy to be depressed. It is raining and dreary. It's near the end of the quarter and we all have papers to do in our classes. Final examinations are coming up, and most of us will soon be going home. Home is always great for a few days, but you know after that your parents will stop treating you like a guest and start trying to turn you into an adult by treating you like their child again. Thoughts like the ones I've just expressed demonstrate that with little or no effort, you can develop thoughts that will make you feel bad and depressed. If you dwell on those thoughts, you will generate other negative thoughts and with little effort you can make yourself unhappy and depressed for the rest of today and for the rest of the week.

Notice what I said, however. I pointed out that you are the one who is responsible for developing these negative thoughts. Today I want to urge you to do the opposite. I want you to make greater efforts to enjoy your life through thinking positive thoughts.

I know that changing negative thoughts to positive sounds too simple and easy. After all, the weather really is depressing, isn't it? The papers you still have to do for your classes are lots of work and usually no fun to write. Examinations are no fun either. Just changing the words or the ways in which we describe negative things doesn't change them, does it? If you decide to call something that's really depressing by a different name, that's just double talk, like calling child abusers strict disciplinarians. But positive thinking does mean changing names and descriptions for many events. We all want to be happier, and positive thinking enables us to be happier. It cannot turn real problems into joyous events. It can, however, prevent us from turning minor problems and setbacks into big problems.

Let me begin by pointing to Snoopy in the Peanuts cartoons as an example of positive thinking. The reason we all like Snoopy so much is his ability to deal with the world in a positive manner. His fantasies that convert his doghouse into a Sopwith Camel for a bout with the Red Baron illustrate how the boredom of the kennel can be transformed into a world of fun and frolic. Inattention by his master can lead him to become a star of the hockey rink or the scourge of the tennis courts. If we think about it, when it comes to people, we like people with those same characteristics— the ability to interpret the mundane and unpleasant in a positive manner.

Contrast the positive approach with the way in which people go about making themselves and others around them unhappy. Many negative thoughts grow out of fallacious thinking. A primary source of negative thinking comes from fallacious ideas many people our age have about the world. Perhaps you have some of them yourselves. J. D. Maurath and R. P. Larsen, clinical psychologists at Ohio University and the University of Illinois, respectively, enumerate those ideas in their guide to dealing with the stress which college students frequently feel.[1]

Would you like it if everyone liked you? When another person makes a negative remark about you, do you feel bad about it and start trying to figure out what you have done wrong or what's wrong with them? Wanting

---

[1]Jerry D. Maurath and R. P. Larsen, "A Self-help Method for Dealing with the Stresses in Living," mimeographed (Athens, Ohio: Counseling and Psychological Services, Ohio University, 1980), pp. 1-6.

everyone to like us is an example of an irrational belief held by many people in our age group. Individuals get upset when they find that someone does not like or approve of them. Maurath and Larsen point out that you will almost always find people who don't like you or approve of you. It is irrational to expect that everyone will find you likable and/or lovable.

Do you believe that most of your unhappiness results from things beyond your control? Do you believe there is little you can do about those forces? Certainly, it is the professor who schedules the examination who is responsible for you worrying about it, isn't it? "No!" say Maurath and Larsen. It is not easy to get into a good mood about a test, but it can be done, and it is you who put yourself in a bad mood, not the professor.

Do you believe that nuclear war or other dangerous things are things everyone should be concerned about? Do you spend much of your time worrying about catastrophic events? Again, the answer is "No!" As terrible as it is, anxiety and worry about nuclear war or other terrible events does not help us discover ways to prevent disaster; it only makes us too fearful to view the threat objectively and thereby creates a situation in which we most certainly will be unable to find a sensible solution.

Do you believe that most of the problems you have and most of your friends' problems have an ideal solution if only you and they could find it? Are you also convinced that unless you find this ideal or perfect solution, the problem is likely to develop into a devastating tragedy? Again, say Maurath and Larsen, you have an irrational belief. Human problems, unlike math problems, do not have perfect solutions. The best you can obtain is a more or less reasonable solution from the list of available alternatives.

I hope you are getting the idea of what I am saying about positive thinking. Many of our negative ways of thinking and many of our beliefs about our problems are errors in logic or rationality. Reworking those thoughts or errors into a positive mold is exactly the way to have a happier life. According to Dr. Aaron T. Beck and Ruth L. Greenberg of the Institute for Rational-Emotive Therapy, when you feel negative or depressed, these are the kinds of things most people do.[2] They automatically generate unreasonable negative thoughts. Though the thoughts appear plausible, according to Beck and Greenberg, they serve no useful purpose. They go on to add that if you are not careful, these thoughts will lead you to interpret almost everything that happens to you as negative. If you stop for a moment and look at what you are thinking about events, you will discover exaggeration and overgeneralization and that you are ignoring positive aspects that do exist. For example, if your professor announces a quiz in class that you've forgotten to study for, you may think an exaggerated thought like "I'm finished in this class." You may go on to overgeneralize, "If I flunk this class, it will pretty well finish my academic career." You've all had thoughts like that in this kind of situation. You also are ignoring the positive fact that the quiz is only a quiz, and that it will count little in determining the grade you get in class and will probably not count at all in determining whether your college years are a success or failure.

[2]Aaron T. Beck and Ruth L. Greenberg, "Coping with Depression," pamphlet (New York: Institute for Rational-Emotive Therapy, 1974), pp. 3-4.

Beck and Greenberg describe this process through a simple three-part formula: (1) an event occurs, (2) you interpret the event in your own thoughts, and those thoughts generate (3) your feelings. It is the thoughts you have about the event that usually determine your feelings about it. More often than not, regardless of the cause of the event, the event is over. It is your thoughts and interpretations of that event that create any problems that occur. Thus, if their formula is right, you should be able to control your negative feelings by controlling your thoughts about the event.

I find the meaning of what I've just explained to you to be one of the most exciting ideas I've ever found. It means that if you or I watch what we think about events, then we can, by controlling our thoughts, control our feelings. There are some who carry this idea to extremes. Just because I can decide that an unexpected quiz has enough positive aspects that I don't have to spoil my whole day because I messed up by forgetting the quiz—just because I can decide to view that positively doesn't mean that I have to try to view a serious injury to a friend as a positive event. That would be foolish. Most of our day, however, events that happen that involve us become positive or negative largely because of what we think about them. That's why I'm trying to inspire you to think and act positively.

What advantages can we all expect if we make greater efforts to turn events that happen to us into positive experiences? There is the advantage that each of us will get ourselves and there is the advantage we will provide to other people. Let me talk first about the advantage that we will get ourselves. I've already pointed out what happens when you interpret things negatively—how that makes you depressed and unhappy. The opposite occurs when you are positive—you feel happier and enjoy your life and world more. Increased happiness is the result of positive thinking. Is there a limit to how far this can go? Yes, there is. Even though we like Snoopy's fantasies, it is probably unwise to go that far in being positive— at least you shouldn't do that much pretending very often. But most people need not worry about going too far. Try to pick one event every hour to interpret positively, and I think you'll be surprised both at how your days improve and how much discipline it takes to interpret one event positively each hour. (When you realize how much you have to work to think positively, you will have a clue to how much negative thinking you are probably doing.)

The second advantage of being positive is the effect that will have on other people we care about and who care about us. When you are negative about a lot of things, then even if you don't express it verbally, your non-verbal cues give you away, and everyone around you is uncomfortable because you are unhappy. They frequently think that they have done something to upset and the result is that your unhappiness is contagious for those around you. Each of us knows at least one person, a friend or relative, who can throw a wet blanket on good times almost, so it seems, without trying. Keep in mind that you are that person in many cases and that if you were more positive, then that positiveness is just as contagious. Other people begin to feel good when you are around and look forward to seeing you. Your positiveness makes them more positive, and before long you and your friends discover that good times are the rule, not the exception.

To end this speech, I want to tell you how far some people who are wise think that positive thinking can go. If I've done a good job, you know why you like Snoopy, and you know some fallacies in your thinking that may create unhappiness for you. You also know that it is your thoughts about events and not the events themselves that produce your feelings, and you know what to do about it. You know that if you become more positive that you will begin to enjoy life more—that you'll be happier. You also know that those around you will be happier and that will in turn help you be even more positive. What is the upper limit on positive thinking? Listen to this quotation from Leo Buscaglia's best-selling book, *Love*.[3] He says, on pages 18 and 19, that psychologists like Rogers, Maslow, and Herbert Otto, are saying, "We could have the ability to feel color! We could have the ability to see better than an eagle, the ability to smell better than a bird dog, and a mind that could be so big, it would constantly be full of exciting dreams." He goes on, "These men and others are saying. . . that it isn't outlandish to say that if we really desire to fly, we could fly!"

Preparing and Giving the Speech to Actuate ————————————————————

Preparing the Speech to Actuate

Moving individuals to act requires that you carry the audience beyond conviction to action. There is an easy way and a difficult way to get others to act. The easy way is to select a topic and a goal of such a nature that the audience will be willing to do what you request almost without your speech. In the extremely easy case, all that is required is that you give a coherent explanation of the basis for the action; this must, however, be coupled with the opportunity to act. Asking students to sign a petition opposing a tuition increase is an example.

Difficulties result when you advocate an opinion that the audience strongly opposes prior to the speech. In the extremely difficult case, you must give, in essence, three speeches. First, you must deliver a speech to convince the audience to change their minds. Second, you must present a speech to stimulate or to inspire the listeners to intensify their acceptance of the new position. Third, you must present a speech that specifies the means of carrying out the recommended action and that also provides the motivation for following through on that action. Some sales pitches are typical of the types of speeches found at the difficult end of the continuum. The generic description of sales talks given earlier in this chapter should demonstrate to you that these presentations really do fall into three sections. When people are sold something that they had no desire for prior to the presentation, the sales pitch usually goes on for some time. The encyclopedia or cemetery-plot salesperson who goes door to door usually spends an hour or two making a pitch and

[3]Leo Buscaglia, *Love* (New York: Fawcett Crest, 1972), pp. 18-19.

even then fails more often than he or she succeeds. Land developers frequently will spend an entire weekend providing room and board for prospective clients. You may have spent weeks or months persuading parents to allow you to take a trip during spring break or to allow you some other privilege that they originally opposed. There are, fortunately, many gradations from which to choose between the easy and the difficult situation. For in-class speeches, you should probably choose a topic from the easier end of the continuum.

Identifying Receiver Needs. With easy and mildly difficult topics, you will face an audience that is leaning in the direction of action. You will, accordingly, want to analyze their needs by using the same methods that are employed in the speech to stimulate or inspire. You will want to know why they hold their current position. You will also want to make sure that you have sound evidence and reasoning to support your position. Weaknesses in this area may give the audience incentives to think up reasons for opposing the action you wish them to take.

Incorporating Pressing and Important Information. It is important for your listeners to have sound reasons for acting *now,* rather than delaying action. In the speech to actuate, it is wise also to identify potential objections and answer them.

Making Recommendations. A problem that frequently arises in speeches to actuate is a failure of the speaker to make recommendations as clear as they need to be to produce the desired action. One of the most consistent findings in experimental research about persuasion is that speakers cannot overdo being clear and specific in their recommendations. Even when it comes to a simple signature on a petition, it is necessary to tell the listeners to write legibly, because those who look at the petition will have to be able to read their names. If you do not indicate clearly where people are to sign, some will sign in the wrong place. So it is with any speech in which you implore the audience to act. If you make your recommendations as clear and specific as possible, then you are more likely to get people to take the action you wish them to take.

Giving the Speech to Actuate

This checklist should enable you to review the major qualities of an effective speech to actuate.

1. Do you have a topic that will lead to an action that the audience can perform with relatively little difficulty at the end of your speech?
2. Have you analyzed your audience to discover exactly which of their needs will be met if they take the action you recommend?
3. Have you made sure that there is a sound, rational base for the action? Do you have evidence and reasoning to demonstrate that base?

4. Have you made sure that you have good reasons for people to act at the end of your speech rather than later on?
5. Have you considered objections the audience might have to acting? Do you have answers to those objections?
6. Have you made your recommendations for action so clear and specific as to be virtually foolproof?

Examples of Actuation Speeches. One student gave an excellent actuation speech on littering. He began by opening and displaying a bag of trash he picked up on the way to class. He proceeded to cite statistics about the cost of cleaning up litter but dwelt more upon the aesthetic effects of litter on the natural beauty of the campus and countryside. His action step involved having the audience practice telling people who litter to pick it up. Similar topics might include speeches in which the audience is trained to recognize and then to respond appropriately to ethnic, sexual, or racial slurs. Another student gave an effective speech on donation of physiological organs for transplant in the event of death. His action step was to ask people to take out their driver's license, and in states where it can be done, to endorse the section on the back that permits the taking of organs for transplant in the event of death. In a similar vein, another student spoke on the "Living Will" and passed out copies for classmates to sign. Speeches urging donation of blood, for which the speaker provides appointment cards, or even in some cases, brings a schedule that enables him or her to schedule appointments for those who become convinced, also work as actuation speeches. One of your authors once taught public speaking to a group of adults, one of whom was a physician who urged renewal of tetanus shots for an actuation speech and who proceeded to give the shots to those who wanted them at the end of the speech. In all cases, the effective actuation speech built a convincing and compelling reason for taking the action and then provided an action that the audience could take immediately or almost immediately.

Summary

1. Topics for persuasive speeches must be presently or potentially controversial.
2. If your inductive search for a topic for persuasion fails, there are lists of possible topics available.
3. The speech to convince relies on primarily rational appeals (sound evidence and reasoning) to change the minds of listeners.
4. The speech to stimulate or inspire assumes that the audience agrees with your position, and proceeds with your attempt to strengthen or intensify that belief.

5. The speech to actuate requires that the audience perform some specific or immediate action at the end of the speech.
6. Speeches to actuate given in the classroom usually are on topics of such a nature that the audience will be leaning in the direction of the action at the beginning of the speech.

Questions and Exercises _____

1. Find examples of each of the kinds of persuasive speeches—the speech to stimulate or inspire, the speech to convince, and the speech to actuate. Use the checklist given in the chapter for that form as a basis for criticism of the speech. Be prepared to present it in class or to discuss what you have found with classmates who have selected different kinds of persuasive speeches.

2. Observe a number of persuasive messages in advertisements in newspapers and magazines or on television. For each, identify the receiver need, the attempts to make the information presented pressing and important, and the nature of the recommendation made. Focus particularly on the recommendation. Is it explicit or implied? Will it really work?

3. Observe a number of persuasive messages made by those seeking public office (watch a "Meet the Candidates" program on local television, for example). Again focus on the persuader's identification of needs, attempts to make those needs pressing and important, and particularly the recommendations made. How do these "real people" compare with the fantasy people in the advertisements? How do their recommendations compare? What accounts for the differences between them (provided there are differences)?

4. Identify the one persuasive speech that you have heard that influenced you the most. What kind of persuasive speech was it? What about it caused it to be effective with you? Do you think your experience was unique? Compare your experience with those of your classmates.

5. With several classmates, brainstorm a list of possible actions for actuation speeches. Try to list as many immediate actions as possible without criticism or comment. Whatever is mentioned should be listed. Then go over the list and try to find one or more possible speech topics to go with each action.

6. Prepare an outline of the student speech on positive thinking included as an example in this chapter. How well does the speech outline? Attempt to reorder the points in the speech to make them follow outline rules more precisely. Do you think the speech could be improved if it were given from your revised outline?

7. Prepare a thorough criticism of the stimulation speech on positive thinking. Pay particular attention to the language and organization. Be prepared to present to the class specific suggestions for improving that speech.

8. Prepare an outline of the student speech on postponing marriage included as an example in this chapter. How well does the speech outline? Attempt to reorder the points in the speech to make them follow outline rules more precisely. Do you think the speech could be improved if it were given from your revised outline?

9. Prepare a thorough criticism of the convincing speech on postponing marriage. Pay particular attention to the language and organization. Be prepared to present to the class specific suggestions for improving that speech.

10. Using the topics and examples given in Tables 17-1 and 17-2 as a guide, prepare brief, three-level outlines (Roman numerals, English capital letters, and Arabic numerals) for a persuasive speech on at least four of the topics. Alternatively, use two topics and develop a persuasive pro-and-con outline for each of the two.

Courtesy of Holland Wemple

Special Forms of Public Speaking

OBJECTIVES

By the time you finish reading this chapter, you should be able to:

1. Describe the purposes and expectations associated with speeches of introduction.
2. Describe the purposes and expectations associated with speeches of nomination.
3. Describe the purposes and expectations associated with presentations.
4. Describe the purposes and expectations associated with speeches of tribute.
5. Describe the purposes and expectations associated with speeches of dedication.
6. Describe the purposes and expectations associated with commencement addresses.
7. Describe the purposes and expectations associated with keynote addresses.
8. Describe the purposes and expectations associated with speeches of good will.
9. Describe the purposes and expectations associated with after-dinner speeches.

Among the first theorists to classify speeches by type was Aristotle, who identified three kinds of speeches: *deliberative, forensic,* and *epideictic.* Deliberative speeches proffered counsel or advice; examples included speeches presented in the legislative assembly or to the public regarding matters of government policy. Forensic speeches addressed matters of prosecution and defense and were generally found in the courts of law. Epideictic speeches were given primarily as exhibitions or displays; they included eulogies and speeches that "praised or blamed" an individual for a particular action.[1] Today we no longer follow such a classification system. Instead, we typically divide speeches into types based on the end that is sought by the speaker. Our approach throughout this text, for example, has been that speakers engage in oral discourse with one or a combination of three basic ends in mind: (1) to create or modify the information base of the audience, (2) to modify thoughts and behavior, and (3) to reinforce thinking and behavior. Some speeches defy classification. Aristotle could not have anticipated that the *hanging speech* would become a popular type of public address for Americans of

---

[1] Aristotle, *Rhetoric,* 1.3.1358b, trans. Lane Cooper (New York: Appleton-Century-Crofts, 1960), p. 17.

the early nineteenth century: the scene of public execution would seem to be an unlikely occasion for speechmaking. Nevertheless, as Bower Aly and Grafton Tanquary report:

> In the early decades of the nineteenth century, executions were plentiful and public. People gathered from the countryside for miles around to see justice at work; and often the hanging of a convicted person was merely a central act in a day of drama. The condemned man, among others, was commonly permitted, if not actually expected, to make a speech confessing or denying his crime.[2]

Happily, the custom of presenting public speeches at executions no longer persists; consequently, we will not advise you about the standards of good practice associated with such oratory. Many less morbid occasions do persist, however, that invite and perhaps require a public speech. What would a retirement party be without a speech commemorating the long and valued service of the retiree? How could a convention be held without a keynote speech? How could a banquet not include an after-dinner speech? Within this chapter, we focus on a number of speeches that do not fall within the usual taxonomic categories. The speeches we deal with are either suggested or required by social conventions or by particular occasions or circumstances. We term such forms of speaking *special forms of public address*. Specifically, we examine speeches that focus on honoring an individual (i.e., at presentations, nominations, and tributes) and speeches that focus on an occasion (i.e., at dedications, commencements, conventions, and after dinners).

Speeches Focusing on an Individual

Many specialized forms of public speaking serve in some way to direct the audience's attention to an individual and the accomplishments of that person. Among the more common speeches that serve such a function are speeches of introduction, nomination, presentation, and tribute. In the following section, we address each of these speech types, describing expectations associated with each speech and suggesting some content considerations.

Speeches of Introduction

When you introduce a speaker, you play a subordinating role. It is not the time to present your own views on the subject about to be addressed. It should not be your goal to dazzle the audience with your wit or otherwise impress them with your ability. The audience did not assemble

[2]Bower Aly and Grafton Tanquary, "The Early National Period: 1788-1860," in *A History and Criticism of American Public Address,* vol. 1, ed. William Norwood Brigance (New York: Russell & Russell, 1960), p. 89.

to hear you speak. At the same time, however, when you agree to introduce a speaker, you accept an important responsibility.

As we noted in Chapter 7, the introduction accorded a speaker can affect the audience's initial perceptions of the speaker's credibility. One of your responsibilities, then, is to do all that your conscience will allow to cast the speaker in a favorable light. Because of this, it may be wise to agree to introduce a speaker only when you personally respect and trust him or her. But such a luxury is not always possible. If you are not in such a position, you will want to be certain that you are treating the speaker in a fair manner. To fulfill this responsibility may require some homework on your part. A wise speaker will provide the individual charged with the responsibility of introducing him or her a résumé that details the speaker's accomplishments (academic degrees, offices held, publications, work experiences, honors, and so forth). But if such a summary is not made available, it will be the task of the introducer to locate such data elsewhere. In short, your first responsibility is to explain to the audience why this particular speaker is qualified to speak on the chosen topic.

Your second responsibility is to generate interest in the speaker's topic. Here it might be wise to check with the speaker in advance. One could easily imagine a circumstance in which an introducer might steal the thunder of a speaker. Suppose, for instance, that you, as the main speaker, are going to talk about the necessity of instituting stiffer penalties for drivers who are intoxicated. You intend to introduce your speech by describing three cases that point to the need for stricter laws. As you sit there anticipating your speech, you hear a well-intentioned introducer describe "your" three cases in great detail. If the person giving the introduction had consulted with you in advance, this problem could have been avoided.

Should you, as the introducer, decide that the situation is such that humor is in order, be certain your chosen humor is appropriate to the purpose and mood of the occasion, the prestige of the speaker, and your familiarity with the speaker. Telling a "knock-knock" joke, ridiculing a foreign ambassador, or relating a potentially embarrassing story about a speaker you hardly know may not be appropriate. Keep your introduction short. Most introductions last only 30 seconds to 2 minutes. The more prestigious the speaker, the shorter the time necessary to establish his or her credibility.

Speeches of Nomination

Most of us belong to some kind of club or organization—fraternities, sororities, Young Democrats or Republicans, a computer-users club, a professional society, and so on. At least once a year, we participate in the election of officers who will administer these organizations. Sometimes the process of election is quite simple. Once the call for nomination occurs, someone might stand and say, "I nominate Mary for president.

We all know her and have seen how hard she has worked for the club. I think she would do a great job." In many circumstances, such a speech is sufficient. If the organization is small, and if people are, in fact, aware of Mary's hard work, qualifications, and accomplishments, nothing else need be said. At other times, the election process is more complex, and the need for a more developed speech of nomination exists. If you have ever observed a national political convention, you have some notion of what we mean by a fully developed speech of nomination. Should the occasion require a formal, fully developed nomination speech, there are four principal points that should be included:

1. The office for which the speaker is offering a nomination and the name of the individual who is being nominated.
2. A description of the duties of the office and a statement of the tasks that face the new office-holder.
3. A statement of the qualifications of the proposed office-holder. This statement should emphasize the high degree to which the nominee's qualifications match the requirements of the office.
4. An appeal to the audience to support the nomination.

To a large degree, the speech of nomination is a persuasive speech that calls for the audience to endorse and subsequently vote for your nominee. With that thought in mind, you should approach it as you would any other speech in which you attempt to shape, change, or reinforce behavior. Audience analysis and adaptation (see Chapter 6) are highly important. If your audience has little previous knowledge of your nominee, you will have to pay particular attention to detailing the candidate's qualifications and noting how they match the requirements of office. Are there audience members who are likely to be less than favorably disposed toward your nominee? Why do they hold such a predisposition? How can you diminish these unfavorable perceptions? Such questions are of considerable relevance as you plan your speech of nomination.

Presentations

It is always a pleasurable experience to recognize the accomplishments and contributions of outstanding individuals. Each year, colleges and universities bestow hundreds of honorary degrees. Such awards are usually presented at commencement ceremonies, where the degree recipient is the featured speaker. The award is actually presented by the president of the institution or another high-ranking official. But it is not only universities and their officials who bestow and present awards. Many organizations recognize the contributions of members and friends by presenting them with a formal award. An effective presentation speech will address four topics. It will:

1. Describe the award. The speaker might explain how the award was created, specifying for whom it is named (if relevant), how long the award has been in existence, and possibly enumerating the past recipients of the award.
2. Explain what the award is intended to recognize. The task here is to be clear and accurate. This need not be a long section of the speech, but it is an important one. Here the speaker specifies the meaning of the award, detailing the personal characteristics being rewarded.
3. Name the recipient and demonstrate how the individual possesses the characteristics embodied in the award. Here it is important to strike the proper balance between too much and too little praise of the recipient. Naturally one should build a good case for the recipient, but at the same time one would not want to go into such detail regarding a person's accomplishments and contributions that the recipient becomes embarrassed.
4. Incorporate a statment of the text of the award (if applicable). With many awards go plaques, certificates, trophies, or diplomas. Typically, these will be inscribed with a statement of recognition. The audience may be curious about the wording.

Tributes

There are yet other circumstances in which the contributions and accomplishments of an individual are recognized. People change jobs and are forced to relocate. When they do so, they may relinquish their membership in many groups, including houses of worship and civic, political, and special-interest organizations. Frequently, the contributions of such individuals to a particular organization have been such that some formal acknowledgement of their leaving is judged to be in order. This formal acknowledgement can occur in a variety of settings. Typical celebrations occur at a banquet, a coffee hour, a formal group meeting, or perhaps an informal gathering in someone's home. Another typical circumstance that sometimes demands a speech of tribute is the retirement of a valued employee. Business, educational, and political organizations are among those groups that formally recognize the retirement of members. Sometimes circumstances are such that one or a series of tribute speeches will be given at ceremonies commemorating an individual's loss to the group. Not atypically, the departing group member will be given a gift by the organization, and one of the speakers paying tribute will be charged with the responsibility of presenting it. Within speeches of tribute, the speaker will want to address the following topics:

1. Explain the nature of the individual's departure. If the departing person has taken a new position in another city or has received a promotion that requires relocation, the speaker should make the circumstances known to the audience. If the honored person is retiring after many years of service, the speaker should detail the

number of years and some of the important positions that were held by the person.

2. Express the group's sense of loss. Here the speaker should be sincere and direct, taking care not to turn the event into a mournful occasion. When an individual leaves one group or community, it frequently is to take advantage of greater opportunities elsewhere. If such is the case, the speaker will want to express a sense of loss but will also share delight in the new opportunities available to the honored individual.

3. Focus on the major accomplishments of the individual. Here the speaker might allude to offices held, committee work, or specific obstacles facing the group that the individual was instrumental in overcoming.

4. Detail some of the individual's characteristics that made him or her a valued group member. If the person was industrious, tenacious, and creative, the speaker should say so. Here it is useful to relate some actual incidents that illustrate these characteristics. If this topic is handled appropriately, the speaker can actually inspire the members of the organization, using one person's accomplishments as the source of such inspiration.

5. Describe the departing individual's impact on other group members or members of some larger community. Here again, some real anecdotes would be useful. However, the speaker must be careful not to embarrass the departing individual.

6. Reiterate the speaker's personal as well as the group's sense of loss, and convey best wishes for the future.

Speeches in Response

Most often, a speaker is on the bestowing end of an award or tribute, but occasionally one is fortunate enough to be the recipient. In such a situation, the recipient is usually expected to acknowledge the award or tribute by giving a speech. As with other speeches, it is important to learn the group's expectations. Will a simple "thank you" be sufficient, or will the person be expected to speak at greater length? He or she must be careful not to violate the group's expectations. Here we are reminded of several Academy Awards we have viewed, in which an Oscar recipient took an unreasonable amount of time to accept the award. The speaker will want to consider the following topic areas when formulating a response:

1. Express thanks simply but sincerely, indicating pleasure at being acknowledged. The speaker should also express the hope that he or she is worthy of the recognition.

2. Acknowledge the contributions of others. Few worthwhile goals are accomplished alone. If there are other individuals who have assisted the speaker in his or her pursuits, the recipient should make those individuals and their special contributions known.

3. Acknowledge the values of the organization. We once heard an award recipient acknowledge an award by saying, "There are a lot of awards in my field, and this one certainly means more than some of them." Needless to say, such a response was not appropriate.

Speeches Focusing on an Occasion _____

At times, it is an *occasion,* not an individual, that invites or even requires oral discourse. As with speeches that honor individuals, these presentations acknowledge values regarded by some groups in society as important and worth perpetuating. In this section, we examine occasions that call for recognition of values. Specifically, we discuss speeches of dedication and commencement, keynote addresses, speeches of good will, and the after-dinner speech.

Dedications

It is a custom to commemorate the completion of major projects with a ceremony. A new highway or bridge opens, and we hold a ribbon-cutting ceremony. We construct a new park or building, and we mark the completion with a formal gathering. Our house of worship pays off its mortgage and holds a "mortgage-burning" party. A charitable organization reaches the goal of its fund-raising campaign and holds a banquet to celebrate. Under many circumstances, a project would not seem truly complete unless it were honored by a dedication ceremony. A featured speaker at such an event would need to include the following topics in an address:

1. A brief description of the project or object being dedicated or commemorated.
2. An indication of the needs that will be satisfied as a result of the completion. If a fund-raising goal has been reached, one might want to specify how the new funds will be utilized. If a new or expanded library is being dedicated, one would want to comment on the services that will be provided and the number of people expected to be served by the facility.
3. A recognition of individual contributions. To build a new city park, a county library, a bikepath, or a new softball field requires the dedication and cooperative efforts of many individuals. These people should be thanked publicly for their efforts. The speaker must keep in mind, however, that it is easy to forget someone who should be mentioned.
4. A statement of the values symbolized by the project. Why do we build new highways, hospitals, schools, parks, bridges, and so forth? What do these projects say about our values? An effective

speaker will identify the appropriate values and relate them to the project being dedicated. A community that spends 2.5 million dollars on a new library must value the pursuit of knowledge. A state that builds a new technical college must value technical education and believe in providing opportunities for those who strive to improve their position in society. New buildings or bridges are more than concrete and steel. A good dedication speech focuses on what the project symbolizes to the people who have been instrumental in its planning and completion.

Commencements

As parents and university professors, your authors have attended many graduation ceremonies. More than once we have secretly hoped that the scheduled speaker would fail to appear, thus shortening the ceremony. At the same time, however, we recognize that graduation would not be the event that it is unless the accomplishments of graduates are recognized. Few of us will ever be a featured commencement speaker, but a number of us may serve in a secondary speaking role. Among those frequently called upon to speak at a college commencement, for example, include the presidents of the senior class and student senate, class valedictorian and salutatorian, officers of various honor societies, and so on. Generally, a commencement speech addresses three principal topics:

1. It offers congratulations. Parents, grandparents, friends, and relatives all need to be acknowledged in some fashion. They are proud of the scholar and appreciate being associated with his or her success.
2. It reviews accomplishments. What obstacles did the graduates overcome? What special characteristics did they exhibit? What were their special accomplishments? In short, this topic develops the significance of the occasion.
3. It issues a challenge. The word *commencement* denotes a *beginning*. Thus, the commencement speaker typically attempts to forecast the future, specifying problems that the new graduates will be called upon to address as they take their place in society. Here the speaker's task also is one of providing inspiration by assuring the graduates that they are ready to take up the challenge.

The commencement address offers a special challenge to the speaker as well, for the circumstances present a dual audience, consisting of the graduates and those who have assembled to honor them. Even though the speaker's focus should be on the accomplishments and future challenges of the graduates, the remainder of the audience must not be excluded.

Keynote Addresses

Many conferences, conventions, and meetings of large organizations begin their proceedings with a keynote address. This speech is typically presented by someone who is perceived as high in credibility by the members of the organization. The keynote speaker is frequently a member of the organization—perhaps a past president or executive secretary—but he or she can also be someone from outside the group who embodies qualities respected by the organization. The keynote address speaks to the theme of the conference or convention; it also indicates future directions. Perhaps you have heard a keynote address presented at a national political convention.

In many ways, the keynote address is similar to the commencement speech, for a primary goal of the speaker is to inspire the organization to address future challenges. The immediate audience is usually favorably disposed to the speaker and his or her ideas; thus, a main thrust of the keynote address is to reinforce existing attitudes, values, beliefs, and behaviors that characterize the group, but the audience for a keynote speech frequently goes beyond those who are physically present. In our electronic age, it is not uncommon to have millions of television viewers watching a keynote speech. In addition, journalists, who will later write for their own audiences, are present at many keynote addresses. These people will abstract and interpret the address for thousands, perhaps millions, of people who will not hear the actual speech. In short, the burdens of the keynote speaker are to:

1. Remind the organization of its goals, objectives, and values.
2. Emphasize past accomplishments of the organization, stressing the group's history.
3. Indicate future challenges that face the organization. Many conferences and conventions have a central theme. Certainly, the keynote speaker will want to develop a challenge to the organization around the topic of the meeting.
4. Inspire the organization to meet the future challenges. The speaker will specify potential courses of action that might be pursued. He or she will outline the possible effects, both good and bad, of those actions.

Speeches of Good Will

You may sometimes be called upon to present a speech of good will. Many organizations maintain speaker bureaus, employees or members of the organization who volunteer to develop speeches on topics relevant to the organization. These speeches are delivered before civic clubs, service organizations, school audiences, and meetings of professional societies. Your authors have had considerable experience in coaching the members of such speaker bureaus on the preparation and delivery of these speeches of good will. Specific speeches take the form of an employee of an electric utility talking to the Rotary Club on "The Safe Use of Electricity," a drug company research scientist speaking to the local humane society on "Controlling Parvo Virus in Dogs," or a state highway official discussing "Litter: An Expensive Problem" with a class of elementary school children. Why would businesses, governmental agencies, and educational institutions commit considerable resources (money as well as time) to keeping the public informed? There are several answers to this question. Some speeches of this type are presented by the sponsoring organization out of a genuine caring for the public. Electric utilities, for example, have had many unhappy experiences with individuals unfamiliar with the dangers associated with electricity—from the homeowner who gets an aluminum ladder too close to a power line to the person who replaces a blown fuse with a penny. But the speech of good will also is intended to serve two less apparent functions: it serves both information-gathering and public-relation functions. Good-will speakers encourage and allow ample opportunity for questions from the audience. Many organizations that sponsor speaker bureaus ask their speakers to keep a log of all the questions asked by an audience regarding a specific topic. By analyzing the logs, the organization learns much about public attitudes, beliefs, and knowledge levels—information that is of considerable value in determining future organizational strategies, policies, and practices. At the same time, sponsors of good-will speeches find that the public perceptions of them may be enhanced through the speeches of their representatives. The good-will speaker, then, has an interesting challenge—informing *and* generating the favorable perception of his or her organization, without making the latter goal obvious to the audience.

After-Dinner Speeches

A luncheon meeting or a banquet of an organization is yet another occasion that invites public address. Many times, civic and service clubs hold their meetings around a meal. Typically, the food is followed by a speech, the primary purpose of which is *to entertain*. The mood of such occasions is most frequently convivial. The listeners do not want to exert great efforts to acquire knowledge; they are not interested in being moved to achieve great goals. They want, instead, to be amused, relaxed, put in a pleasurable state of mind. This is not to say that an after-dinner speech is frivolous and devoid of substance. Like any other good speech, it will have a definite thesis, clear and unified organization, and an abundance of supporting and amplifying materials. The speech also will have a clear purpose; this will consist of one or a combination of the three primary purposes on which we have focused—*creating* an information base; *changing* attitudes, beliefs, and behaviors; or *reinforcing* them. But what, then, distinguishes the after-dinner speech from other speeches? The distinction resides primarily in the manner of the speaker's style and delivery and, to a certain extent, in the choice of topic. Language choices, voice, and physical activity should convey excitement and suggest amusement.

Topics for after-dinner speeches do not always have immediate practical value. A colleague reported to us that he had heard a most enjoyable speech at a meeting of his Kiwanis Club: a local physician spoke on the maladies of our nation's early presidents and the treatments inflicted on them by their doctors—cures that almost killed them. Even though the audience delighted in the physician's speech and did learn something of the history of medicine, they were more *entertained* by the speech than informed or moved to action. The goal of the after-dinner speaker is to move the audience to what we earlier identified as a state of nonvoluntary (effortless) attention (see Chapter 19). If the listener is forced to work hard, to make a conscious effort to attend, the after-dinner speaker has not fully realized his or her purpose.

Summary

1. Special forms of public address can be divided into speeches that focus on an individual (introductions, nominations, presentations, and tributes) and speeches that focus on an occasion (dedications, commencements, keynote addresses, speeches of good will, and after-dinner speeches).
2. Speeches of introduction have two fundamental purposes. They should serve to cast the speaker in as favorable a light as circumstances allow, and they should generate audience interest in the topic.
3. Speeches of nomination are to a large degree persuasive in intent. The nominator must change the perceptions of some audience members who are not favorably predisposed to the candidate. The speaker must also maintain the support of those who already are favorably disposed.
4. A good presentation speech has four major topics. It will describe the award to be made, explain what the award is intended to recognize, name the recipient and demonstrate how the individual possesses the characteristics embodied in the award, and incorporate a statement of the text of the award.
5. Speeches of tribute explain the circumstances surrounding an individual's departure, express the group's sense of loss, focus on the accomplishments of the individual in question, detail valued characteristics of the person, describe his or her impact on the group or larger community, and provide a sense of loss and best wishes.
6. Speeches in response express thanks and acknowledge the contributions of others as well as the values of the organization bestowing recognition.

7. Speeches of dedication explain how the object or project being dedicated will satisfy needs not previously met. It recognizes individuals who have contributed to the project and clarifies the values symbolized in the object of dedication.

8. Commencement addresses offer congratulations. They review accomplishments and issue a challenge.

9. Keynote addresses remind an organization of its goals, objectives, and values. They emphasize past accomplishments while issuing future challenges. They serve to inspire the organization.

10. Speeches of good will meet audiences' need for information, but they also provide a means by which the sponsoring organization can learn about public attitudes, beliefs, and knowledge levels. Sponsors of good-will speeches also expect that the public perception of them will be enhanced through such speeches.

11. The usual purpose of an after-dinner speech is to entertain, but it can and frequently does have more than frivolous intent. The after-dinner speech typically makes a serious point while simultaneously bemusing, teasing, and delighting.

Questions and Exercises _____

1. Choose some public figure known to your classmates. Assume the person is coming to your class to make a speech that falls within his or her field of specialization. Prepare a five-minute speech to introduce the person to the class.

2. Assume that there is such an office as president of your public-speaking class. Identify a classmate who would be a good candidate for such an honorific role. Present a short speech nominating the individual for this high office. Be sure to review the requirements for the speech of nomination.

3. Assume that you are to present an Oscar to your favorite actor or actress. Prepare a speech through which you present the Oscar in the best actor or actress category. Be sure to review the requirements of a presentational speech.

4. Choose an individual (known to your classmates) who has recently retired from some societal role. Prepare a speech of tribute to the individual.

5. What advice would you give the keynote speaker at the Republican or Democratic National Convention, who must simultaneously address two audiences: an immediate, partisan group and several million television viewers who may not share the enthusiasm of the immediate audience?

6. Recall an effective after-dinner speech you have heard. What made it effective? Contrast this speech with another than you judged to be ineffective. What accounts for the different degrees of effectiveness?

General Considerations

UNITED STATES

Courtesy of Jean Kirkpatrick

19

The Audience as Individual Listeners

OBJECTIVES

By the time you finish reading this chapter, you should be able to:

1. Offer a definition for the listening process.
2. Explain how selection and storage operate within the listening process.
3. Differentiate between aural, verbal, and vocal data.
4. Characterize involuntary, voluntary, and nonvoluntary attention.
5. Describe how information processing occurs within the human conceptual system.
6. Explain what it means to suggest that the human conceptual system is hierarchically organized.
7. Distinguish between listening performance and listening capacity.
8. Explain the thought and speech differential and how it can retard listening comprehension.
9. Distinguish between denotative and connotative meaning.
10. List a number of poor listening habits that might be practiced by audience members and explain how a speaker might compensate for them.

In Chapter 6, we examined the nature of audiences and demonstrated that listeners can be categorized based on their degree of involvement. In addition, we observed that not all audience members are equally important for the achievement of the speaker's purpose. In this chapter, we explain how individuals listen to and process information. The speaker who understands the listening process is better able to compensate for any listener inadequacies that may exist.

The Listening Process

We define listening as *the process by which the human organism selects, processes,* and *stores aural data.* Our definition restricts listening to a human activity, although we recognize that other animals and even some electronic machines also have listening capabilities. *Selection* is the name we use for the process that determines which of the multitude of potential stimuli within our perceptual field actually stimulate thought. Information processing occurs after sound waves strike the eardrum, are transformed into electrical energy, and finally enter the central nervous system. It is the phase of the listening process in which neurological impulses are assigned meaning. *Storage* is the process by which the organism retains data for either short- or long-term use. *Aural data* are perceived by the ears and are of three types: *verbal data* (sounds that are recognizable as words), *vocal data* (vocal cues, such as inflection, pitch, and vocal quality, that aid us in our interpretation of verbal data), and *other kinds of sounds* (a book striking the floor, lights buzzing, a phonograph playing music, an automobile engine running, etc.).[1] In Figure 19-1, we have visualized the listening process.

FIGURE 19-1   The listener. [Reprinted by permission from Richard Whitman and Paul Boase, *Speech Communication* (New York: Macmillan, 1983).]

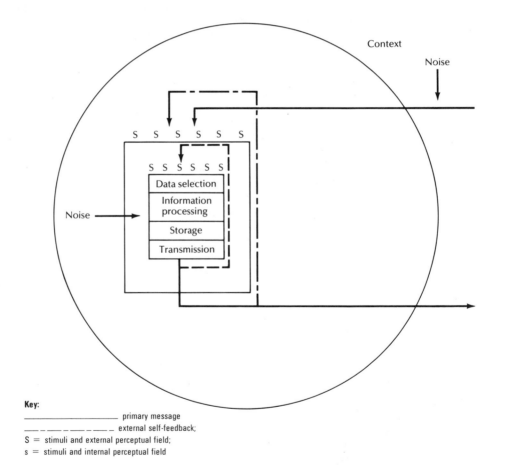

Key:
_____ primary message
— — — — — — — — — external self-feedback;
S = stimuli and external perceptual field;
s = stimuli and internal perceptual field

[1]Carl H. Weaver, *Human Listening: Processes and Behavior* (Indianapolis: Bobbs-Merrill, 1972), pp. 6-7.

Data Selection

At any given moment, the members of your audience will be bombarded by a multitude of stimuli, some that are be a part of their external perceptual field and others that are located within the listeners and that are said to be a part of their internal perceptual field. Think of the choices that are available to your audience members. They can focus their attention on you and your speech, a pretty woman or handsome man sitting nearby, noise emanating from the next room, or the sounds of a band passing by the location of your speech. Such stimuli are a part of the listeners' external perceptual field. These influences exist outside or apart from the mental and physical functioning of the listener. Your listeners' internal perceptual field is composed of stimuli produced either by mental activity (thought), or as a result of other physiological functioning. Here again, the listeners can decide to listen to your speech or to think about being tired, hungry, cold, or hot. Your listeners also may worry about whether or not they will have a ticket on their illegally parked automobile, wonder whom they should invite to an upcoming party, or reflect on tomorow's history exam. All such stimuli are generated by the listeners and are a part of the internal perceptual field. The speaker's task, obviously, is to make his or her message the most attractive, the most compelling stimulus in the listeners' perceptual fields. An explanation of the exact mechanisms employed in the selection of data goes beyond our present purposes, but in Chapter 14, we do discuss some techniques that the speaker can employ to direct favorable attention.[2]

With every moment, dozens of stimuli will compete for your listeners' attention. Individuals cannot, however, attend or respond to all stimuli. To do so would overload the central nervous system, resulting, perhaps, in complete disorientation. Researchers have consistently demonstrated that the number of stimuli that can receive simultaneous attention is very limited and that the span of absolute attention—our ability to focus completely on one and only one stimulus without wavering—ranges between 2 and 24 seconds, with most research suggesting the shorter time period as the more plausible. In the public-speaking context, it might be useful for the speaker to consider listener attention from a broader view. Floyd Ruch, for example, identifies three types of listener attention: *involuntary, voluntary,* and *nonvoluntary.*[3]

Involuntary Attention. This is the type of attention that your listeners will accord to certain types of stimuli that demand their attention. Because of the strength or uniqueness of these influences, the listener will automatically perceive and focus on them above all others.

[2]For those who would like a comprehensive account of the listening process, we recommend Carl H. Weaver, *Human Listening: Processes and Behavior* (Indianapolis: Bobbs-Merrill, 1972); Larry L. Barker, *Listening Behavior* (Englewood Cliffs, N.J.: Prentice-Hall, 1971); and Andrew D. Wolvin and Carolyn Gwynn Coakley, *Listening* (Dubuque, Iowa: Wm. C. Brown, 1982).

[3]Floyd L. Ruch, *Psychology and Life* (New York: Scott, Foresman, 1937), pp. 453-454.

No matter how engrossing a presentation is, the audience members would notice if the lights were suddenly to go off, leaving the room in complete darkness. With these dramatic cases, listeners will automatically divert their attention from the task at hand. We frequently hear people suggest that the purpose of an introduction to a speech is to gain attention. This is not entirely true, because as you rise to speak and approach the podium, you stand as a change in the environment, a novel and attractive stimulus, a stimulus likely to produce involuntary attention.

Voluntary Attention. Once your audience initially attends to you, they are likely to be thinking something like "Well, so that's the speaker. As long as I'm here I might as well listen to find out if there is anything of value for me in the speech." Revealed in such listener thought is the decision to exert voluntary attention—a form of attention that requires effort and conscious intent. It is the type of attention that the listener accords when he or she judges that it is in his or her best interest to do so. No matter how boring one of your professors might be as a lecturer, you are likely to force your attention on what is said, particularly if you suspect that the lecture materials may eventually appear in a final exam.

Nonvoluntary Attention. How often have you sat in a class, expecting to hear a boring lecture on, say, the causes of the French Revolution, when suddenly you discover that the whole class period has passed and that you were so immersed in the lecture that you were not conscious of the passage of time? This phenomenon illustrates how a skillful speaker can change voluntary attention to the form that is nonvoluntary. In certain situations, we discover that the required effort to concentrate diminishes, perhaps to the point where attending is pleasurable, requiring no effort. Such attention is called *nonvoluntary*.

As a public speaker, you should keep in mind that you are likely to hold the attention of your audience until you do something to lose it. Your goal should be to move your audience along an attention continuum. As you rise to speak and serve as a new and novel stimulus, you will have your listeners' involuntary attention. As you begin your address, you can be assured that the majority of your audience will make an effort (expend voluntary attention) to see if you will state something of value to them. Your task, then, is to provide valuable data to make listening a pleasurable experience and to move your listeners from the voluntary form of attention to the nonvoluntary.

Information Processing

As we have already suggested, the human organism is always being exposed to multiple stimuli but can attend to only a few. Several researchers suggest that the reticular formation of the brain stem serves as a center of attention that receives all incoming data from our *receptors,* sense organs that are adapted for reception of either externally or internally generated stimuli. The reticular formation appears to screen incoming stimuli, assigning them a value and determining which ones will be allowed access to the brain for additional processing.[4] But it is within the cortex, our top command post, where electrical energy is converted into meaningful symbols that become the raw materials of thought. Exactly how this process occurs is not known, although research suggests that once the cortex receives an impulse it has the capability of searching the conceptual system for an impulse match, with the previously stored meaning assigned to the new impulse.

Researchers believe that the cortex's search for a match is greatly facilitated by the manner in which data are stored in our conceptual system. Many investigators suggest that our cognitive system is hierarchically structured, that concepts at a high degree of generality subsume those of greater specificity. In Figure 19-2 (a composite of classifications suggested by Brown and Hollingworth),[5] we have depicted a partial illustration of the hierarchical nature of subcategories of the term *collectivity*. Reflect for a moment on what happens to you when you hear the word *collectivity*. Once the brain recognizes *collectivity* as a valid configuration of sound by finding that sound or a similar sound on file, the meaning that we accord to the sound is likely to be either the

FIGURE 19-2   A Partial Illustration of the Hierarchical Nature of Subcategories of the Term *Collectivity*

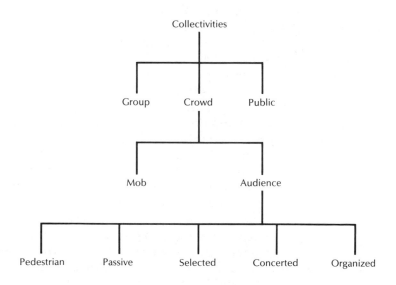

[4]See D. E. Broadbent, *Perception and Communication* (London: Pergamon, 1958).
[5]Roger W. Brown, "Mass Phenomena," in *The Handbook of Social Psychology,* vol. 2, ed. Gardner Lindzey (Cambridge, Mass.: Addison-Wesley, 1954), pp. 833-876. See also Henry L. Hollingworth, *The Psychology of the Audience* (New York: American Book Co., 1935), p. 17.

meaning associated with all concepts subsumed under the concept *collectivity* or the meaning associated with a subcategory with which we might have special familiarity.

But usually we do not hear single words. Instead, we hear groups of words that compose phrases and sentences. Examine the following sentence:

The large crowd applauded wildly.

The words *crowd* and *applauded* are the two primary concepts involved. *The* and *large* are adjectives that serve to isolate or particularize a certain category of crowd; these modifiers facilitate our evocation of only those meanings associated with a certain level of a hierarchy that has *crowd* as its immediate, subsuming term. Likewise, we have various categories of action that we group together under the superordinate term *applauded*. The adverb *wildly* again helps us to locate a subcategory of applause behavior. Quite likely, then, the two specific subcategories of *crowd* and *applauded* would be merged and would be assigned a meaning.

It also is useful to note that meanings are assigned to concepts on at least two levels. These two levels, or perhaps types, are referred to as *denotative* and *connotative* meanings. Denotative or explicit meanings are provided by dictionaries, whereas connotative meanings are more personal and unique, produced by our past experiences and associations. To one individual, a *crowd* can be "a large number of persons gathered together,"[6] but for the individual who has survived the panic of a crowd escaping from a fire, the concept will take on a much more individualistic association or meaning. In Chapter 12, we observed that meanings reside in message users as well as within the words themselves. Thus, for any given concept it is conceivable that we can assign both a denotative and a connotative meaning.

Of equal significance is the observation that the way in which individuals store and process a stimulus is undoubtedly associated with the purpose that the individual has for attending to the stimulus in the first place. These storage and processing decisions are tied to an assessment of the degree to which the incoming information will have to be recreated at some future time to assist the individual in accomplishing a given task. Sometimes we listen and attempt to make verbatim recordings of what we hear. At other times, we listen to find fault, to locate fallacious reasoning or inadequate evidence. Frequently, we listen because it produces pleasurable reactions within us. Think about a lecture class you have taken or are taking from an instructor who was initially unfamiliar. As the class began, were you concerned about how you should listen to the lectures? Most probably, you attempted to create a listening (information-processing) mode that would produce your best

[6]*The American Heritage Dictionary of the English Language,* ed. William Morris (Boston: Houghton Mifflin, 1976), n.p.

performance on examinations. To do so, you had to know whether the examinations were objective or if they took essay form. You had to discover if the instructor looked for specific facts or for generalizations. You had to ascertain if you could reproduce exact definitions of concepts or if you could define in your own words. These factors determined your listening mode.

Implied within our discussion has been the concept that information processing is more than a neutral process. During this process, we also make evaluative judgments about the information or data to which we attend. We make decisions about its present and potential value. We decide whether we agree or disagree with a position, whether data are true or false, good or bad, just or unjust. Later, we will observe that the public speaker must recognize that his or her audience is involved in such evaluative activities.

Storage

Information that is processed must be stored, with some facts retained for future use. It is the memory system that serves to store the data. Individuals are not very effective at this process of information storage. Most people are not good listeners. Listening theorists point to the existence of what they term the differential between listening *capacity* and listening *performance.*[7] In general, researchers have discovered, at least in laboratory situations, that as individuals increase in either age or sophistication, their capacity to listen also increases. Specifically, as listeners acquire wider data bases, they are able to understand a wider array of messages. This positive and linear relationship between age or sophistication and capacity to listen holds until the upper age levels, at which point the capacity to listen diminishes as a function of physiological deterioration. Outside the laboratory, this specified relationship does not seem to be quite so apparent. Try to recall last week's sermon. How much of it can you remember? Ninety percent? Fifty percent? Ten percent? What about the history lecture you heard last week? Undoubtedly, your recollections of these two events will be tied to the purpose you had for listening to each. We expect that you remember more from the history lesson than from the sermon, because you will be tested on the material covered by the lecture. Seldom are we tested over sermon content. But even in the classroom setting, evidence suggests that we do not always listen as capably as we can. Ralph G. Nichols and Leonard A. Stevens report that in some environments listening performance seems to diminish with age and grade level.[8] These researchers asked teachers at various grade levels to interrupt their lectures and have their students respond to the following question: "What was I talking about

[7]Weaver, *Human Listening,* p. 14.

[8]Ralph G. Nichols and Leonard A. Stevens, *Are You Listening?* (New York: McGraw-Hill, 1957), pp. 12-13.

before I called time out?" The following list shows the percentages of students who were apparently listening to their teacher at the time of interruption:

> 1st Grade—90 percent
> 2nd Grade—80 percent
> Jr. High—43.7 percent
> High School—28 percent

Even though studies have shown that the capacity to listen theoretically increases with age, data such as these suggest that actual listening performance does not improve. Some factor interferes. In your role as public speaker, it will be useful to remember that you and your message are just a small part of the stimulus complex available to audience members. You must be an attractive and useful part of that complex if you expect your receivers at least initially to attend to you and your message. But remember, attention is at best momentary. The good speaker recognizes this and continually makes efforts to capture and recapture the attention of audience members. If you expect to affect others, you must provide them with something of immediate or future value. Ask yourself this question: "Why does my audience need to know this?" If you cannot answer that question satisfactorily with regard to potential speech topics, another approach may be in order.

Listener Characteristics of Interest to the Speaker _____

Listening is an activity that requires considerable energy. But listeners will most likely not expend the amount of energy necessary to comprehend your message. They will usually have good intentions, initially according the voluntary attention to which we alluded earlier, but will often be distracted by stimuli that require less effort or that will produce more pleasure.

Thought and Speech Differential

It should be obvious that each of us has the capacity to process information at a much more rapid rate than speakers typically present it—in some circumstances up to four times more rapidly. As a public speaker, you will most likely present your speeches at between 125 and 140 words per minute (wpm) and produce, if you are lucky, approximately a 60 percent comprehension level in your audience. With the advent of compressed speech (an electronic technique for increasing the speed of speech while producing minimal distortion), it has become possible to study what happens to comprehension as speed increases. In one such study, Grant Fairbanks, Newman Guttman, and Murray

Miron taperecorded a message at 141 wpm. They then compressed the tape by 30, 50, 60, and 70 percent and tested subjects for comprehension of the message. At the base rate (141 wpm), subjects averaged 63.8 percent comprehension. At the 50 percent compression rate (282 wpm, or twice as fast as normal conversation), comprehension did drop, but only to 58 percent, which, for many purposes, is a rather insignificant reduction.[9] Other research has shown that humans can cope successfully with messages that are produced at 400 wpm.[10]

For the public speaker, this differential between speed of speech and speed of processing suggests a special problem: even your most devoted listeners will have a kind of built-in spare time that they will attempt to occupy. In other words, they might listen intently to you for a time, but when they find processing easy, they will tune out and focus on other stimuli in either their internal or external perceptual fields. After a period of time, they will again concentrate on your speech. This in-again and out-again behavior might occur throughout your speech. Furthermore, you must be aware that some of those additional stimuli may be so attractive to the listeners that they may never return to you and your speech. It is also possible that as the listeners keep checking up on your speech, they may develop a false sense of security. That is, the listeners may allow the tune-out periods to become longer and longer, until the receptors miss important ideas. Consequently, organizational devices such as previews, transitional phrases, and internal summaries (see Chapter 15) become useful. These devices, which alert your listeners to where your speech is going and where it has been, help diminish the problems associated with the speed-of-speech and the speed-of-thought differential.

Speaker Mannerisms

Your listeners expect that your vocal and nonverbal behaviors will in some way serve to clarify, amplify, or support your verbal message, but this does not always happen. We have all observed the nervous speaker jingling keys or coins, pacing rapidly across the front of the room, rubbing his or her wrist, or gripping the lectern so vigorously that fingers turn white from lack of circulation. Likewise, we have noticed the speaker who fills his or her speeches with filler expressions—"kind of," "sort of like," "ahh," "and ah," "umm," and so on. Such expressions add little, if anything, to a speech and eventually can distract the listeners' attention from the message. Here we are reminded of a professor who prefaced almost every comment with the expression "We find." His lectures would be filled with statements such as "*We find* that

[9]Grant Fairbanks, Newman Guttman, and Murray S. Miron, "Auditory Comprehension in Relation to Listening Rate and Selective Verbal Redundancy," *Journal of Speech and Hearing Disorders, 22*: 23 (1957).

[10]David Wood, *CRCR Newsletter* (Louisville: Center for Rate Controlled Recordings), *1*: 3 (1967).

in 1952. . . ," "*We find* that the Democrats. . . ," and "*We find* that the economy. . . ." It was not long until students began to focus on the expression instead of the message. Some listeners occupied their time by counting how often the phrase appeared in a given lecture.

Our advice here is simple. Do not provide your listeners with an excuse for not listening. Do not give them the opportunity to say, "Anyone who talks like that (or has those mannerisms) must not have anything worthwhile to say."

Multiple Meanings

Words are symbols. In the oral communicative process, they begin as sound waves originated by one individual. Another individual receives the sound waves and decodes them, assigning some meaning to the electrical impulses generated by the sounds. Therefore, it seems legitimate to suggest that the meanings we assign to words are meanings that reside in message users and not in the words themselves. Words mean what they do because we have agreed upon their meanings and have recorded our agreements (at a denotative level) in dictionaries. Consider the word *horse*. What image comes to your mind? Do you envision a large, hoofed animal with a mane and long tail galloping across a green pasture? Or do you think of the gymnastic device having four legs and an upholstered body that is used for vaulting? Most of you probably decoded the sounds (in this case light waves) associated with *horse* by assigning the first of the two dictionary definitions, but some, perhaps because of their association with a gymnastic team, assigned the latter definition or meaning.

In most instances, we do not have difficulty deciding on the right definition. Chances are that if someone were to say to you, "Bring the *horse* over here," you would bring what is appropriate and not an *equus caballus* when a vaulting device is required. Frequently, because of the context in which words are used, we are able to recognize the appropriate meaning. However, this is not always the case. The public speaker needs to recognize that words have multiple meanings. Possibilities for misunderstanding exist whenever the listener assigns his or her own meaning to a concept. The effective public speaker is highly aware of the potential ambiguity of language and makes every effort to establish common understandings.

Emotive Response

Not long ago, your authors participated in a situation in which a speaker referred to an audience member as "the young gal in the back." The speaker had no apparent ill intent. To him, *young gal* was a perfectly acceptable way to refer to a member of the female sex in her early twenties. But the *young woman*, as she preferred to be called, took exception to the speaker's terminology; she considered the label to be an insult. She is not unusual. When we listen, we do so with our emotions and prejudices, our attitudes and beliefs. We filter everything others say through our own experiences. Some words and gestures trigger strong emotive responses in others. Racial, ethnic, and sexual slurs, profanity, slang, and sexual suggestions all are capable of producing undesirable responses in your listeners. Their desire to listen and understand may then be replaced with a desire to retaliate.

Listener Response

By nature, the responses of the public-speaking audience are relatively ambiguous. We mean by this that the audience provides few clues as to how they are really perceiving a speaker and his or her speech. Social conventions are such that audience members sometimes nod approval even when they disagree. They may also pretend to understand when they are, in fact, confused. Many professors will close their lectures with the query, "Are there any questions?" Frequently, there are no questions, but what does that mean? Was the lecture so clear that no questions remain? Does no response signify a lack of desire to learn more about the subject? Or does this absence of questions reveal that the listeners are in such a state of confusion that they do not know what to ask or where to begin? In a given circumstance, each of these interpretations, and others, might be plausible.

The responses of the audience are symbolic too. That is, they are subject to multiple interpretations. We encourage you, in your role as public speaker, to be highly aware of your audience's responses. In Chapter 13, we recommend an extemporaneous mode of delivery in which the speaker delivers a speech from an outline, rather than from a complete manuscript. The speaker will then depend on the inspiration of the moment for exact word choice. One reason we recommend such a method of delivery is that it provides a maximum opportunity for the speaker to monitor the audience and to adjust the speech accordingly. But here again we caution that some audience response will be hard to interpret. Be cautious. Recognize that multiple interpretations of audience behavior are frequently possible.

Listeners as Notetakers

In many circumstances, your listeners will attempt to take notes during your speech. It would appear that notetaking might facilitate subsequent comprehension, but this is not always the case. Many of your listeners will be poor notetakers, who copy down the less important information. From what we know about attention, it seems clear that the number of stimuli to which an individual can simultaneously attend is very limited. Suggested by that observation is the probability that when a listener takes the trouble to record an observation, he or she is no longer attending to the speech. To put it another way, when a listener takes a note, he or she does so at the expense of attending to some part of a message. A good notetaker is alert for the right opportunity to take notes, but you as the speaker must provide these opportunities.

A good speech will have a number of redundancies built into it. In other words, the speaker will frequently restate and amplify in an effort to make an idea clear. The speech will have an abundance of good transitional phrases that tie off one idea and show movement toward another. In addition, the good speaker periodically reminds the audience of the ground that has been covered: he or she will offer appropriate internal summaries of ideas and arguments. During these redundant periods, the good notetaker does his or her work—without missing new information. If the speaker fails to supply such redundancies, large portions of the message will be missed or confused by the listeners.

Summary _____

1. Listening is the process by which the human organism selects, processes, and stores aural data.
2. *Selection* is the name for the process that determines which of a multitude of stimuli will actually stimulate thought.
3. Storage is the process by which the organism retains data for either short- or long-term use.
4. Aural data are perceived by the ears. They consist of verbal data, vocal data, or other kinds of sound.
5. Stimuli existing outside or apart from the mental and physical functioning of the listener reside in an external perceptual field.
6. The internal perceptual field is composed of stimuli produced either by mental activity (thought) or as a result of other physiological functioning.
7. Attention can be described at a macro level as involuntary (uncontrolled), voluntary (requiring effort), and nonvoluntary (requiring little effort, if any).
8. Many theorists believe that the conceptual system is hierarchically organized, that is, that concepts at a high degree of generality subsume those of greater specificity.
9. A considerable gap exists between individuals' capacity to listen and their actual listening performance.
10. The listener will display numerous poor listening behaviors for which the speaker must compensate. They will not use their listening time wisely; they will allow the speaker's mannerisms to detract from a message; they will not respond to words as symbols; they will respond emotionally to words; they will be relatively passive and nonreflective; and they will be poor notetakers.

Questions and Exercises _____

1. Review the definition of listening (see p. 305). Offer definitions for each of the key terms in the definition.
2. Differentiate between the terms *internal* and *external perceptual field*. Provide examples of stimuli that might appear within each type of field.
3. Provide examples of *involuntary, voluntary,* and *nonvoluntary* attention.
4. Numerous researchers suggest that the human cognitive system is hierarchically structured. Explain their position and indicate how a public speaker might organize information to take advantage of this structural feature.
5. Explain how one's purpose for listening might affect what the individual later is capable of recalling.
6. Researchers have observed a gap between what is termed listening *capacity* and listening *performance.* Define each term and describe the nature of this alleged gap.
7. One barrier to effective listening develops from what is termed the speed-of-speech and speed-of-thought differential. How does this differential influence effective listening?
8. Describe a speaking experience you have observed in which the speaker's mannerisms detracted from your listening performance.
9. Your authors maintain that notetaking can have an adverse effect on comprehension. Why might this be the case? Have you had an experience that supports or contradicts this position?
10. Refer to Figure 19-1 for your authors' visualization of the listening process. Try your hand at designing a model of this highly complex activity.

20

Humor and Speechmaking

OBJECTIVES

By the time you finish reading this chapter, you should be able to:

1. Enumerate a set of theories that explain or account for what we regard as humor.

2. Explain the biological, instinctive, and evolutionary theories of humor.

3. Explain the superiority theory of humor.

4. Explain the incongruity theory of humor.

5. Explain the surprise theory of humor.

6. Explain the ambivalence theory of humor.

7. Explain the release and relief theory of humor.

8. Explain the configuration theory of humor.

9. Formulate your own theory to explain laughter and humor.

10. Specify guidelines to follow when a speaker incorporates humor into a speech.

Given the appropriate time, place, and circumstances, people enjoy a good joke or a humorous anecdote. But individuals do not always agree about what constitutes the appropriate time, place, and circumstances. Perhaps you recall how Earl Butz, Secretary of Agriculture in the Ford administration, forced himself from office by telling what many considered to be a tasteless and demeaning joke about blacks. Then, in 1983, President Reagan's Interior Secretary, James Watt, held a news conference in which he announced the formation of a coal-leasing review commission. Attempting to refer humorously to affirmative action policies, Watt described the commission as composed of "a black, a woman, two Jews and a cripple."[1] America was not amused. Repercussions from Watt's witticism were of such a nature and magnitude that he was forced to resign. James Watt, like Earl Butz before him, lost public confidence through the injudicious employment of humor.

Not all humor produces negative outcomes for the public speaker. Frequently, just the opposite is the case. In a recent essay, *Time* magazine cited Ronald Reagan as a sometimes effective practitioner of the art of comedy. At a ceremony to commemorate a new highway project, President Reagan took to the podium and apologized for Secretary Watt's absence from the event, explaining that Watt would have been present had he not been on assignment stripmining the White

---

[1]"Why Reagan Is Funny and Watt Not," *Time*, October 17, 1983, p. 100.

House Rose Garden.[2] The President's remark produced much laughter, obviously signaling that the audience perceived his comment as humorous. Knowing that intended humor can produce responses of pleasure as well as pain within an audience, public speakers must give very serious attention to the issue of what is funny and what is not. Later we suggest some guidelines to follow when utilizing humor, but first it is useful to consider some theories that attempt to explain humor.

Theories of Humor

Humanity has long enjoyed the pleasurable state produced by humor and for an almost equally long time has attempted to state reasons why certain circumstances or events are humorous. As might be expected, numerous theories have been offered to explain the production of humor or laughter. In one text, for example, Edmund Bergler, a psychiatrist, listed eighty such theories.[3] A more manageable set is offered by Jeffrey H. Goldstein and Paul E. McGhee, who organize the circumstances under which humor exists into seven categories.[4] Goldstein and McGhee observe that many of the theories are only descriptions of conditions under which humor may be experienced. Their classification system provides a convenient system from which we can better understand the nature of humor.

Biological, Instinctive, and Evolutionary Theories

Many theorists suggest that humor and laughter are built into the central nervous system and serve an adaptive function. Such theorists observe that laughter appears very early in life, long before complex mental processing begins. Even before infants can speak, they express, through laughter, their amusement at a comic face or a peculiar sound produced by a parent, grandparent, or sibling. Laughter and humor also are observed to be universal; that is, all humans, from Africa to suburban America, have the capacity to laugh—to perceive and express the humorous. This class of theory hails humor as good for the body; it cites how humor and laughter "stabilize blood pressure, oxygenate the blood, massage the vital organs, stimulate circulation, facilitate digestion, relax the system, and produce feelings of well-being."[5] Some theorists suggest that what we consider as humor and laughter are adaptive behaviors of long standing. Could it be that laughter served a communicative function in prelingual times, signaling good news,

---

[2]*Time,* p. 100.

[3]Edmund Bergler, *Laughter and the Sense of Humor* (New York: International Medical Book Co., 1956).

[4]Jeffrey H. Goldstein and Paul E. McGhee, *The Psychology of Humor* (New York: Academic Press, 1972), pp. 4-13.

[5]Goldstein and McGhee, p. 5.

safety, or group unity? Could it be that laughter is a relic of struggling, biting, physical attack, and ultimate conquest of a victim? Is present-day ridicule a substitute for the physical assaults of prehistoric man? Evolutionary theories of humor and laughter would answer such questions in the affirmative.

Superiority Theories

Not long ago a "friend" and native of a state that borders ours asked us, "Do you fellows know what's the best thing that ever came out of Ohio?" When we confessed that we did not, our friend's eyes began to twinkle as he announced, "An empty Greyhound Bus." As residents of Ohio, we were amused, but not to the extent of our friend. In a similar vein, one of our female colleagues was asked, "Do you know what they call a good-looking woman in Athens, Ohio [our home town]?" Our colleague replied that she did not, to which she received the answer, "A tourist!" Somehow, such humor always seems to bring greater joy to its source than to its receiver. Such stories support superiority theories of humor and laughter. These theories maintain that it is triumph over others that produces the humorous. Summarizing this class of theory, Goldstein and McGhee observe, "Elation is engendered when we compare ourselves favorably to others as being less stupid, less ugly, less unfortunate, or less weak. According to the principle of superiority, mockery, ridicule, and laughter at the foolish actions of others are central to the humor experience."[6]

Incongruity Theories

What makes Don Rickles funny? Why do we laugh when we notice that our prim, proper, and stodgy history professor is presenting his lecture with the zipper of his trousers at half-mast or lower? Why are we amused when we see the 7′2″ center on the basketball team and his date—a 4′11″ coed? Although superiority theory certainly could be utilized in answering each of the three questions, proponents of incongruity theory would observe that humor arises from the ill-suited pairing of ideas, events, and situations. These pairings are divergent from habitual customs or expectations. We do not expect a stand-up comic to build his entire routine around insulting the audience. Our history as audience members is such that we expect speakers to praise us, not to insult us. We are amused when Rickles violates these expectations of praise, particularly when we believe that his insult is only theatrical and not indicative of his true feelings. Likewise, it well may be incongruity that explains the amusement evoked by both the proper professor lecturing with an open zipper and the members of a couple who are greatly different in height.

[6]Goldstein and McGhee, p. 6.

Surprise Theories

Many theorists regard surprise, suddenness, or unexpectedness as necessary if not sufficient to evoke the humorous experience. Here we are reminded of the antics of comedian Sid Ceasar. In one vignette, Caesar was cast as a nineteenth-century British officer attending a party in India. After walking out into a garden adjoining the house where the party was held, Caesar and his sweetheart stood talking, when suddenly the dashing young officer drew his revolver and fired in the direction of his lady. Realizing the shots were intended to protect her, the young woman rushed into her hero's arms, asking, "What was it?" To the query, Caesar replied, "It was a cobra." At these words, the young woman's face took on an expression of great relief. But Caesar continued his response to her question by adding, "And I missed it!" Whereupon he again drew his revolver and fired twice more, this time more successfully. Clearly, this was a case when surprise did, in fact, evoke humor. Some theorists posit a blend of surprise and incongruity to explain humor. Reflect on President Reagan's remark that his Secretary of Interior would have been present at a ceremony had he not been stripmining the Rose Garden. Given the source of the remark, we are at once surprised and struck by the incongruity of the situation. Under certain circumstances, surprise theories do seem to account for humor, but many unexpected circumstances nevertheless fail to evoke laughter. The unexpected alone is not sufficient to produce the humorous experience.

Ambivalence Theories

"I didn't know whether to laugh or cry!" At some time, each of us has probably uttered some variant of this expression. Ambivalence theories, as Goldstein and McGhee observe, "hold that laughter results when the individual experiences incompatible emotions or feelings."[7] Or as another theorist, D. H. Monro, puts it, "We laugh whenever, on contemplating an object or situation, we find opposite emotions struggling within us for mastery."[8] Among the incompatible emotions said to produce laughter are the pleasure and pain resulting from envy and malice, joy mixed with hate or shock, love modified by hate, playful chaos mixed with seriousness, and sympathy accompanied by animosity.

Release and Relief Theories

Yet another group of theorists suggests that what we know as humor functions as a means through which we release our stress and strain, our repressions. Those holding to this view suggest that the human

[7]Goldstein and McGhee, p. 10.

[8]D. H. Monro, *Argument of Laughter* (Melbourne: Melbourne University Press, 1951), p. 210.

organism, on occasion, builds up an excess of purposeless nervous energy, and it is the humorous experience that alleviates the tensions associated with the excess of energy. Of the "release theorists," Sigmund Freud has to be considered the most eminent.[9] Freud believed that the human mind was complicated by the existence of three characteristics: the *ego,* the *id,* and the *superego.* In his view, the *ego* is our rational being, the mind's contact with the realities of the world. The *id* is the source of all instinct energy, guided entirely by the pursuit of pleasure and the avoidance of pain. The *superego,* Freud argued, consists of inherited moralities and taboos as well as moral views acquired from parents. It functions as a regulator of the amoral impulses of the *id.* To a large extent, the *superego* can be regarded as our conscience. Freud wrote extensively on humor, maintaining that when energy builds up in certain psychic channels, it cannot be released due to the censorship of the *superego.* In these cases, the energy was pleasurably discharged in laughter. Humor, according to Freud's view, can be considered the triumph of the *ego* over the sometimes immoral impulses of the *id.*

Configuration Theories

We once heard a research scientist tell the following amusing story:

> Thanks for the fine introduction, John. Most of you probably do not know that John is something of a scientist himself. As a young man, he once took a summer job as an assistant at a research laboratory in southern Florida. The lab was experimenting on a drug that retarded aging—an elixir of youth derived from the yolk of young seagull eggs. One of John's jobs was to take the lab's truck to a distant city and haul the young seagulls back to the laboratory, where they were located in breeder houses to lay their eggs. John also had responsibility for the feeding and care of a group of porpoises—the recipients of the experimental drug. One day on his way back to the lab with a load of seagulls, John was driving through a state game refuge. Suddenly, a lion darted in front of John's truck. Not able to stop in time, John ran over the lion. Police who arrived on the scene were appalled at John's actions and arrested him. The charge—"Crossing the state lion with young gulls for immortal porpoises!"

Those holding to a configuration theory maintain that the humor associated with such a story results when listeners combine elements that were originally perceived as unrelated. N. R. F. Maier, a configurational theorist, maintains that a thought configuration that makes for a humorous experience must:

1. Be unprepared for.
2. Appear suddenly and bring with it a change in the meaning of its elements.

[9]See, for example, Sigmund Freud, *Wit and Its Relation to the Unconscious* (New York: Moffot Ward, 1916).

3. Be made up of elements which are experienced objectively.
4. Contain as its elements the facts appearing in the story, and these facts must be harmonized, explained, and unified.
5. Have the characteristics of the ridiculous in that its harmony and logic apply only to its own elements.[10]

Summing Up Humor Theories

Which theory of humor is best? Which has the greatest explanatory power? According to one theorist, Charles Gruner, the most useful explanation is found in the works of Thomas Hobbes—a superiority theorist of the eighteenth century. In his *Treatise on Human Nature,* Hobbes maintains as follows:

> The passion of laughter is nothing else but *sudden glory* arising from a sudden conception of some *eminency in ourselves* by comparison with the infirmity of others, or with our own formerly: for men laugh at the *follies* of themselves past, when they come suddenly to remembrance, except they bring with them any present dishonour.

In Gruner's view, "The two words 'sudden' and 'glory' make up the two elements necessary for evoking of laughter."[11] We agree. Much of what we perceive as humorous suggests our superiority over some person, institution, animal, and so forth. The suggestion that all laughter requires "sudden glory" implies that to have laughter there must be a victim or loser, someone or something over which one might triumph. Larry Wilde, comedian and best-selling author of thirty humor books (e.g., *The Absolutely Last Official Polish Joke Book* and *The Complete Book of Ethnic Humor*), claims, "Something or somebody has to be the butt of a joke, or it's not a joke. No matter what you do, you're going to put somebody down, whether it's doctors, lawyers, mothers-in-law, Polish people or Ronald Reagan. That's what humor is and I see nothing wrong with it. It's what you might call 'a human phenomenon.' "[12] Reflect on the case of James Watt. He most likely intended to criticize rigid affirmative action policies, but many perceived the victims to be women, minorities, and the handicapped. A sense of humor can be a great asset to the public speaker, but it also can be misinterpreted. Reflect carefully on how you choose to evoke humor.

[10]N. R. F. Maier, "A Gestalt Theory of Humor," *British Journal of Psychology, 23*: 73-74 (1932).
[11]Charles R. Gruner, *Understanding Laughter: The Workings of Wit and Humor* (Chicago: Nelson-Hall, 1978), p. 30.
[12]Larry Wilde, cited by Kathy Hocker, "Are Tasteless Jokes a Laughing Matter?" *Family Weekly*, November 27, 1983, p. 11.

Evoking Humor: Some Guidelines _____

It is not our intent to discourage you from using humor in your speeches. Humor can provide just the right kind of seasoning for nearly any type of speech. Too much or inappropriate humor, however, can seriously impede the speaker. Accordingly, we offer some guidelines relating to the use of humor.

Announcing Humor

Do not announce your humor. Perhaps you have heard a speaker say something like "Now let me tell you this really funny joke." Introducing a joke in such a manner usually ensures that the joke will be greeted with no more than forced, nervous, or polite laughter. To announce a joke is to remove the element of surprise. According to noted comedy writer Bob Orben, announcing your humor is "the worst thing a nouveau humorist can do," because it challenges the audience and inspires an "Oh yeah, make me laugh."[13]

Exercising Control

The late Jack Benny was so successful a comedian because of his ability to deliver the most humorous remark from behind the most deadpan of expressions. Laughing at one's own jokes discourages the audience from joining in. Let them decide if a remark or story is humorous. Wait for your audience to signal their perception of humor. Then you may join in, but with self-control. No one likes to see speakers convulsed in their own humor.

Avoiding the Risqué, Off-Color Story

The double entendre and off-color story have no place in a public speech. All too frequently, such attempts at humor are only counter-productive, as they cause the audience to perceive the speaker's credibility negatively. Why risk embarrassing or offending members of your audience?

Determining the Victim of Humor

As we have indicated, much humor involves the triumph over a victim. We delight when Lucy pulls the football away from Charlie Brown as he attempts a field goal; this is because we believe that we are not as stupid as "that loser." People in Minnesota tell South Dakota jokes ("What do you call a chicken, a broken tractor, and a tomato?—

---

[13]Bob Orben, cited by Clive Lawrence, "He Helps Politicians and Businessmen to be Comedians," *Christian Science Monitor,* September 24, 1973, p. 7.

The South Dakota State Fair"), and we suspect South Dakotans have equivalent retorts. Henny Youngman became famous with his one-liner, "Take my wife. . . please!" A list of individuals, groups, or institutions often cast as victims in attempts at humor includes women, wives, mothers-in-law, brothers-in-law, Norwegians, Poles, blacks, Irish, the handicapped, Republicans (or Democrats), ministers, rabbis, priests, golfers, fishermen, professors, students, and fraternity or sorority members. The list could go on and on. Should you decide to employ humor at the expense of a victim, reflect on the matter carefully. Your attempts at humor should offend or embarrass no one. Avoid humor that hurts or cuts. Frequently, it is effective to cast oneself as victim. This is known as self-directed humor.

Providing Relevant Humor

The most effective humor a speaker can employ relates directly to the circumstance or situation in which the speech is presented or to some serious point the speaker is attempting to make. One time, we heard a student begin his speech by saying, "This has nothing to do with my speech, and before I begin it, I want to tell you this really great joke." In our view, this speaker made two mistakes: announcing attempted humor and utilizing irrelevant humor. Humor that has no bearing on the aim of your speech is seldom effective. Should you decide to include humor in your speech, it should relate directly to your purpose and theme.

Presenting More than Words

Mark Twain was famous for his "salty speech." Determined to rid her husband's vocabulary of vulgarities, Twain's wife, as one story tells us, devised a plan to cure him. Her plan was to shame Twain into adopting more appropriate speech by adopting his favorite cuss words in her own speech. In response to one of his wife's four-letter diatribes, Twain responded by saying, "Woman, you know the words, but you don't know the music." So it is with humor. Many know the words of a humorous anecdote, but they do not know "the music." Facial expressions, timing, and vocal variety are all part of the music (see Chapter 13). Getting the right response to a humorous anecdote depends as much on how the story is told as on the substance of the anecdote.

Summary _____

1. Humor can be a valuable addition to speeches, regardless of the speech purpose. But humor must be used in right amounts and in appropriate circumstances.

2. Numerous theories have been proposed to account for humor. Some theories attempt to explain the mechanisms that produce it; others describe the conditions that lead to the humorous experience.
3. Biological, instinctive, and evolutionary theories suggest that humor is built into the central nervous system and that it serves as an adaptive function.
4. Superiority theories argue that humor results when the individual is able to compare himself or herself favorably to others.
5. Incongruity theories maintain that humor results from the ill-suited pairings of ideas, events, and situations. These pairings are divergent from habitual customs or expectations.
6. Surprise theories suggest that sudden change, sometimes coupled with the incongruous, produces the humorous experience.
7. Ambivalence theories observe that laughter and humor result when an individual experiences two incompatible emotions.
8. Release and relief theories suggest that what we know as humor functions as a means through which we release our stress and strain.
9. Configuration theories maintain that when elements of a situation originally perceived as unrelated suddenly fall into place, the result is humor.
10. Your authors take the view that much of what we consider as humor does, in fact, involve a victim. Accordingly, the speaker must exercise care when employing humor.
11. When using humor, your authors suggest the following: Do not announce humor; do not take greater delight in your humor than the delight shown by the audience; avoid risqué or off-color stories; embarrass no one with your intended humor; choose humor relevant to the purpose or aim of your speeches; remember that evoking humor requires appropriate use of voice, gesture, pauses, and timing.

Questions and Exercises _____

1. Provide an example of a tasteful joke that supports the superiority theory of humor.
2. Tell three or four humorous stories to your class. With your classmates' assistance, attempt to explain what makes the stories humorous. Try to explain the humor in terms of one or more of the theories presented in this chapter.
3. Your text suggests that it may be *sudden glory* that accounts for most of what we find to be humorous. What theory of humor is most associated with this position? Do you agree? How is the humor of a pun accounted for within the sudden-glory explanation of humor?
4. Specify at least six guidelines to follow when attempting to evoke a humorous response from your audience.

5. Frequently, speakers like to portray themselves as the victim of their own humor. Why do you suppose they do so? Can you think of any ways in which such an approach might backfire?

6. Observe a stand-up comic in action. How do facial expression, timing, and vocal variety contribute to the humorous impact of the presentation?

7. Your authors advocate the use of what they term *relevant humor*. What do they mean? What is their position on this topic?

8. Think back on a situation in which you observed a speaker fail in an attempt to provoke humor. What went wrong? Was the failure attributable to the substance of the material or to the manner in which it was presented?

9. Why do you suppose it is generally ineffective to announce humor?

Index